THE BOOK KEEPER

THE

A MEMOIR OF

BOOK

RACE, LOVE, AND LEGACY

KEEPER

Julia McKenzie Munemo

SWALLOW PRESS / OHIO UNIVERSITY PRESS

ATHENS

Swallow Press

An imprint of Ohio University Press, Athens, Ohio 45701

ohioswallow.com

Printed in the United States of America

Swallow Press / Ohio University Press books are printed
on acid-free paper ⊗ ™

30 29 28 27 26 25 24 23 22 21 20   5 4 3 2 1

Library of Congress Cataloging-in-Publication Data
Names: Munemo, Julia McKenzie, 1974- author.
Title: The book keeper : a memoir of race, love, and legacy / Julia
   McKenzie Munemo.
Description: Athens: Swallow Press--Ohio University Press 2020. | Includes
   bibliographical references.
Identifiers: LCCN 2019040686 | ISBN 9780804012218 (hardcover) | ISBN
   9780804041065 (pdf)
Subjects: LCSH: Munemo, Julia McKenzie, 1974---Family. | Authors,
   American--21st century--Biography. | United States--Race relations.
Classification: LCC CT275.M865 A3 2020 | DDC 920.073--dc23
LC record available at https://lccn.loc.gov/2019040686

for Ellen, who knew how to live

and for Gogo, who knew how to love

Author's note: This is a work of nonfiction. In some cases, I have changed names and identifying details to protect the privacy of people who never asked to be in this story.

Love takes off the masks that we fear we cannot live without and know we cannot live within. I use the word "love" here not merely in the personal sense but as a state of being, or a state of grace— not in the infantile American sense of being made happy but in the tough and universal sense of quest and daring and growth.

—James Baldwin, "Down at the Cross"

Contents

Prologue

I'd like to show you a snapshot of my family. It will reveal a fact you need to know. Otherwise what follows doesn't matter. No, that's wrong. It does matter, but without knowing this—without seeing this Polaroid I keep on my fridge—you won't know why it matters quite so much to me.

We're all dressed up for a wedding. Our elder son is four, and he leans against his dad's hip, squinting unsmiling into the camera in a sharp seersucker suit. The baby is one and I'm holding him. His considerably more rumpled seersucker is all bunched up around his neck, and he looks cross. I want to reach back through time and pull it down, let him breathe a little better.

My husband and I stand a hairbreadth apart—there's a slash of green grass hill between us. My pale white skin looks washed out in the October sun, but my thick brown hair falls nicely against my face and my rust-colored dress is fabulous and I'm smiling at the camera. My husband isn't smiling, but not because he's unhappy. He never smiles for a picture. His suit is dark gray and his tie matches my dress and he looks fabulous, too. I don't know if it's the quality of the film or the slant of the sun, but even after all these years on the fridge, in this picture the shades of light and dark on his black skin are perfectly rendered.

There it is. The fact you need. Why didn't I just come out and say it? I'm a white woman married to a black man—our children are mixed race. My intention wasn't to fool you, but to take you there slowly. Normally, you'd just see us on the street and know. You'd decide whatever it is you're going to decide. And this is a story about how some things take time to come clear.

PART I

WINTER SKIN

1

LATE ONE NIGHT the winter our children are nine and twelve, I settle on the green couch in the den of our rural New England farmhouse holding an old softback book in shaking hands. Its title is *The Wrath of Chane,* and the teaser copy promises "the most shocking portrayal of slavery ever written," but the image under those words reveals a tale as old as time. There's a tall, muscular black man trying to pull his wrists apart, but his chains don't allow it. He's got no shirt on and his pants are unbuttoned. A white woman in a yellow dress with carefully curled blonde hair clings to his arm and gazes up at his face. I keep looking at the author's name and trying to pull out a memory from the distance. I know it's one of my father's pseudonyms, printed there on the cover of this thick piece of pulp, but I can't remember ever hearing it spoken out loud. Tonight—with my family sleeping upstairs—I open it for the first time.

My father wrote this book, and I know very little about my father.

Right away I see the name of my mother's mother penciled in the right-hand corner of the first page. It's handwriting that brings back birthday cards and grocery lists, handwriting I haven't seen since childhood. My father's mother-in-law didn't just keep this book he wrote, she marked it as hers. Laid claim to his work, even when it was slavery porn. Her tidy name in the corner of that brittle yellow page softens me to the book, softens me to my dad. It allows me to begin.

"The young black man sat for a long time within sight of the house of the overseer. It was almost morning when he first stirred, changing from a sitting to a kneeling position beneath the large cypress tree hung with Spanish moss like a shroud," I read. These are the first words of my writer father's I've ever read. "The chorus of spring stars was still loud in eulogy in the heavens," I read. "Loud in eulogy." I run my eyes over the phrase again, there at the bottom of this first page. It's not *so* bad, I tell myself. I can do this, it is time to do this.

But then there are torn clothes. There is a "wide forehead." There's a "thick chest." There is Chane, speechless and superhumanly strong. A slave with sex appeal.

> His large black nostrils flared and his heart pumped fury through
> the veins Iwana had given him. The son of Iwana and the high
> medicine stood in the Louisiana night and felt a great pounding
> beneath his forehead and behind his eyes. He remembered the
> white woman who was asleep not fifty feet from where he stood
> and tasted the heavy saliva that was collecting on his tongue.

When Chane finds that woman, her "white fingers [run] over [his] coal black skin," before he takes her head in his huge hand, "grasping it like a fruit" to "fling her to the ground by it."

He is an animal, this man with a vaguely African-sounding mother. He is an animal, this man in Louisiana where the "high medicine" made him, and not a mortal father. I can't understand why this man is shown to be an animal in these opening pages.

The white woman he's come for doesn't see yet that he's here to kill her. She thinks he's looking for something else. "She lifted her night-dress up to her thighs and said, 'Gonna get me some poison ivy like as not, but it's goin' to be worth it, ain't it, you?'" and I have to close down a memory that threatens to rise up—a story about a woman my father had sex with in the woods one night, how she became covered in a rash from poison ivy afterwards, how he wasn't allergic to it—and I give my head a shake, remind myself why I'm here. Look back at the book.

> He knelt, took her neck in one powerful hand and began to
> choke the amazed, half naked, throbbing woman. Her eyes

swelled in her head, a strange small sound left her throat and when he stood up, still holding her by the neck, she was dragged up with him. Her nightdress fell, covering her body again. She shook violently for a moment and then died, a foot off the ground, held in the powerful grip of the infuriated slave.

AT FIRST I sit dumbstruck and wonder what my tidy WASP of a grandmother thought when she read her son-in-law's words. How Joan McKenzie from Albany, New York, felt about writing her name in that book after all.

Then I wonder what it takes to dream up that violence. What parts of a person have to be accessible for him to reach in and find *that*. How the plot the author puts down on the page is informed by the contents of his heart.

I think about my family sleeping above me and put the book down. I climb the stairs and creep into first one kid's room and then the other's. I linger as long as I can, press my lips onto warm foreheads until their bodies shift and resettle. Stand in the hallway and listen to them breathe. Worry about what I have done, opening this door. About what I will tell them when they ask where they come from, who their grandfather was.

Then I climb into the bed I share with my husband and lie as still as possible. I don't want to wake him, I don't want to ask him to hold this truth with me, I don't want to burden him with these fears. I lie as still as possible in the bed I share with my husband and wonder how my father's imagination could have been so filled with racial stereotypes about couplings like my own. I lie as still as possible and think about how much I want to crawl out of my skin. Out of my marriage from the guilt I feel, because if this is who my father was, who am I?

2

THE FIRST TIME I saw Ngoni, I was eating lunch in the Bard College cafeteria. I looked up from my soup and there he was across the room, a point of stillness in the surrounding mêlée. Framed by the cafeteria's wide-open doorway, he didn't move while people pushed their way by and around him. His face was filled with uncertainty and confusion and confidence despite being out of place. He wore a round, flat-topped felt hat that didn't cover his ears and a tan cotton jacket with a pattern that, from a distance, looked like a map of the world. His lavender pants didn't reach his ankles, and I worried what was protecting him from the upstate New York winter that raged out the window behind me.

Looking at him made me shy, embarrassed, so I turned back to my soup. As I did, I thought I felt an invitation in the crinkling near his temples. A light behind the trim wire-rim glasses on his face. Picking up my spoon, I chided myself. He didn't smile at me. He can't see anyone particular in this sea of white faces.

The next day I rushed into the cafeteria for a quick lunch between classes. A South African student I hardly knew ushered me to a table and introduced me to the man I would marry. He told me his name but I couldn't hear it, he named his country but I couldn't place it. He made a joke but I couldn't follow it. I just looked into his soft brown eyes and smiled. When I walked away, my whole body vibrated.

In my bed that night, I turned off the light and closed my eyes and saw his profile as if in silhouette—the curve of his chin and lips, the round of his nose, the tall forehead and the spot where it met his hairline. I followed that line in my memory, tracing it to the tidy crush of curls on the top of his head. I still didn't know his name.

I opened my eyes some hours later into a darkness I couldn't change. I was too surprised by the contents of my dream to find the light switch. This dream had recurred throughout my childhood, but I hadn't had it in years. Its premise was always the same—my father is really alive—but the circumstances changed every time. In this one, we were speaking on the phone. He said he was living in New York, writing under a pseudonym. When he named it, I recognized the author—a literary hero I'd been reading for class—my God! That's really you?

But eyes open in the dark, the name was smoke.

SATURDAY NIGHT, THE first party of the semester over. Ngoni accepted an invitation to the local diner. Liz—my closest companion since our first day on campus—drove us over the bridge and across the Hudson, started interviewing him from our side of the booth. I sat across from him, really seeing him now that I could be still and watch. His eyes were set wide apart in a face shaped like an owl's. His nose was broad and—I noticed when he removed his glasses and wiped his hands across his eyes—marked on either side by dark spots where those trim wirerims rested. He didn't smile much, and when he did I couldn't tell if it was because he thought something was funny or because he was tired of the talk, thinking of ways to escape.

"Do you have any siblings?" Liz asked.

"A sister."

"Older or younger?"

"Younger."

"What do your parents do?"

"My father passed when I was sixteen."

"I'm so sorry," I interjected. Our eyes met for a moment. My dad is dead, too, I wanted to say. I wanted to take his hand.

Liz again, though not unkindly, "And your mother?"

A pause. "My mother's not around."

Too personal too fast. I changed the subject, asked for the bill, got us out of there. Back on campus, we left Liz at her room, found our own spot in the lounge down the hall.

I asked only the safest questions.

"What will you do after this year?" was one.

"I want to attend graduate school to study colonialism," he said, as though this were perfectly obvious. I had to stop myself from asking why a young black intellectual from Africa would want to study the first thirteen colonies of the United States, my only definition of *colonialism*.

"The best programs are in the U.K. and the States," he said.

It was a physical jolt, my relief that he might return.

At some point I took his hand, led him back to my room. We talked late into the night. We started, then, to draw the lines of similarity, the lost fathers, the ties that would bind. The bright fluorescent hallway lights were sharp in my eyes when he opened the door to leave. I leaned in and kissed his cheek. He says now that's when he knew.

When he was gone, I slipped into the bathroom that separated my room from Liz's and took down the small laminated U.S. map she'd tacked up on the wall, flipped it over to see the other side, on which was drawn the world. I put my finger on Africa and quickly found Zaire—I'd written a report about it in sixth grade, and its familiar shape marked the only country I recognized on that continent. I searched all around and then drew my finger south before landing on a country shaped like the head of a rhinoceros. Zimbabwe. Landlocked, with a river following its northwestern border, Botswana and South Africa along the southern one, Mozambique curled around it to the east. I hung the map back on the wall, leaving the world side showing, and held my finger on Zimbabwe awhile, tracing the rhinoceros horn and thinking about Ngoni's place on the planet—a place I knew nothing about.

WITHIN A COUPLE of weeks, Ngoni and I had established the routines of college lovers. We knew the times and locations of each other's classes, knew which nights were best for sleepovers, didn't have to ask about when we would eat dinner, where we would sit at breakfast.

One night he told a story to the ceiling as we lay side by side on the futon I'd dragged from home to replace the narrow dorm-room bed. "My father was mentally ill," he said. "But in Zimbabwe, we don't think illness comes from nowhere. We believe there's been a possession."

I conjugated the word and realized a beat too late that he meant a spirit had possessed his father. I thought of *Poltergeist* and snow on a TV screen, had no frame of reference for what he meant. He was describing a culture so unlike my own, a place where even mental illness had a different name, a different definition. A world I was sure I would never understand without my own handles to hold it by. A world without the guideposts I'd grown up requiring.

There's been a possession.

◆   ◆   ◆

IT'S JANUARY OF 1980 and I'm five and a half years old and my father is just dead. The house on State Street is full of love and fear and confusion and lasagna. I stand in the dining room loud with people, looking for my mom. My hand rests on the warm haunches of our loyal black Lab, Shandy. She hasn't gone on a run in a while. Her haunches are getting thick.

The light in the room comes from a large paper globe that hangs over the dining room table, which itself is round and has lion claws for feet that scare my toes when I eat. We haven't sat at that table since Dad left for the loony bin. I consider crawling under it now to hide from all these people—maybe Mom would look for me then?—but the lion claw feet.

I need Mom because I have a question in my heart that I don't know how to ask and I think maybe with all these people around I'll be brave enough to speak. Why hasn't Dad's picture been in the corner of the screen when Channel 3 Eyewitness News is on in the mornings yet, the way other dead people's pictures are in the corner of the screen? When are they going to come on the TV and explain why he's dead? Because I would really like to know.

I've been watching the news every morning since he died, crawling up onto the stool at the long kitchen counter across from Mom and her thick black coffee, no toast. "Tea and toast?" she asks me, and

I nod. But my throat hurts when people talk to me these days, so I just turn and watch the TV that sits on the counter and wait for Dad's picture to appear.

But right now there are all these people who knew him and Mom is nowhere and I'm not sure where to look for her and I'm afraid that if I take my hand off Shandy's back I'll lose my balance and fall through the holes I have just learned are all over this house. There are so many dark corners.

Behind me is the living room with the red couch Dad napped on, and my older sister and brother are sitting there with plates of food on their laps and grown-up hands on their shoulders. At least that's what I think they're doing, but I haven't been able to look at them the last few days because I don't recognize their eyes anymore and I can't tell if they know how to talk. I don't want to talk.

In front of me is the kitchen with cooking aunts, and the knees of one of the aunts look just like Mom's knees, and I'm scared if I see them I won't be able to stop myself from hugging that knee, and what if it's the wrong knee? So I just stay in the dining room. I just stay between.

Then someone says my name, and I look up and swallow, and the giant paper globe light is blocked out by a man's bald head. It comes down to my level before he speaks.

"When will I see your first novel, Jules?" the man asks. "You're always watching everything. You're sure to become a writer, just like your dad."

THE SUNDAY MORNING before my college graduation, the phone on the floor by my futon startled me awake.

"Julia?" said my grandmother Rose, my father's mother. She said my name as though she might've called someone else by accident. As though if she had, it would have been their fault.

"Hi, Grandma," I said, trying to sound awake, alert. Alone. She called me most Sundays. I was mostly at the library. Mostly let the answering machine pick up.

"What's new?" she asked. The question was code for *Do you have a boyfriend yet?* I sat up in bed, placed my feet on the cold linoleum floor. Felt a door open somewhere dark.

"Actually, Grandma," I said, "I have news." I turned to Ngoni and smiled, hoping to communicate to him to keep quiet, stay still.

"Oh?" The hope was in her voice now.

"I've met someone."

"What's his name?"

"Well," I said, wondering if she was wearing her hearing aid, hoping not to have to shout, "let me spell it for you."

"What?"

"Let me spell it, you won't recognize it if I just say it." I took a breath. "He's from Zimbabwe."

13

There was a silence then. In it, I knew the folly in that hope I'd held like a shard of glass.

"Colored?" Defeat thick in her voice.

"Yes, Grandma," I said, shifting on the bed so even my profile was hidden from Ngoni. "He's black." I wished I'd said something radical, I wished I'd communicated to my grandmother that my loyalty was to this man next to me in bed. I wished I'd challenged her language, ideas, assumptions. But I didn't know how to. I only knew how to change the subject, so we started making plans for the upcoming weekend—one I was now dreading.

And when she arrived for it, with my aunt and uncle and their children, they all seemed foreign and I couldn't place why any of them had come to my graduation when I hadn't seen most of them in years. I couldn't place how I was meant to treat them. My mother and sister, Ngoni and I, stood in a clutch by their car as they gathered their things and got out. Cold embraces, quiet hugs.

"This is Ngoni," I said to everyone, reaching out my arm to draw him near.

He was elegant and reserved, extending his hand to Rose first, as the eldest. "It is so nice to meet you, Mrs. Wolk," he said.

She turned her face away. Offered him her left hand, in which she clutched a Kleenex. He shook it as though this were the common way, but when he turned and looked back at me, I saw a shadow cross his forehead. I took his hand in both of mine, as though I could rinse it clean of her touch.

"I'm not surprised," my mother said after dinner, as we watched them drive away. "The black woman who cleaned her house was forty years old if she was a day," my mother said, "but Rose called her *the girl.*"

I held Ngoni's hand but couldn't look at his face. I didn't know how this information would settle on his shoulders, if he would be able to join a family with people like that in it. By now I very much wanted him to join my family.

As we lay on my futon late that night, I held his face and apologized. For Rose. For my inability to confront her. For my inability to know what he felt and to help him through it.

"Your grandmother is from a different time," he said to me. "She'll come around."

I nodded at Ngoni, smiled a little. But I wasn't so sure she would.

◆ ◆ ◆

THAT SUMMER I rented a small apartment deep in the woods, bought a frame for the futon and a used dining room table, pots and pans, a few mismatched plates and glasses, and borrowed the old red couch from my mom. It felt like playing house, but I was determined to make it a home. Determined to make it Ngoni's home for his final semester in the U.S. before he returned to Zimbabwe forever. I'd found a job in the college admissions office so I could stay close.

One evening I sat on the couch staring at my hands. Wishing time would stop, wishing this warm night would last forever. Wishing Ngoni would never leave. I'd waited all my life to find my person. I didn't want him ever to leave.

Ngoni came over and held out his hand, leading me to the window. "Look," he said. "Look outside."

"What? I don't see anything."

"Look into the woods."

"I am."

"Look harder."

Then I saw her. In the woods through which we'd crashed an hour before, a small brown deer blended in with the trees. She was standing in the light from the sinking sun, and her white tail caught it. She was not ten feet from me, and yet she was a wild thing. I watched her ears twitch and her head turn as though she knew I saw her. She looked at me and I stood very still and for just one moment closed my eyes. I was playing the game I played as a child—if I don't move a single muscle and close my eyes and can't see you, you can't see me either. If you're peering into our car windows on the highway as you pass, or sitting next to me on the worn red couch after my father's funeral, or standing before me with a book in your hands trying to teach me to read, you cannot see me. I am not here.

When I opened my eyes and let them adjust to the light, the deer had gone back to her meal. I noticed the fading white spots on her back—she was a baby. Then I saw the rest of her family and started to count in my head.

"Eleven," Ngoni whispered. He had seen all of the deer from the beginning. He pointed with his eyes to the buck, larger again by half than the baby. His antlers stood on his head like tree branches that grew from velvet fur, and I understood why I hadn't seen him before. He was at the edge of the group, alternately bending down to chew the blades of grass marking the spot where lawn turned to wilderness and looking up to keep watch. His whole body was alert, even when he ate. Several does stood behind him, their tails flicking as they chewed.

I thought of asking Ngoni if that's what fathers do—stay always alert to the dangers—but my throat hurt the way it hurt at my father's funeral, and I was scared to speak the way I was always scared to speak when I was little. I hoped Ngoni didn't see the tears on my cheeks, and I was almost glad when the spell was broken and something startled them and they ran away in different directions. But the baby was the last one to leave, slower than the rest, and I was sure she went the wrong way.

4

MY FATHER DIED in a psychiatric treatment center in the Berkshire Mountains, one month after his admission. My father died in a place my mother called "the loony bin," and every Saturday morning I watched Looney Tunes and tried to make the world match up.

My sister remembers visiting him in his room at Austen Riggs. Talks about all of his things, his "personal belongings" standing bare on the shelves and windowsills, naked and alone. She says those things on the shelves were what made her so sad. His things, separated from him and home and set there in that space, apart.

Nan says she looked at the things. She doesn't remember if she looked at him. She doesn't tell me now what they were, and at first I picture a television jail cell with pinup posters of pink ladies, a Bible, an awkwardly placed toilet. I have to blink to come back to this place, wipe the slate clear, and put the things of his that she remembers inside the room I know I was in. I see arranged against the backdrop of white walls and windows: toothpaste, shaving lotion, a framed photograph tilted so I can't see who is in it, several little bottles of booze.

It's another conversation and another sister—his—who tells me Riggs allowed its residents to drink. She calls them "residents" and not patients, as I expect. She is, after all, an analyst herself. She says she has learned things about Austen Riggs since his admission, things that would have given her pause had she known them before. That there were no locked wards. That the residents were free to come and go as they pleased. That there were no rules about what they brought into their rooms.

"I thought it was the Bellevue of the Berkshires," she says. "I thought we were putting him somewhere safe," she says. "I thought they could help him," she says. And then, after a moment, she says, "This was a preventable death." As though it's the fault of those lenient laws or those tiny bottles of booze.

All I remember about Riggs is the thick red carpet and the brown rounded tips of my beat-up winter boots.

THE FACTS I learned about my father in the years before and just after his death were spare. He grew up in Brooklyn, the first child of a Jewish couple whose parents fled Poland and Russia early in the persecution. He was smart, went to Cornell when he was sixteen. After he met my mother—a WASP from Albany—at the Riviera Bar in the Village in the sixties, they traveled by boat to Tangier and then by train to Rome, where they lived for six or seven months. When they returned to the States, they eloped to the shores of Lake George in part because his parents would never accept my mother as his bride if she didn't convert; Judaism is passed on to the children from the mother, not the father. And they eloped in part because it wasn't the first wedding for either of them.

I knew he suffered from eczema, which sometimes covered his body from his head to his feet. I knew he was funny. I knew he was handsome. I knew he had a thick red mustache despite the black mop on his head.

And I knew he was a writer who had published some novels under his own name—George Wolk—and many more under various pseudonyms. I don't remember a time when I didn't understand that word, or that pulp fiction was called that because of the thick, cheap paper it was printed on, revealing its true worth. Did I know that when they lived in Rome, both of my parents wrote trashy novels under names not their own? Of course. But that was just something to talk about at a dinner party with loud laughter and tarnished sentimentality, my siblings and I squished along the top stair, elbows on knees, chins in hands. It was just part of the fabric of the past and, like any child who thinks her family is the only kind of family, I assumed it was nothing unique. *You mean your folks didn't write novels under pseudonyms in the sixties? Are you sure?*

I knew that my father had renounced Judaism and was seeking en-lightenment when he went to a Buddhist retreat in the mountains—a trip of ten days, from which he returned transformed indeed, but not in the way he had hoped. I knew that after some time—a year and half, maybe—of trying to live with those transformations, he allowed him-self to be admitted to Austen Riggs. And I knew that when that place was unable to quiet the voices or the depression, he hanged himself in his hospital room.

◆   ◆   ◆

THE TATTERED YELLOW quilt is tucked up to my chin. It's dark out-side Nan's bedroom windows. I've never been in here this early in the morning. Josh is next to me on the bed, our backs up against the wall, the quilt pulled high around us, my head on his shoulder. Why were we called here? Nan scoots back to sit up but stays under her own blanket. Apart. The quilt is soft against my face. My thumb is in my mouth, my eyelids are droopy. I don't hear the words Mom says, but when she speaks them we know he is dead.

5

AFTER NGONI RETURNED to Zimbabwe, our connection was dependent on weekly phone calls and nightly letters. This is how I learned about the demonstrations and strikes raging on his university's campus, how I learned that one day tear gas forced him back from the campus gates. Soon classes were canceled, and he described his days alone in the house where he grew up, trying to find a plan. No university to attend, no diploma in reach, no graduate school applications he was qualified to fill out, no way out. Just a love across the ocean who thought she saw a possibility. With a crackling phone line covering the distance between us, a conversation in which each word arrived a beat after it was spoken, I could hear something new in his voice, which typically betrayed so little. It sounded like fear.

"How long can I sit around doing nothing?"

I squeezed the phone to my ear and took a breath before speaking. "We could get married," I said, my voice quieter than I intended.

A pause. So I filled it. "You could come here and marry me."

Another beat, so I said, "We would figure out school from here."

"Yes," he said, though it felt like hours waiting. "Yes," he said, and I could hear a new sound now—was it hope? "We could get married."

It was the only thing I ever wanted anyway.

ONE SPRING MORNING when everything was decided and the paper-work all but completed, when families on either side of the world were clapping at the news, I climbed into my car and drove a couple of hours south to see my father's mother for a conversation that had to happen in person. My grandmother Rose stood in her black slacks and silk blouse, her old lady flats, her short gray hair, her compact five feet no inches, at the head of the tarmac path that led to the front door of her retirement village condo. It could have been 1978, this scene was so familiar.

"You're delicious," she said, and squeezed my cheeks like I was tiny. Except now there was no one behind me waiting to be squeezed and made to squirm. I was here alone, heavy with my task.

I followed her into the air-conditioning and sat on the couch in her icy-white living room. The coffee table was made of glass. There were glass sculptures backlit on bookshelves. There was a glass door to a patio I'd never stepped on. When I was little, I'd wander from here into the bathroom to pee, linger there and lift every cloisonné clamshell lid in search of treasure. Pause at the bookcases in the back hallway and check for her footsteps before crouching down on my knees to read the names of the authors of the books on the bottom shelf. Josh said they were Dad's, and I worried that if I didn't memorize them on these visits, Dad really would disappear. Cheryl Nash. Barney Parrish. Walter Bond. I didn't know then that Dad's most prolific pseudonym was miss-ing from his mother's shelves, I didn't know then that my father wrote more than these titles to pay the mortgage.

I'd sneak further back into her bedroom to scare myself at her shrine. Giant portraits of my grandfather and my dad hanging on the wall by her bed. Grandpa's hair was gray but his skin was smooth, and there was his nose like a mountainside on his face. I'd peer in as close as I could get to see if I could spot the scar—Mom said he'd tried to cut it off with scissors when he was little. Cecil died a year after his son, died of esophageal cancer a year after his son hanged himself. Died of esophageal cancer after not smoking a day in his life.

Dad's portrait was different. It was taken outside in the snow, and his puffy seventies jacket and transition lenses and slight smile ached because I knew them so well. This picture was meant to appear on the back flap of a book he never published. Even as a kid I knew where Mom kept the negatives. I used to search them for clues. In high school I got one printed, kept it hidden between books in my bedroom. He's sitting on the top of a picnic table in a yard I don't recognize, he's smiling like there's something funny. How can Rose bear to have these portraits hanging on the wall, looking at her all night long? Doesn't she want to forget?

"Where shall we eat?" Rose said to me when I sat on her couch. It was a trick question, because there was only one place she thought good enough.

"That place you like," I said. "But before we go, there's something I need to tell you." My hands shook and my face was too hot. I was ready for the slap this time. She took her round pink plastic glasses off her face and looked at me steadily. "Ngoni and I are getting married."

There was a pause before the tears. I sat with my hands in my lap, tea cold on the table, and felt myself get distant from that place, from her pain. I almost wanted to laugh. If this was going to make her sad, I decided in that moment, I was sad for her. But I was not sad. *This is a ridiculous thing to cry over,* I wanted to scream. *I've found my person after all my life not having my person! If this makes you cry,* I wanted to tell her, *then cry. But I will sit here next to you and smile.* I saw her then as if she were very far, and I didn't come back to meet her.

After a while she got up and walked to the kitchen, so I got up too, and found her standing at the counter with something large and glass in her hands. A vase or a bowl. It looked heavy.

"Where will the children be?" she shouted as I walked in. "That is what I want to know!"

She slumped into a chair at the table, her back hunched and heaving, and I didn't know where to put my body, where to put my eyes. So I focused on the large glass bowl in her lap. She was curled around it like a baby. It was clear and the glass looked very thick. I'd never seen anything like it, but it reminded me of the thick glass countertops in the bank my mother used when I was little. As she filled out small rectangular strips of paper with a pen attached to a chain, I stood with my eyes just exactly at the counter level, staring into the thick green glass edge. I'd then pile onto tippy-toes to see that from the top all was clear. Back and forth, thick green glass edge, all clear on top. A magic trick, an illusion. I repeated it again and again, rolling up and down on my toes. The bowl in my grandmother's lap held this same illusion—purple edging curled into handles like a basket, clear from another angle. I focused on the edges, the thick purple edges I couldn't see through. They were the color my skin turned with a bad bruise.

"Where will the children be?" she said again.

I sighed.

"That's what I asked your father," she said quietly.

"That's what I asked your father!" she shouted.

"But Grandma," I said, thankful now for a script. Thankful for her reference to what she considered the other mixed marriage in her life— my parents'. "Look at me! I'm fine. I'm happy and I live in a world that doesn't wonder what I am. By the time we have children, their world won't be as divided as yours has always been." How naïve to think this, but how could I have known?

She wouldn't look at me. She just shook her head. Continued to cry. Was it an hour before she spoke? A day?

"There's nothing I can do to convince you?" she asked finally, and I watched her free hand fold and refold a cloth napkin on the table. I looked at her clear nail polish, her papery white skin. Wondered if the bowl would tumble out of her lap onto the floor and smash to bits. Wondered who would clean it up.

"Convince me?" I asked.

"Because if you marry him," she said and looked at me, her round eyes narrowed to slits, "don't ever come to me. Don't ever come to me again."

I knew then that I never had to eat soggy chicken parmesan at a crappy Italian restaurant again in my life. I saw the exit map and I wanted to follow it. I could get out of this condo, forever. I pushed my chair back and stood up. Walked to the door.

"Julia," she said behind me.

I turned and saw her there, small and sour. Did I want her to take it back? Did I want her to come through herself and back to me? Did I turn because she was my grandmother, because she was my father's mother, because once when I was small we stood together at his grave and cried? She could have made it right with a word.

But instead she shoved the glass bowl into my hands. I grabbed onto it because I didn't want it to smash my toes. I grabbed onto it because I didn't want it to smash her toes. I grabbed onto it because she shoved it into my hands and I couldn't do any other thing.

We looked at each other for a moment, but there were no more words. So I turned and walked out the door with my gift. But once out onto route 84, I pulled into a rest stop, opened the driver's-side door, and placed the glass bowl on the black pavement. Looked at it in the rearview mirror as I drove away, an illusion of light in the afternoon sun.

BY THE TIME I joined the Taconic Parkway an hour later, almost safely returned to my apartment in the woods, singing along with Joni Mitchell with the sun shining and my eyes alert for deer in the median, I felt a familiar tap on my shoulder.

"It's just a muscle spasm," I said aloud, though I'd never before pretended to believe the tap on my shoulder was anything but what I knew it was. My dad, reminding me he's here.

I steadied my hands on the wheel and pulled myself up a little so I could see the backseat rather than the road behind me. I startled hard and swerved into the other lane, looked back to the road to right the car. Took a deep breath.

"No one was there, Jules." I said this out loud, too. But I saw him there in black lines and fuzzy shapes and tan cloth-covered car seats. Was he in the car with me, or hovering just outside?

I pulled into a rest stop that invites tourists to park and gaze at the view. Turned around in my seat and looked bravely into the back, convinced I'd be able to tell that he had been there, certain I'd see mustaches and transition lenses and a mop of curly black hair. Lying in the backseat maybe, giggling like a girl.

But of course the backseat was empty. So I stepped out and walked around the car a couple of times, held tight to the bike rack and stretched my arms long, arched my back to open it. "It was just a fucking muscle spasm," I muttered under my breath before I got back in the car and pointed it toward home.

6

"TURN IN HERE," Ngoni said as he touched my elbow to steer me into a small restaurant with tables and chairs lined up along a narrow window, a counter at the back. "This is the place I learned about fish and chips."

We were just off the bus from Cardiff to Llantwit Major, in Wales, where Ngoni went to high school. Our fiancé visa application required forms signed by city officials in each of the places he'd lived, and we managed to make a reunion out of this one. We hadn't seen each other in six months, and it seemed worth the credit card debt to meet here for a week to spend some time together before the wedding. Make sure we meant it.

I looked around at the people in the little Welsh café and thought about Ngoni's uncle Dakarai, if he'd ever eaten here. If any of the people here knew him. Dakarai had married a Welsh woman he'd met at Oxford, but all I knew was that it didn't last. All I knew was what Ngoni had written to me about Dakarai these last months.

"Me being here helps my grandparents' burden with Dakarai," he wrote in one letter. I'd not known there was a burden with Dakarai. "Dakarai talks to himself sometimes now," he wrote in another. "Dakarai broke down the door in his bedroom," in a third. I sensed fear in Ngoni's tidy blue cursive words but didn't know how to hold it. This wasn't a topic we could talk about on the phone, Ngoni standing in the hallway of his family home. So in my private thoughts about Ngoni's uncle I used words I'd applied to my own father, and which Ngoni sometimes used to discuss his—mental illness, schizophrenia. But I didn't know if Dakarai's illness was like that of his older brother Donal, Ngoni's dad. If he was, did that mean the illness snaked through this family I was marrying into, as it snaked through my own?

"Tell me more about Dakarai and Cati," I said to Ngoni as we sat in that Welsh café, unable to ask what was really on my mind.

"There isn't very much to tell." His face looked weary. "They met at university, at Oxford. They got married in Zimbabwe."

Now I had different questions. What was that wedding like? How did his grandparents, who raised Ngoni and whom I had not yet met, treat *that* white daughter-in-law? I looked across at my fiancé, his soft face, his stoic eyes, the newspaper greasy in his hands, but I couldn't ask any questions at all because thoughts about race and mental illness were mixing up inside me and I wasn't sure which topic to pursue, wasn't sure which topic I really wanted to know more about. Nothing felt safe.

"When they moved back to the U.K., he couldn't find a job, the marriage fell apart. So he returned to Zimbabwe."

That conversation we'd had in my dorm room about Ngoni's father came back to me in a solid beat. How his grandparents had sent him—a child in grade school—to a traditional healer in the bush whom they'd hired to heal his father. Father and son spent weeks there, drinking and expelling medicines, hoping to also expel the evil spirit, because "the spirit that possesses the father possesses the son as well," he had told me. I wondered now if the family took Dakarai to a traditional healer to expel his spirits, too. If the spirit that possesses a man also possesses his brother. Dakarai went to the best private high school in Zimbabwe, was its first black head boy, studied at Oxford. As Ngoni reminded me of this, I realized that maybe my future in-laws didn't believe in just one thing. Maybe they lived in two worlds. They'd blamed spirits for possessing Ngoni's father, but maybe this time they'd blamed something else.

"If he'd been able to find a job, become productive," Ngoni said, "he and Cati would have been fine. He would still be living here." He stood up, wiped his hands on a thin paper napkin, wrapped up the newspapers with our other trash, and tossed it all into the overflowing bin. "It's as simple as that."

It didn't seem simple, but something stopped me from saying so. The same thing that stopped me from asking about the first interracial wedding in his family or what it was like to live with Dakarai now, even though we were alone in Wales and I could have asked him anything. What kept me quiet that day? Fear of admitting that I was scared for our future and what we might pass on to our children? Anxieties about not having the right language for our racial and cultural differences? Naïveté and my assumption that everything would be fine because we loved each other?

◆   ◆   ◆

HERE IS A list of what I carry: One of my father's cousins killed himself when he was twenty-four. One of my father's cousins lived in an institution most of her adult life. One of my father's cousins died of cancer but took pills every day to quiet the voices. One of my father's cousins mixed cyanide with orange juice and fed it to her son, to her dog, to herself.

Some of the survivors whisper that the disease followed their parents from the shtetl. Some of the survivors whisper that the disease can't be traced because it died in the camps. Some of the survivors whisper that the disease started after the war. Some of the survivors whisper that it lingers now in our blood.

One of the survivors called me when our first son was born and told me that now my worries would really begin.

7

THANKSGIVING 1998. My sister kept me company in my mother's upstairs bedroom in the house on State Street, where we'd grown up.
She was laughing and telling stories as we waited for the cue that the
wedding could begin. I looked in the mirror and pretended to check
my hair, but really I watched the room behind me and the memories
it held. The big white bed I slept in most nights for most of my childhood, afraid that if I wasn't with her, my mother would die in the dark.
The old pine bureau that made me smell mothballs just looking at it,
where I knew the neatly folded wool sweaters were waiting their turn
to be pulled over her head. The windows were cracked open a bit, letting in the sounds from the street below, busier now than it was when
I was little. And then Nan's pretty face smiling at me, holding up the
dress she helped me choose and telling me it was time to put it on. As
I stepped in and she zipped it up, I heard the click of a camera and saw
that my sister-in-law had come in, all smiles and warm embraces and
loud laughter.

"What's the holdup?" Michele called from behind the camera, loud
even though I was right there, in front of the mirror attached to the
inside of the closet door. When I was little, what I loved best was that
my mother's closet was a tunnel that led to the other side of the house.
A much shorter walk from my bedroom to hers, the push of hanging

clothes rough then smooth against my face, the smells of the silks and wools and velvets she hadn't worn, even then, for years and years.

"James isn't here yet," I told Michele, naming the one guest on Ngoni's side besides his best man, the only other African in attendance, one of twenty people at that small wedding at my mom's house. We had no money to bring his family over from Zimbabwe for this day. We told ourselves we'd celebrate there as soon as we could. "The bus from Boston is late," I said. "We'll wait."

I looked out the window and saw it was getting dark, saw we should be married by now. I could hear the sounds of the gathering party downstairs and wondered what Ngoni was doing, who he was talking to, if he was nervous like me. The women around me laughed and told stories, and I loved them but they were far away. Something was missing, and it wasn't until I said it that I knew what it was.

"Can someone get Mom?" I hadn't seen her all day.

She came up trailing the smell of the white lasagna she was cooking, her lavender dress creased where the apron strings were tied. She was filled with family, happy to have all of her people there, excited for an excuse to celebrate.

Mom said, "Yes?" as she walked toward me, in the way she used to say, "Yes?" when I'd called to her from my sixth-grade bedroom wondering if the laundry was clean.

"I just thought you might want to say something to me before . . ." It was hard to say the words. She looked at me and smiled. Her sea-blue eyes were clear, open, guarded. I wondered how my hazel-greens matched up.

She paused before saying, "I do." And then it was too late to stop her. "I want to tell you that you don't have to do this if you don't want to."

This wasn't what I meant, this wasn't the story I wanted to hear, but of course it was the only story she could tell me in that moment, and I should have known better before asking. I'd heard this story so many times I could have told it to myself.

"No one ever said that to me before I got married, and I want to make sure someone says it to you. Do you want to do this?"

WHEN MY PARENTS met at the Riviera, a bar in the Village, early in 1967, they were both still married to other people. Mom was a "copy girl" at the publication she still calls *Sporty Illustrations,* and Dad was an editor at Tower Books, a "factory of paperback originals." He saw contracts go out to writers he was sure he could best, and he soon hatched a plan to get one himself, to fund a trip to Africa and Europe where he could become "a real writer." It had worked for Hemingway. He got my mom a contract, too, and they typed their way across the Atlantic on a freighter with cheap fare. I have a picture of them leaning against the railing, the wind blowing my mom's long straight hair across her face, my dad's white shirt flapping against his tan skin, his sunglasses dark on his face.

They spent some weeks living in Tangier before settling in Rome, where they wrote novels to fulfill the first contracts and got new contracts to write more. It seemed this could be a great way to make a living. Letters from Mom to her parents from that time reveal plans to live there indefinitely. Those letters don't mention the annulment my mother's father helped her organize before she left, but they do make it sound as if Mom and Dad kept separate apartments, as if it were a funny and sometimes irritating coincidence that George was also living in Rome. Really they shared a rooftop apartment above a restaurant. Had their mail delivered to the American Express office.

Six months into the trip, something happened and my mother returned to the U.S. alone. Sometimes she says she was expected home for Christmas. Sometimes she says she was fleeing a failing relationship. She says, "Anyway, your dad wanted to stay in Europe to *confront his art,*" using air quotes so I know it's not her phrase. She says, "Anyway, I was just sure it wasn't going to work out with us."

But my father had another idea. Within a few months, he'd returned to New York with plans to win her back. She says when he emerged from the airplane "he was covered from head to toe with eczema," and the implication is that this manifestation of his heartbreak on his skin softened her, broke *her* heart, brought her back to him.

By the time she took him to Albany to meet her parents, it was summer. Dad's skin had cleared up and his position in her life was safe. My grandmother—black sleeveless dress, black stockings and pumps—stood tall in the doorway of her suburban home as my folks climbed out of the car. My dad had a good six inches on her, but that didn't make her short. He approached slowly and stayed on the lower step.

He bowed low before exclaiming, "My God, it's Mrs. Robinson." She loved him from the first.

I wonder what my trim, silver-haired grandfather thought of this charming stranger, his mop of untamed black hair, his thick rusty mustache. Was he as quick to hand over his firstborn again so soon? I can almost see him there, just inside the house mixing a gin and tonic and muttering to himself about this stranger's saccharine words seeping through the screen.

After dinner that night—I picture smoked salmon on simple white china—Mom and Dad headed north. They landed at a motel on the shores of Lake George and eloped in the morning.

"I WANT TO do this," I said to my mom in her bedroom. My voice was smaller and less confident than I intended. Maybe she hugged me before she headed back to the party. Watching her go, I felt a familiar yearning, a wish to call her back to me, to ask her to take me up into her arms and tell me that everything was going to be all right. But just as I'd learned to do when I was little, I shut that feeling out, turned to my face in the mirror, pasted on a smile.

Then it wasn't long before someone told me that James had arrived, that it was time. I walked to the top of the stairs and stood where we used to sit and listen to their dinner parties when we were tiny, and I could hear Dad's deep voice and loud laughter wafting up at me through the years, and for a moment I lost my balance and thought the heels on these stupid shoes were too damn high. I grabbed the banister with my shaking left hand, looked down and saw my brother smiling up at me. His face blurred and he was Dad, hair longer and smile broader and shoulders wider.

When I reached the bottom of the stairs, it was Josh's voice that whispered, "You look beautiful," but maybe it sounded like Dad. I smiled and blushed and Michele snapped the camera, but the flash didn't go off and I knew the picture was lost, the one picture I ever would have seen of me and my dad. Tears sprang to my eyes as I rounded the corner and there was my aunt Libby in her striped dress.

"Does anyone have a Kleenex?" she asked. "Jules and I have this thing." Her voice wavered as she, right there in the middle of me

walking down this makeshift aisle, reminded us of all the Thanks-
givings during which we've cried when we caught each other's eye as
someone spoke aloud the Robert Burns poem before the meal. I realized no one said it this year—we were so preoccupied with the wedding
a few days away—and as if to make up for the neglect, or to bring
myself back into this moment, I said it in my head as I crossed my
childhood living room:

> Some hae meat and canna eat,
> And some wad eat that want it,
> But we hae meat and we can eat,
> And sae the Lord be thankit.

But do I have meat or do I want it? Which one am I in the poem? Because how it feels is that something is missing, and even when there's a
feast on the table I'm hungry and alone.

When I arrived at the front of the room, the windowsills heavy
with purple day lilies, Ngoni, Kathleen the priest, my beautiful sister
Nan, and Dave the blond best man were each looking my way, and
I had to shake out those thoughts and return. I focused on Ngoni's
herringbone suit, his black hair cut short to his head, his tidy wire-rim
glasses, the deep browns of his skin and eyes coming together in a shy
smile. His cheek twitched just a little.

Kathleen looked at me long before she told what she said might
be an apocryphal story. "In antiquity," she said, "when a marriage procession and a funeral procession came together at an intersection," she
said, "the marriage procession had the right of way."

I was conjugating verbs in my head, left turns and triangles and
ceremonies not my own. She saw my confusion, Kathleen the priest,
and so explained it to let me catch up.

"The story tells us that love is more powerful than death." She joined
our hands there in front of the family who knew what she meant.

Then it was Ngoni's turn, and he took out the papers on which
he'd typed up some words from the book of Ruth: "Intreat me not
to leave thee, or to return from following after thee: for whither thou
goest, I will go; and where thou lodgest, I will lodge: thy people shall
be my people, and thy God my God."

I was too hot and couldn't focus my eyes and my head was thumping and pumping. I turned to Nan and asked for the John Donne book she was holding, opened it to the page I'd marked, but the book shook in my hands and I couldn't see the words, so I took a deep breath and tried to get steady.

> If ever any beauty I did see,
> Which I desir'd, and got, t'was but a dreame of thee. . . .
> My face in thine eye, thine in mine appeares,
> And true plaine hearts doe in the faces rest,
> Where can we finde two better hemispheares
> Without sharpe North, without declining West?
> What ever dyes, was not mixt equally;
> If our two loves be one, or, thou and I
> Love so alike, that none doe slacken, none can die.

Dad wasn't mixt equally, I wanted to scream. Our loves be so alike, you and I, I wanted to whisper. But when I looked across the space that separated me from Ngoni, I couldn't tell if he saw me anymore. If he wanted to take my hand.

Kathleen burned brimstone, filling the house with smoke and the smell of sulfur. Rings were exchanged, vows spoken, our hands were wrapped together in a colorful stole as Kathleen declared that those whom God has brought together no man can put asunder. But when I kissed him, for the smallest moment, it felt like make-believe.

Until my aunt Annie said, "Doesn't it make you want to clap?" and there was loud applause and we stood in the living room closed in by walls my father Sheetrocked, surrounded by the people who raised me or came up with me there in that house on State Street, and I came back into myself and then I clapped, too.

When it came time for the toasts, Ngoni gathered me up by his side and wrapped his arm around me, and the people in the room formed a circle around us. He said, using his teacher voice, "In Zimbabwe, where I'm from," as though anyone there didn't know where he was from, "it is believed that when a person dies, his soul goes to the wind."

I heard Annie moan just a little. I felt Ngoni's arm tighten around my shoulder. "I would like to toast the winds that brought us together."

And then I knew that he felt it too, our dads blowing by in the November night. They were there for me and they were there for Ngoni, and we couldn't see through them to us but we knew that everyone was there to help us try to see through them to us. We knew that we would try to see through them.

THAT NIGHT IN the hotel room I had the dream again. The one I had the night I met Ngoni. The one where my dad is really alive. This time he was a homeless man in my hometown. I came upon him in the dark cold entranceway to the old record store on Main Street. I'd walked by him my whole childhood and not seen him.

We talked for hours, and by the end I understood why he had to do it, why he had to make us believe he was dead. I promised to keep the secret and I walked around the next morning proud that he chose me, proud of this secret only I could hold.

8

THREE YEARS LATER, Ngoni and I sat huddled on an airplane hurtling ever closer to Harare for my first visit to Zimbabwe. His immigration status was tenuous even after we got married, and until his paperwork was in order it didn't seem wise to leave the country. We had brought his grandparents—Gogo and Sekuru, who'd raised him—to visit us a couple of years before, so I knew there would be some familiar faces when we arrived. But for the most part I spent that plane ride wondering what these weeks would hold. What it would feel like to see Ngoni in his place. What it would feel like to be the outsider.

The plane was filled with Zimbabweans, and I watched them talk to their children and their spouses and their elderly parents thinking about where they'd been, if they were returning to stay. I listened to their voices when they spoke Shona and tried to discern syllables I recognized from Ngoni's phone calls with his grandparents. I listened to their voices when they spoke English and tried to hear words that would answer my questions. I lowered my eyes when they caught me looking and wondered what they thought about me, white and American, by Ngoni's side. If they were angry, if they saw me as having taken one of their own.

Ngoni flipped through a loose stack of pictures of home I didn't know he'd stowed in his carry-on, and I was eager to see, too. I leaned closer and looked first at a picture of a house made of red bricks painted white. Then one of large grassy grounds that I would call a lawn, but when he pointed at it, he said, "I miss that garden." There was a banana tree ripe with fruit, a bed of pink and yellow and maroon flowers circling it, a swimming pool in the background. Next I saw a wide-angle shot of the whole grounds and noticed two small buildings near the main house and tall corn plants growing in a plot behind, a cement-colored wall surrounding the property.

As the plane got closer to the ground, I shifted my focus to where I was going and gazed out the window at a patchwork of fields and farmland cut into squares and rectangles and trapezoids. It wasn't as tidy as those in the Midwest I'd flown over, but each plot seemed monstrous from here, bigger than any land I could imagine. There were clusters of trees in some spots and brown lines long across the land marking roads. It was all so flat and extended out so far.

When we landed and were allowed to stand and pull our bags onto our backs, my legs felt weak underneath me. Like they might not know how to carry me through the exit tunnel and into the airport. A wave of exhaustion and fear of everything I did not know almost took me under, but I clapped my eyes on Ngoni's back and followed, and once through I saw high glass walls and a sharp dark carpet on the floor and tourist booths advertising adventure trips. The customs lines were separate, and Ngoni with his Zimbabwean passport went one way while I went the other. I was supposed to be ready for this but still worried that one of us wouldn't come out the other end. I counted and recounted the cash in my wallet, certain I would be wrong about the expectations and not have the exact change I'd heard was required for the entry visa. But the customs agent was polite and didn't stumble on the contradiction of my Shona surname and white skin, and when he stamped my book and told me to enjoy my stay in Zimbabwe, I walked out and there was Ngoni, waiting.

"We have nothing to declare," he said as we passed through a wide, open door with our luggage piled onto a cart, and I thought of the different ways to interpret that phrase. Ngoni just meant we weren't carrying anything valuable, but I wanted him to mean that I didn't need to explain my presence in this country. I wanted him to mean I would fit here.

On the other side of the doorway was a woman in a business suit who knew Ngoni. I watched him greet her as though they saw each other every day. I waited to be introduced, but instead he just stopped talking for a moment and in the empty space she said, "Hello, Julia."

"Hi," I said, confused. Who was this? No one was offering hands to shake, so I took a moment to watch, to see if I could figure this out on my own. This woman who knew my name wore her hair in long, neat braids pulled back into a bun. Her skin was darker than Ngoni's, and she had high cheekbones and sparkling, almond-shaped eyes. Her laugh was loud and inviting, and I wanted so much to know her, to know who she was. But we hadn't been introduced, and I didn't know enough about Shona culture yet to understand the reason for that. I just assumed that if she knew me, I should know her. So when they walked toward the large open doorway and the bustle beyond, I grabbed the handle of my suitcase and followed. Outside, I was surprised by the bright sun and how fast I had to walk to keep up, searching in my hand-bag for sunglasses I knew were packed in my suitcase. My winter skin was tight in the heat.

When we got to a car and the woman climbed into the driver's seat and Ngoni into the passenger's, I realized this must be his aunt. She was just a couple of years older than we were, but her confidence and her connection with my husband intimidated me. As we drove out of the parking lot, they spoke to each other in Shona, and I tried to push aside the worry that this was how it would feel here. Tried to push aside that familiar fear of being left alone. I felt around in the backseat of the dusty old sedan for a seatbelt, and when I couldn't find one I looked up front to see Ngoni wasn't wearing one either. Decided to stop looking. The windows were down and the hot air pushed into my face and blew my hair back, and soon we were driving fast enough that I couldn't hear the sounds from the front seat, so I distracted myself with what was out the window, this landscape like nothing I knew.

Ngoni had told me what to expect. He'd warned me about Ameri-can stereotypes of thatched-roof huts, pervasive poverty, AIDS every-where. He'd told me instead about swimming pools and large houses on large grounds, about beautiful suburban streets lined with jacaranda trees and a modern city center. He wanted to help me shake out the images of Africa I'd grown up hearing, but the result was a different kind of surprise. When we left the multiple-lane highway that led away from the airport and entered the outskirts of the city, I saw townships lining the street, wooden slabs of wall hitched together, canvas roofs, house after house after house lined up and falling down. Crowds of people walking along the sides of the road, their feet bare even when they wore business suits.

The road from the airport took us straight through downtown, and I gazed up at tall buildings and into shopping centers curled around parking lots filled with people. Soon we passed rows of white clapboard apartment buildings lined along side streets, then into suburban neighborhoods with houses I couldn't see because they sat behind cement-colored walls like those in the photos, wide gates at each driveway. Now there were fewer pedestrians, fewer cars, and I thought it looked like a dusty Santa Barbara without the mountains or the sea. Though the jacaranda trees lining the roads weren't in bloom, I could imagine their lacy lavender petals shading our drive if they were. And there were all kinds of other flowers exploding out of their leaves and lining the streets despite the dry heat, light yellow blossoms that looked like cowbells and bright red bursts that sat on bushes otherwise plain. It looked tropical and felt like a desert, the abundance of color tamped down by the dust tracks on the road.

I knew we'd arrived at the house on Marlborough Drive when we turned off a quiet, winding road and idled before a large black metal gate. Ngoni's aunt tooted the horn and I looked at my husband's face for signs that he was home, that I would finally see him in his place. But he wasn't smiling. He was waiting.

Soon there was a loud rumble and clatter and the metal wall in front of us began to move, though I couldn't see by whose hands. As the gate yawned open, it revealed the wide lawn I recognized from the pictures, the banana tree and the flowers, and a metal cage exactly the size of a sedan in the middle of the driveway. It looked like a birdcage, and it took me a moment to realize that the need to protect a car from the elements is a luxury, but protecting it from thieves, a necessity.

As I climbed out of the backseat of the car, I thought that the house seemed smaller than it had in the photos. The swimming pool was empty and cracked and filled with dust from disuse. I tried not to look at it for too long, tried not to reveal my disappointment or ask if we could get it fixed before we left. It was so hot here, and a pool would give me a place to be if I started to feel unsteady. Water has always connected me back to myself. Instead I turned back to the gate to see who'd let us in, and there was a tall man, skinny in his jeans and sweatshirt. Ngoni's uncle Dakarai.

I wanted to introduce myself, thank him for letting us in, but he was making himself busy relocking the gate. He stayed apart from the group and looked down at the plants that lined the driveway as though the red and green leaves might hold a message. His hand reached up to his mouth and I thought I saw his lips moving behind it.

When I turned back toward the house, there was Gogo walking with her arms outstretched. She sang to herself, unable to contain her excitement. She was bold and glittering in a pink-and-gold-patterned dress and matching headscarf, bracelets tinkling on her arms, skin shining, lips pursed in ululation. She walked past her grandson as though he wasn't standing there and grabbed me up into herself. Rocked me back and forth, back and forth, in the same welcoming dance she'd led me in at JFK the day we met. She said into my ear in her deep soothing voice, "Julia! Julia! You are finally here," and this was a welcome so big and bright I didn't know how to respond. I surrendered to her laughter, joined in, stopped trying to figure everything out and just let myself be in this new place. Over her shoulder, I saw Ngoni smile. Sekuru stood next to his grandson, smiling too, and soon made his way over to me. I remembered just in time that in Shona culture, women don't hug men they're not married to, and so, despite the connection we formed when they visited us a couple of years ago, I could only shake Sekuru's hand now. He wore black pants and dress shoes, a button-front shirt and a tie. The circle of dyed-black hair that wound around his head like a crown was slightly narrower than it had been when we first met, and as I looked into his face I remembered how much it reminded me of Ngoni's. Although Sekuru's face was round and Ngoni's narrow, although his cheeks formed apples under his eyes when he smiled and Ngoni's stayed flat, although he was shades darker than his grandson and didn't wear glasses, there was something in the way they each extended their bottom lips when they were finished making their point, and in the unison of their voices and their hands when they spoke. How when they looked at your face it felt as if their eyes went all the way through.

Soon we were ushered into the house, and I followed Ngoni through a dining room with an oval table and mismatched chairs, paint peeling from the walls by the ceiling but otherwise a pretty Easter-egg green. Then into the living room, which was large and dark. It took a moment for my eyes to adjust, and when they did, I saw Dakarai sitting with the woman from the car, Ngoni's aunt. They were arranged on the dark green couch like teenagers, and soon Gogo and Sekuru joined them. Ngoni led me from one to the next for my formal introductions. I started with Sekuru and Gogo, whom I knew but whom I still needed to greet. I stood in front of them for a moment, took their hands in mine, thanked them for inviting me here. Then I turned to Dakarai, who shook my hand and said it was nice to finally meet me. When I came at last to Tendai, she shook my hand too, but didn't say anything much. It was in her eyes, the message that we were in this together. *We already know each other,* she seemed to be saying with her bright smile and wink. *We go way back.*

Gogo told me to sit down, and I watched as everyone in the family bowed their heads together and prayed a prayer of thanks for our safe arrival. When they looked up, Gogo kept her hands together but clapped them slightly, pointing them first to Ngoni and then to me, thanking us for coming. This was our formal welcome—a scene that would repeat in living rooms in Zimbabwe and the U.S. in the years to come. A scene that always seemed, to my American eyes, to come a beat too late. I was so used to welcoming people in kitchens or across the passenger seats of cars, wild hugs and hoots of laughter at the reunion, at the return. The Shona people, I was coming to see, had a formality I'd previously only attributed to Ngoni's personality.

9

A WEEK INTO the trip I found myself disoriented and unsteady between two walls of a florist's shop near the cemetery where Ngoni's
father was buried. There was the surprise of darkness, of cool air,
and the scent of damp dirt under the thatched roof. There were three
women working there, two with babies strapped to their backs with
beach towels, each with what I saw as a sadness in her eyes. They were
seated on three-legged stools, and behind them were wooden shelves
tacked to the walls. On each shelf sat clumps of red carnations pulled
together in small wooden baskets. Zimbabwe exported roses and asters
and chrysanthemums, but in this shop there were only carnations. An
ugly flower. But what did I know, maybe carnations are the traditional
flower for cemeteries. I don't live in a world where we visit the dead,
where we bring them presents.

As Ngoni paid for his basket, I watched the women watch us.
Wondered how they thought we fit. They'd probably seen our wedding
rings, guessed that I was American, that Ngoni lived there with me. But
did they guess at the warmth Gogo and Sekuru, lingering in the shadows by the door, showed me when we were at home? Could they tell I
wanted to melt into the walls of this place, wanted to blend in and fit in
and stop standing out? From where they were watching, could they see
if I might become part of this family?

When we climbed back into the car with our basket, I looked out the window and saw that the cemetery stretched for miles. To my right there was no grass, just land pulled into long, dark mounds. At first I thought it was a garden with small labels describing the crops beneath. But then I realized the tin sheets lashed onto metal stakes marked graves. The land had been recently dug into; the mounds and rows would flatten in time. I couldn't see where it ended. On the horizon, almost too far to see, there were gentle slopes of hills and a burning sunset and the sense that this planet was too big to hold us.

"When people started dying so fast, graveyards expanded in-formally like this," Ngoni said. To my left was the formal cemetery, where the grass was tall and plentiful in spite of the drought. It wasn't green, but a living brown color I didn't recognize, maybe like what wheat looks like before it's mown, vast and tall and windblown. But this wasn't wheat, and it wasn't standing on empty soil. Some graves—those that had been recently visited—were cleared of the long grasses. It was a patchwork quilt. "The Shona don't cremate," Ngoni said. "We have to put our dead in the ground." I imagined the entire country sitting on top of graves some day in the future, the dead taking up all of the available land, houses come alive as in *Polter-geist*, possessions of everyone lucky enough to live past their people. I imagined the whole earth encompassed by ghosts. We pulled in and parked, and the hot air smashed into my face as I stood up in the dusty lot. Despite the heat it was suddenly winter 1980 and I was five years old.

◆ ◆ ◆

I SIT AT the edge of the pew of the college church—the only one that would perform services for a suicide, I heard my mother say into the phone one hundred times this week. I can't look forward, so I look back. Crane my neck around and see the room full of faces. Spot my kindergarten teacher and wonder, *Who's teaching school?*

Later I stand in the cold next to my grandmother, at the foot of the open grave. Her whole body shakes as my grandfather shovels the first dirt onto the coffin. I can't look forward, so I look back. Nan's small face in the triangle of the backseat window of Mom's friend's station wagon. Peeking out. Driving away. Where is she going?

Can I come?

◆ ◆ ◆

I SHOOK MY head to focus on the line we were walking in. Sekuru was in the lead and I was at the back, and we were following a narrow path cut into the grass. I could tell by their murmurings that they didn't see the usual landmarks. Didn't know where to look for their son. I watched Gogo's face to see if she knew where Donal was and wasn't telling, was letting Sekuru find the spot. But her face revealed no secrets, and we kept walking. At last Sekuru saw something familiar and signaled to the groundskeeper, who came with his scythe. I watched Sekuru watch the man and thought *He looks old today.* His eyes were bloodshot, his belly hung over his belt. As if he knew I was watching, he stood up taller, shifted his weight. I wondered if it was shame he was shouldering. If visiting that place that preserved his son's memory also preserved his sadness, his illness, and his defeat. I wondered if it looked the same on me. If the reason we never visited Dad's grave was the fear that people driving by the cemetery would see by the set of our shoulders that he was a suicide. I wondered how Sekuru handled it, his family broken. I wondered how I did.

It would take some time for the groundskeeper to clear the grave, even though he was being careful to clear only Donal's spot. As he settled into the task, Ngoni and his grandparents went in one direction, to visit the grave of a more distant relative, and I went in the other. I walked along the red clay pathways peering at the ground. Separated stalks of grass in search of a rock. It was a Jewish tradition I wasn't raised with, didn't understand, had never done before. But it was a tradition I seemed to need to do then. Find a rock to place on the grave. I would just need one, but soon realized the entire cemetery was built on clay, so I reached down and picked up what I hoped was a substantial enough clump of red earth and joined them at the foot of Donal's grave.

I bowed my head when they did, but couldn't close my eyes. It was a lie I was unwilling to tell in Gogo's presence—pretending to pray. I wished I could answer her questions about Jesus. About if I believed. Instead, I squeezed my lump of earth to make it firm and focused on my unpainted toenails exposed in my sandaled feet and listened to Gogo speak to her God. She bowed her head, and her wire-rimmed glasses slipped down her delicate nose. Grief kept her voice quiet, and I wanted to reach over to soothe her, I wanted to steady her. But I stayed still as she prayed. Gogo clutched her small purse between fingers wrinkled and dark with age, her thin wedding band loose on her finger. But my eyes couldn't focus, and it was Mom's ring I saw through tears, a diamond and two sapphires tipping to the wrong side of her hand as she stirred the sugar into her cup of black coffee. I was ten.

◆   ◆   ◆

I'VE ASKED MY mother one hundred times to bring me there, but each time the answer is the same. "He's not at the cemetery, kiddo."

I'm smart enough not to ask where he is, then. Because I would go anywhere. Instead I bide my time, and when my grandmother Rose visits, I climb on wobbly legs into her car. It's a wide Oldsmobile with red pleather seats and it smells like an old person, and she makes me slide all the way across the front seat until I am right up next to her in that spot where the gearshift is in Mom's car. She pats my knee in a rhythm that I think means she loves me, but I can't tell because it makes me want to jump out of my skin and run. She pats my knee in a rhythm that I think means she's trying not to cry—not yet, because she has to be able to see to drive us to her son. She is the only person who will take me to this place, and it's my job to stay stoic and brave beside her or I'm scared she won't let me come along, so I focus on the stripe across the top of the windscreen where the glass is tinted blue. No matter the weather, things look sunny up there. I'm scared of what will happen when we get there, when we won't have the blue tinting to protect us from the rain.

Now we're at the foot of the grave, and just like that day when we put him here, her body shakes with sobs and she pulls me tight and tighter against her. Her straight wool skirt scratches the backs of my bare knees. Her large plastic glasses dig into my shoulder where she grasps them. A Kleenex balled in her other fist is a knot at my neck. We stand at the foot and stare at the stone. I read the words and wait for him to appear. I read the words and try to call him forth. But this is no magic trick, and I can't make him come and attest to why he left. His mother can't make him come and demand from him an answer for his absence.

How long do we stand there waiting?

Does she place a rock on his grave?

◆　◆　◆

I LISTENED TO Gogo pray for her lost son. Thought *I am lost*. Felt something shift and start to loosen. I didn't know where I was, was not safe. I didn't know this man at my feet and shouldn't be mourning him. But was this mourning? Was it grief? My hands shook and tears fell and the lump of clay resisted the squeeze of my fingers. I tried to breathe. Gogo scrunched her nose and sniffled, pushed up her glasses and sighed. She'd said what she came here to say and she walked now to the car. I watched her go but my feet were cement. Sekuru followed her and I watched him go too. After a time, Ngoni turned and held out his hand to me. I couldn't move. He let me be.

Some time later—minutes? hours?—I walked to the stone and placed the lump of red clay on the rounded granite top of it. Lost my balance and grabbed the headstone so I wouldn't fall. Hot air filled my lungs, my vision blurred.

◆　◆　◆

I'M TINY. I climb up onto Dad's monstrous lap, an ocean of legs for a little girl. "Can I sit in your square?" He bends his leg, places his right ankle on his left knee. Puts me there.

"You can always sit in my square."

10

AT THE SOUND of my approach a few days later, Gogo came to the open door of her second-grade classroom and stood in the fading sunlight, clapping quietly in greeting. She made this now-familiar gesture to welcome me to this place, the last school she'd teach in before her retirement in a couple of months. Her eyes met mine without wavering, with neither pride nor reticence, just an understanding between us that it mattered I'd come. Mattered that I could accept and return her welcome. So I clapped shyly, and smiled.

Everything was tidy and in its place in Gogo's classroom, and while there were no children at the desks that late in the day, evidence of them wasn't hard to find. Stacks of books piled neatly here, art supplies and drawings over there, a chalkboard at the head of the class with the day's agenda carefully transcribed. Gogo walked over to her desk to push in her chair and collect her purse and said, "Shall we take a walk around the grounds before going home?" It wasn't really a question, and I welcomed another chance to see the sky.

We soon came upon the headmaster on his way to his car, and Gogo introduced me with actual pride in her voice. "This is my *muroora*," she said, rolling the first *r* and extending the middle syllable for emphasis, so he knew she meant it, and so that I did. The Shona word for "daughter-in-law" wasn't one I thought she'd ever use for me. There are just some words that don't apply to white people here. But after she had held my hand on the way home from the cemetery the other day, something had shifted between us, and now she got to announce it, make it formal. My body relaxed at the sound of that word, and I shook the headmaster's hand firmly, didn't look away from his gaze.

But I didn't know if there was a new term I should start using for her. I've always called her what Ngoni does, *Gogo,* a term borrowed from the Ndebele, the other main ethnic group in Zimbabwe. It means simply "Gran," though she is more of a mother to my husband than a granny. When Ngoni's father became ill, his mother left, and for a short time Ngoni and his little sister lived alone with Donal. There were scary days, ones Ngoni doesn't talk about much, but in time Gogo and Sekuru—which is Shona for "Grandfather"—took them in. They nursed Donal in his illness and raised the kids alongside their own. Their youngest child, Tendai, is only a year older than Ngoni. Technically his aunt, she feels more like a sister to him. In those early days of our acquaintance, she was starting to feel more like a sister to me as well.

Once the headmaster went on his way, I turned to Gogo, hopeful I'd find a way to talk openly with her. I felt I owed her an explanation for what happened to me at the cemetery, the place where Ngoni was meant to finally, formally mourn his father, and instead it had been me who wept. But I didn't know how to tell Gogo about my dad, about how he died. I didn't even know how to explain that he'd been an unobservant Jew. It somehow made more sense to start with my grandmother Rose, how she'd forced me to decide between her and Ngoni.

"Listen to me, my daughter," Gogo said when I'd finished, taking me by the crook of my arm as we walked toward her house. "When you married Ngoni, you became one of us, you became a *Munemo.*" She emphasized the surname, made it sound royal. "And from now on, when I need something, I will come to you."

I smiled, but I didn't know what she meant.

"In our culture, when the mother—or in this case, the *grand-mother*—needs something from her son, she cannot go to the son. Once he is married, she must go to the *muroora.*"

I tried to imagine what sorts of things she might need from me, from Ngoni, and it took me a moment to realize this wasn't about things—or it wasn't only about things. So I said, "I will be here," and squeezed her arm with mine.

"This is one of the ways that we tie a family together," Gogo said, her eyes steady on the road ahead of us. "This is how we create bonds. When I need something from Tendai, I go to her husband. He speaks to her, and in this way we become more closely tied together. It will be the same with us."

I didn't know why this was her response to my admission about my own grandmother and how she'd hurt me, but I'd been learning in Zimbabwe that here it made sense to stay quiet, to wait for the connections to come clear.

Gogo paused for several beats, for several steps. We were almost home now—I could see the gray Durawall and the black metal gate just around the bend in the road—and Gogo stopped walking and turned to me. "People will study your heart." She put the fingers of her right hand on her own. "They will study it, and they will know who you are. This grandmother of yours, she knows she has hurt you. And now anytime you want to speak to her, you will worry she will hurt you again. She has broken that bond. She is your only connection to your father, and just like that, she cut it." Now Gogo pointed up to the sky and her face broke into a wide smile. She laughed as she said, "Maybe she doesn't know that there is no racism in heaven."

I bristled at this, though I tried to hide it from her. I've never been comfortable talking about God, and I can't pretend to believe in a race-free afterlife—or in any afterlife, really. "But we are one," Gogo said, and I smiled at her. I wanted it to be true. "Racism will really break your heart, but she has made her decision, and you can move on confidently now, knowing that *we* are tied together." With this she hooked her arm back in mine and we walked toward the house. "It does no one any good to come between two people who love each other," she said as we waited at the gate for someone to come unlock it and let us in. "That is why I welcome you, my daughter, that is why we are tied together."

As we walked through the gate and into the house where she raised my husband, I felt a warmth I hadn't at our wedding. I thought maybe this conversation was a threshold, one I needed to cross to really become married to Ngoni, to join his family.

11

"IF WE NAME him Augustine," I said one snowy night in early December 2002, nine months after returning from Zimbabwe, "we could call him 'Gus!'" I hoped this would be what convinced Ngoni. Gus! What a great name. "Sekuru *is* Julius Augustine, after all."

"I hate 'Gus.'"

"Okay," I said. We sat on the worn red couch my mother gave us in our small New York City apartment. The red couch from the living room on State Street. It was so old by then that it had shrunk—or maybe they made couches lower to the ground in the seventies—and when friends came to visit they'd fall the last few inches, expecting the cushion to meet them earlier. We were huddled there with plates of chicken curry and brown rice and salads on our laps. Well, my plate was on my knees because I didn't have a lap by then. NY1 told us what happened that day in the city outside our windows, but I wasn't watching. I was worried about naming our baby after someone still alive and if that would doom Sekuru to an untimely death. I was worried about giving our baby a name that would make the school bully think he was named after his mother. I was worried about what it means to become parents and if we were capable. I was worried about whether our boy would inherit his grandfathers' mental illnesses. I was worried what it would look like, how we'd know.

"We could name him Julius, but give him a different middle name and call him by that one," I said after a while.

There was a patient pause before Ngoni spoke, and for a moment I thought I'd convinced him. "Since I was a little boy and Sekuru took me in, I have wanted to name a son after him," Ngoni said, enunciating every syllable. "It's the best way I know to honor him for taking care of me when no one else would."

This wasn't the first time he'd said this to me, but I finally saw how much more it mattered to Ngoni than Jewish traditions I wasn't raised with and didn't understand mattered to me. It was the first time I saw that my worries about potential playground taunts years away were manifestations of my anxiety about becoming a mother. It wasn't the first time I surrendered to a plan of Ngoni's before it had become my own, but it was the first time I felt my body shift into it. He'd thought about this more than I had, with a clarity I lacked. He could see the potential positives and the potential negatives and had weighed them. His vision was crisp, and I glanced out the window and watched the snow collecting on the fire escape for a moment before deciding to trust him.

You're Julius, I said silently in my head to my baby. *I'm sorry if kids think you're named after me.*

"Let's go get a Christmas tree," Ngoni said as he gathered our plates and headed into the kitchen. I stood up with a grunt and pulled on the thick wool sweater that was the only thing that fit around me by then. Ngoni put on the gray peacoat Sekuru had given him when he moved here and we walked hand in hand to the corner of 113th Street and Broadway to find a tree. We passed the aging white man with greasy gray hair, packing up his table of used books before the snow got too heavy. He glanced from side to side as he did so, expecting someone to run up and grab something from him. I smiled and waved as I always did when I passed. His eyes twitched nervously behind thick glasses, and he almost smiled back. I stopped at his table most nights on my way home from work, looked through his offerings, picked up a title I didn't have. He seemed to always be taking the temperature of our block, and I thought I recognized something in the way he wrung his hands, in the speed and cadence of his voice. As we passed him that night I realized my dad would be about his age and it occurred to me

I might have tethered myself to his book table not because I loved to read but because he connected me to a past I didn't understand.

The tree salesman, a tall black man with a Jamaican accent, was set up a few feet beyond the book table. He stopped talking to the other customer at his kiosk when he saw my belly. It'd been big enough since August to attract attention.

"Oh, let's get you a tree quick before the baby comes!" he laughed. When we chose one and paid for it, he asked if we needed help getting it home.

"Nope," Ngoni and I said at the same moment, and he took the thick end and I took the tip and we walked back home with our tree, a little slower than we had the year before, but with a sweet snow dusting our shoulders and heads.

That night I had a dream I used to have when I was little. There was a pen filled with alligators in the front yard of our house on State Street. Usually in this dream the dark green animals slithered in the stark white of the pool as I stood behind a glass wall with my mother and sister and brother. Dad was always lurking in the shadows, and it was my job to find him and tell him to take this thing away—it's here because he isn't. But on this night my pregnancy changed the dream and Dad was nowhere and the beasts wouldn't stay behind the wall and I was alone with no one to help me and I couldn't move, couldn't run.

When I woke up I was sweaty and thirsty and had to pee. I tiptoed out of the room, then stopped by the closet on the way back. Opened the door and found my old bear, Edward Tedward, on the top shelf. Lay him in the middle of the crib we'd spent the weekend putting together, covered him with a baby blanket, and stood there with my hand on his back like he was alive until Ngoni woke up and saw me and told me to come back to bed.

It was a magic trick he performed, my husband. Without words, he reminded me of this life we were building, that it wasn't my father's life, that the baby in my belly wasn't me. I fell asleep curled around that belly, holding onto Ngoni's arm like a life raft.

12

WE'VE PLAYED IN this scene before. Hot sun hit winter skin in the airport parking lot. Tendai talked and talked as she drove us to the house. The city, the suburbs, rushing past us in a blur. The gate on Marlborough Drive, the toot of the car horn, the clatter and clink of Gogo's bracelets. Julius, swept into her embrace, was the only new piece. It was November 2003, and he would be one in a month. We were in Zimbabwe to stay this time. Six months, a year? As long as it would take for Ngoni to finish the research for his dissertation into Zimbabwe's responses to drought in the previous decades. I had a few freelance projects in my bag to bring in some money to supplement his grants. I listened to Gogo's loud laughter, I looked for Sekuru in the shadows.

When I stepped into the cottage we'd stayed in before, I realized I was looking at it with new eyes. I was a mother now. I saw things I hadn't seen the first time. I toured the small kitchen, opening windows as I went to create a cross-breeze and cool the baby down. I walked into the bathroom and looked at the water heater strapped to the ceiling above the tub and wondered how safely it was hitched up there, if it might fall on my son in the bath. What other dangers had I been oblivious to before he was born? What other aspects of this place, of this life, was I only awake to now?

In the bedroom, I pulled back the curtains above the headboard to let in the breeze and settled Julius into the king-sized bed for his nap. Decided I needed to lie down for a while, too, so I settled my own body around his. No one expected me to sleep away from him here, and I couldn't sleep away from him because since he was born something had shifted and I needed to always be near him. My new tiny family filled an emptiness I'd carried my whole life and quieted the fears in my head and opened up places in me I thought had died with my dad. When we were all three together in a bed I didn't feel his ghost, could focus just on what was in arm's reach, just on what was real. Right now what was real was me and my boy in a bed in Harare, Zimbabwe, across the world from everything I knew.

Some hours later Ngoni came in and said we should unpack. Time to wake the baby and start getting used to the time change. My eyes were foggy, but I thought I saw something on the floor. I squinted to focus, and there, in a room in which food had never been served, were hundreds, maybe thousands of small, red ants. All over the spot on the floor where I would put my feet if I were getting out of bed. Right in the place where I would put Julius down, urging him to walk on his own, after his nap. Right in between the bed and the wardrobe, where I would stand if I were getting dressed in here. Blending into the dirty carpet, which was once beige, I almost didn't see them, but all of my verbs were now subjunctive and I wanted to run away. The carpet was moving.

I called to Ngoni who had gone to get our bags. "I don't remember these from last time," I said, trying to keep my voice calm. My mother's eyes quiet. "If we stay here, we'll need to do something about them."

"These aren't the kind that bite," he said, frustration hardening his brow.

Apparently I should have known that, and apparently their biting was all that should trouble me about ants. I was not allowed to be worried about this thing at this time. I was weak, and American. So I squared my shoulders and slid on my sandals and unpacked, treading over ants each time I moved from the bed, where my suitcase lay open and exposed, to the dresser, where Ngoni put newspaper down on each shelf so that our clothes didn't touch the wardrobe's wood. And I'm the American?

By morning, Ngoni had dug out the lavender-oil bug spray he teased me for buying four bottles of before we left New York. Maybe the long night's sleep had softened him to my worries, or maybe the ants had started to bother him, too. I held Julius on the bed and watched as Ngoni sprayed the oil all over the carpet and swept up piles and piles of ants as they ran away from the smell, which didn't kill them but did repel them—for as long as it lasted. Later we learned that scouring powder repelled and killed them, so the next scene involved white powder all over the floor, and more piles of ants being swept up by my tired husband, who was now muttering about newspaper apartment listings.

As we whispered plans in bed that night, I almost didn't notice that Ngoni had leaned one of Sekuru's old golf clubs against the wall next to his side of the bed. I made myself not ask about it, and doted instead on the sleeping baby between us, grateful again that there was no crib. I was exhausted, and even my worries started to shift into dream. When I woke up, it was very dark and I heard a dog barking. I couldn't tell how close, or if it was the dog that lived there. I could see that Ngoni's eyes were open, too, and I put out my hand to feel Julius's body, still soundly asleep. Did something need to happen, were we worried? But Ngoni rested his hand on my hair and like a child I was soothed back to sleep, letting him worry if worrying was necessary. I drifted back into dreams, listening to the dogs.

◆　◆　◆

IT'S 1978 and Dad has just pulled into the driveway after his trip to the *sesshin*. I'm tucked into the corner of the faded white wing chair in the living room, rubbing my fingers up and down the red piping on the chair seams, worn and shabby. I look through the dining room and its heavy round table with lion's claw feet. I see past the large paper globe over the table, the Persian rug underneath, the tall wooden cabinet with glasses that clink when we run crashing through, that clink when he just walks. I see into the kitchen and he is, at first, just a shape passing by the window. Thumb in my mouth, eyes on kitchen shadows. I wait for the squeak of the door on its hinges, and as soon as I hear it he's inside. He doesn't call out right away, like usual. He doesn't hang up his coat but just stands there, like he's wondering if this place looks different to him now.

Then he's walking toward me. Can I see the difference in his stride, or have I inserted it? Do I burrow deeper into the folds of fabric? What happens next?

◆ ◆ ◆

SOME DAYS LATER I poured boiled water from the teapot into a thick plastic container that I set on top of the fridge to cool. Inside the fridge were six of these thick plastic water bottles, white and canteen-shaped, with a short bottleneck. Also a loaf of bread, a fat chunk of margarine, a package of bright pink sausages called Vienna dogs that when sliced into revealed regular hot dogs under the colorful casing, and five eggs resting on a plate. Everyone told me you didn't need to refrigerate the eggs in Zimbabwe, but old habits et cetera, and it wasn't as though they were taking up precious space.

I reached into the cabinet for the peanut butter, remembered I'd forgotten to buy jelly, and realized we were out of milk. I glanced at Ngoni and Julius reading on the couch as I went out the door, headed to the big house with an empty cup in my hand to borrow some. The walk took about three seconds. About as far away from the house, but in the other direction, was another, slightly smaller cottage. If the yard were a face, the cottages would be the uneven eyes, the big house would be the nose, and the broken, empty pool would be the not-smiling mouth. The back porches of each house all faced each other in a sort of courtyard; the centerpiece was the banana tree. Ngoni's uncle Dakarai had lived in the smaller cottage since 1995, when he returned from Wales, after his marriage dissolved. He didn't come out much, and I'd hardly seen him since we arrived.

On my way across the yard I saw the household dog run out of the big house. Close behind her was Dakarai, about thirty pounds lighter than last time we were here, throwing his shoe at the dog and shouting "Fucking asshole." There wasn't a lot of swearing at this house—the God channel on the television served as a constant reminder. As I walked toward Dakarai from the porch I remarked that I too found this dog annoying. She was too eager to be petted, too slobbery with her licking, and, I'd heard, had a habit of sleeping through break-ins.

Dakarai repeated that the dog was a fucking asshole and, as we passed one another in the wide doorway, he shoved his body against mine, knocking me into the doorframe before rushing back to his cottage. It could have looked like an accident, it could have been an accident, but I saw his wide-open eyes as he neared me, I saw him measure the space between us before his shoulder and hip hit mine. All of my muscles squeezed together as I ran in for the milk and raced back to my cottage quick as I could. The fact was, I was fine. Nothing happened. It could have been an accident. I kept repeating this to myself as I finished making lunch, which I did in a hurry, my eyes darting around the room. Should I tell Ngoni what had happened, or was I being ridiculous? Would Dakarai storm into our cottage in a rage, or had I made the entire thing up?

When I could quiet myself, I saw Ngoni clearly. He sat with Julius on the floor with a puzzle. He was calm and quiet, maybe quieter than usual. When he looked up at me standing in the doorframe with plates of peanut butter sandwiches in my hand, there were circles under his eyes. He looked as though he had become suddenly exhausted. But I also saw resolve set into his forehead. Ngoni, I realized, knew that Dakarai was having a bad day. He knew what that looked like and was readying himself to wait it out.

He stood up and motioned me outside, persuading me that eating inside, no matter how much more private, was intolerable with the heat and the ants. I wondered, though, if he just felt better with Dakarai in his sight line. As we ate our sandwiches, Ngoni and I tried to talk and play with the baby. It was hard to ignore, though, Dakarai straddling the back of a wooden chair on the porch of the big house, smoking as he glared at us. I wondered if we reminded him of what his life could have been with Cati, if it was my race that brought about this episode. If he'd have been fine if I'd never come. I thought about my father then, and if he would have been fine, too, if I'd never come. If everything was moving along just great in his family before I was born. I tried to picture Dad's episodes, plaster this scene in Harare onto a map of State Street to see if they fit. Did my father ever shove someone into a doorframe? Did any of his cousins who struggled with mental illness ever shove someone into a doorframe? And what about here in this family I was now entering? Did Ngoni's father ever shove someone into a doorframe? If this is what madness looks like, will we recognize it if it comes again?

A few hours after lunch, Ngoni went to check on Gogo. He knew she suffered during Dakarai's episodes. And because it was quiet now, because I didn't expect to see Dakarai at the big house, I squared Julius on my hip and we walked over, too.

But the kitchen was empty, which was weird. There was normally at least one woman—sometimes a maid, more often Ngoni's grandmother—in there preparing dinner by that time of day. We walked through the small dining room and no one sat at the table. I took a breath, looked Julius in the eye and smiled, and walked through the doorway into the dark living room, committed now to being there even with these warning signs that something was off. The forest-green couches, the brown carpet, the heavy wood tables all resisted the glare of the sun at the windows. There was a large cross hanging over the doorway I was standing under now, and I thought of it as mistletoe. I wanted it to protect me, or anoint me, or bring me a happy surprise.

Two nephews of Ngoni's grandparents—college kids living here while they went to school—were watching a soap opera on the TV under the window. They sat in front of it on the floor like children, awkward smiles on their faces. It took me a moment to see that they were shell shocked. That these boys had seen something I hadn't, and were scared. They watched this show because they needed to laugh. They needed to look at characters on a screen. When Ngoni headed into the back of the house to find Gogo, I didn't follow. Though I'd been let into the back bedroom several times by then, it was still a place with boundaries, a place I knew only to enter if invited.

Julius and I stood behind the kids on the carpet and kept our attention on the stupid show on the TV. We were all laughing when Dakarai walked in.

"You think this is funny? I haven't eaten in two days and I'm starving and they're cooking that crap they know I won't eat. You think this is funny?"

"No, Dakarai," I started to say. "We were watching—"

"I wasn't talking to you! I was talking to my nephew."

Ngoni had silently returned to the living room and was standing closer to me than I knew. He said, "Shall I make you something warm, Babamidiki?" The word means "small father," and Ngoni used it to show that this uncle was his father's younger brother. There's another word, also based on the root *father*, for an uncle who's older than your dad. The Shona language, I realized standing there, allows fatherhood to be flexible, to fit around various forms, and for a moment I didn't understand. I thought about my uncles and how they never filled the holes for me, never took away the loneliness. How did Ngoni know to let Dakarai be his small father? To play this role of son? Did having a small father all his life help him when he couldn't have the real one?

"That would be nice." Dakarai's voice was angry, challenging.

Ngoni headed into the kitchen and I looked first at the TV, then at my baby. I didn't want Julius to worry, so I smiled at him again. I laughed a little. *It's okay. Don't be scared.*

"So you do! You do think this is funny! I'm starving and they're making that crap I can't eat and you're laughing at me!"

Hadn't the kitchen been empty when we walked in? What crap was he talking about? I wanted to say, No, Dakarai, I'm sorry. I wanted to tell him that I was watching the TV, laughing for the baby. No Dakarai, I'm sorry, it wasn't you. No, Dakarai, I'm sorry. I'm sorry.

I couldn't see Ngoni in the kitchen, but I knew the sounds he was making. He cooked his uncle a lunch of tiny dried fish fried with onions. Put it on a plate with fried white potatoes. Placed on the table a glass of Mazoe, the syrupy orange drink ubiquitous in Zimbabwe. I listened to Dakarai eat in the dining room, the scraping of his fork and knife across the plate. The glass brought to his lips and set back down with a bang. Ngoni sat across from him, his elbows on the table, his hands folded in front of his face.

"HE SPEAKS SOMETIMES of killing himself," Gogo told me the following morning, Christmas Eve. We were sitting side by side on her bed, and I knew I was there to bear witness. I was there for the story of these illnesses and how their legacy might last, but it wasn't a message

I wanted to hear. While Gogo spoke, I gazed at her wardrobe, tracing the worn wooden corners with my eyes and looking longest at the spot where a hinge was loose. The door wouldn't ever sit plumb to the frame.

I sighed but couldn't say anything because it's work, trying to remember that suicide isn't the answer. Trying to remember what it would do to the people who love him. What it did to me. I hugged her and excused myself and walked back to the cottage in the hot morning, the sun big in the sky, white wisps of clouds across the blue. As Julius napped and Ngoni ran errands with Sekuru, I was supposed to be cooking. It was my job to cook the chickens for the party at Tendai's new house that night, so I pulled them out of the fridge, took the knife out of the drawer, and began to cut and clean them the way Ngoni taught me to in New York.

Ngoni said Dakarai was fine, said he wouldn't leave on errands without me if he weren't. But I could still hear the banging on the gate when he got home the night before. He'd forgotten his keys in his hurry to escape the house after Ngoni's lunch, and the gate was locked. Without a car horn to honk, he could do nothing but scream until we heard him. I was too scared in my bed to move. Ngoni didn't get up at the sound. Soon we heard Gogo go to the gate and let in her son. We heard the noises he made at his cottage door, also locked—by morning it was in ruins. We heard him crying with his head in his mother's lap as she sat on the red earth and tried to hold him still.

I couldn't cook. I washed my hands, dried them on a dish towel, dropped it on the floor as I crawled into bed with my sleeping son. I lay next to Julius's hot body, listened as he sighed and resettled himself around my shape. Thought about this lineage coming at him from both directions. Turned over and saw my pale face in the mirror.

Twenty-four years ago on this day my father walked down State Street to Child's toy store to buy us each an Edward Tedward, a bear to stay with us after he was gone. Twenty-four years ago on this day my father was visiting from the loony bin and getting ready to die. Twenty-four years ago on this day the voices in his head were so loud I couldn't recognize him when he passed through the rust-colored kitchen door.

But it had been twenty-four years, and when we were in the States, my sister and my brother and my mother and I laughed at the notion that diseases like his can pass along the genes, laughed at the idea that they could bounce through the generations, could affect the babies born long since.

That was harder to hold in Zimbabwe, with Dakarai outside my door, there with that family who discussed it. Whether they called it possession or an episode or a bad day or the voices, they didn't hide from the fact that this disease had snaked its way through the family, had popped up in Ngoni's father, and now here it was again, in his uncle Dakarai. They didn't hide from the sadness that caused, or the anger. Didn't hide from the legacy like I do.

13

WHEN I WAS LITTLE and imagined the mysteries of a family trip to a place like Niagara Falls, I pictured tall rocks with water tumbling over them, separate and far away. I imagined stairs leading to a cement-floor lookout, and maybe a glass wall for us to press our noses on. At least a sturdy fence that doesn't let anyone drop. I pictured piles of people who stood and looked, far away from the water, safe and dry on their platform. When we went to Zimbabwe, a trip to Victoria Falls felt a little far-fetched to me. I didn't want to be a tourist on a cement platform, looking at the water from behind the protective fence. But there we were, anyway, just before Julius turned two.

"You can't get away this time without visiting the Falls," Ngoni's grandfather told me. "There are just some things you have to see in this life."

At all of the other places we'd visited, Ngoni had shown us around himself. But despite taking a school field trip to the Falls when he was a kid, he didn't feel confident enough in his knowledge of this place to be our guide. So after paying the entrance fee at the gate, he waved to a fellow leaning against a post to negotiate a fee. Fungai, the guide, was slightly taller and trimmer than Ngoni, dressed in an army-green T-shirt and jeans, with flip-flops on his feet. He led us down a paved cement path with plants and flowers I thought belonged in a rainforest, not dry Zimbabwe. Julius was tight to my hip in a sling over my shoulder.

"That fence," said Fungai, pointing to the right at a tall chain-link contraption that separated this place with the plants and the pathway from the wooded wild beyond, "was erected to keep out the elephants." Julius squealed at a monkey who followed a few feet behind, and his feet climbed my thighs in glee and fear. We passed what I thought was a boulder on the ground, but Fungai stopped and pointed and said, "Elephant skull." As it came clear, I saw the eye sockets and the places where the tusks once fit. It was as high as my hip.

We next followed Fungai down a small and slippery path. "Be careful," he said, reaching out for my hand. "Look," he said, turning around when we were safe. Rainbows, three or four, crisscrossing each other. A deep, deep gorge. Water rushing into it from somewhere I couldn't see. A small, wooden, handmade fence at shin level.

"How would this rickety thing hold him back?" I asked Ngoni with my eyes as I squeezed the sling tighter across my shoulder. We stood for a while, vaguely impressed and ready to leave if this was all. Ngoni snapped some pictures and I thought, *Okay, this is the cement-floored lookout. Let's go.* But then a group of tourists came around a corner, drenched and laughing, and there was something in their eyes that revealed they knew more about this place than I did.

"Come on," Fungai beckoned, handing me an umbrella.

We turned a corner and when I looked up I saw we were in for a long walk. The path in front of us didn't show its end, and I was grateful I'd chosen sneakers back at the hotel. As we walked in, the mist I'd ignored before became a downpour and I opened the umbrella, thankful for Fungai. I laughed at my image, only minutes old, of a glassed-in lookout. I got braver, excited.

"Can I walk in front for a while?" I asked Fungai, and let him tell Ngoni about the flora and fauna of this place. Rainbows formed around me and Julius, ferns and plants and rainforest thickness, and the sound of the Falls was now a roar above which I couldn't hear my kid on my hip. I walked through a rainbow at knee level and felt cold pass through my bones like a ghost.

I turned around to Ngoni. "Carry him?" I asked, pulling my head out from under the sling. I wanted to move ahead, I wanted to get wet in this water. "Here's the umbrella."

"Some of these lookouts are too dangerous to walk out to," Fungai told me before I set off.

"I'll be careful!" I called over my shoulder as I ran ahead, certain I'd know what was safe. I turned into a lookout I could see clearly—there was no mist at all now. It was a flat slab of rock surrounded on either side by plants and trees, a window into the cataract of the river. Across the way, miles of water rushed down the emptiness and fell to a bottom I couldn't see. But I wanted to see the bottom. Another short, rickety wooden fence marked the place to stop, but I didn't even come close to it. As the mist shifted again, I inched as near to the edge as my fear allowed and stood very still while I thought about the illusion of the ground at my feet, which I could no longer see. I was blind and wet in the middle of water as thick as mud, the mist rising higher up my body. I held my hand in front of my face to see if that old saying was true and could see nothing at the end of the arm I knew was there. Water sprayed in all directions, a deep wet covered me. The Falls now took over the space in front of me, my whole entire rocky platform, and the longer I stood there the more sure I became that the Falls would soon take over the world behind me as well. I would be an island here on this rock, the only living creature left in the world.

The enormous rush of water was loud in my ears. The depths to which it fell were longer and more powerful than my mind could bear. I was paralyzed, no longer sure which direction to walk to get back to the path. I knew that if I yelled to Ngoni and Fungai they wouldn't hear, and I was sure they didn't know which lookout I'd turned into. I could see nothing, hear nothing, feel nothing but my drenched wet body balancing on the rock.

And then there's a tap on my shoulder and I turn to look and Dad's beside me, his arm pressed into mine, his voice in my ear. *This is what I sought,* he says. *This isolation is what I needed,* he says. I long to sit down and ground myself to this place, this spot, this wetness. I long to tell him to sit down with me. We can be together here, Dad. This place—so far away from our old place with its sadnesses—is the place for us. Dad! I want to call. I get it now! We'll just sit here and you can tell me everything and no one will ever find us because it's so dark in this whitewater mist. I want to lower myself to sit the way he used to sit in the middle of the living room carpet with his ankles resting on his knees and his bottom on a hard round black pillow. I want to lean on his shoulder next to mine. I long to lower myself to sit just the way he used to sit when he was looking for that solitude that I've finally just found for us. Safety at the center of the universe. It's here! If I could sit and ground myself to this place, he would stay with me. I would bring it to him, this place, this solitude, this understanding. If I could sit and ground myself to this place, he could bring it to me, too.

But Julius was over there and I couldn't hear him or see him or feel him but I knew he was waiting for me. He was looking over Ngoni's shoulder at the last place he saw me and he'd keep on looking until I came. So I can't sit, Dad. I can't stand the choice I would have to make to get up again. When I turned, the path was clear in front of me. It was bright in the sun and the mist was gone. The fern fronds beckoned me to come back from the edge, and when I turned the corner, there they all were. And Julius, relief in his eyes as I jogged to catch up. And Julius shouting, "Mama!"

I came back into myself. Returned.

THAT NIGHT IN the hotel I had the dream again, the one where Dad is really alive. We were on the phone this time, too. He told me everything. He's gay! Of course he couldn't live a false life. He'd run off with his lover, but he and my mother had agreed it would be easier if the children thought he was dead.

"It was the seventies, kiddo," his voice boomed across the crackling line. "Things were different then."

He told me the pallbearers were in on the secret, pretending the coffin was heavy.

He sounded happy, telling me about the life he'd made without us.

"And what about you?" he asked, laughter loud in his voice. "Do you have a family?"

I started to say it—*In college I met a man from Zi*—but my tongue tripped over the syllables and I stuttered.

Then the call dropped.

He was gone.

14

WE'D BEEN BACK from Zimbabwe for a couple of months when the first of my father's slavery porn landed on my kitchen table. My cousin had seen them when she was packing up our recently deceased grandmother's Albany apartment. Someone told her who wrote them and she brought them to me.

"I thought you would want to know about this," was what she'd said as she pushed them across the table into my hands. I didn't take a moment to wonder at the circuitous pathway these books had traveled to get from my father to me—first into his mother-in-law's hands, then into my cousin's, and now here in this home where we were raising a toddler.

Julius was playing at the sink with bubbles, and my eyes darted to him standing on a stool before I checked to see if the shake I felt in my hands, now clutching a mug of tea, was visible. *The Wrath of Chane* was not a title I knew. Norman Gant was not my father. These weren't books I grew up with, they did not sit on our bookcases in the back hallway of the house on State Street, as the four books he wrote under his own name sat on our bookcases in the back hallway for me to study. These books were also not on the low shelves of my grandmother Rose's carpeted corridor. Norman Gant was not one of the names I memorized on my way back from her bathroom.

This was no family I knew.

"Oh my God," I said, my voice tight in my throat.

I flipped *Chane* onto its face to hide the cover—from my son? From myself? And saw underneath it a similar one, called *Slave Empire*. Another muscular black man. Another sultry white woman. That's when something switched off. In my mind, or in my heart. It wasn't something I could feel—this switching off. It was a long-practiced skill of seeing the world through a pragmatist's eye. I learned it at my mother's knee. I learned it at my father's funeral. I will, I told myself, be reasonable here. I will take in what I see and categorize it in my mind. That way I won't have to categorize it in my heart. I'll file it away with my few other facts: *This* is what my father was. And this is a fact I need to hide.

"Let me put these away," I said to my cousin as I gathered the books in my hands. "I couldn't bear it if Julius saw them." Or Ngoni, I thought. He'd be home any minute from the library.

FLASH FORWARD ONE year, to the night our second son is born. I sit on my hospital bed and whisper to him. "Maybe if I tell you now," I say, "I won't have to tell you later. Maybe it will become a protective sheath around you. A superstition of protection, if I tell you on the day you are born."

His soft black hair lies flat and thick on his head. There is a red circle covering most of his forehead, but his skin—darker by several shades than his brother's—is still a little red from his exit, so I can't tell how prominent the mark will be. My legs stretch out under the blanket on either of side of him, this perfect person, twelve hours old. We are alone and it is dark out my window and the TV nailed to the ceiling is off and the door is closed and Julius's favorite toy lion is guarding the faucet in the bathroom. I worry he won't sleep without it, but already the torn choices between children are beginning and I know I can only focus on this one for a time.

"Your grandfather was not a good man," I say to my brand-new son. "He wrote disgusting books I hide in a closet because I'm scared of what they reveal about who I am—I'm scared of what they show I will pass on to you."

I look at him to see how this information is sinking in.

"But that isn't all," I force myself to keep going. "He was crazy. He killed himself when I was five." Now that these words are out, I'm freer. I say the rest. "But we're naming you after him anyway. And I'm scared that if I name you after a lunatic you will also lose your mind. I'm scared that if I name you for a suicide you will find a way also to leave."

◆   ◆   ◆

THEY NAMED MY sister Susannah because my mother was Susan and she had always wished her name was Susannah. My sister became Nan when the boy down the street couldn't say Susannah, so he called her Susan-Anna, and somehow that got sliced down to Nanna and then eventually just to Nan. They named my brother Joshua because Dad's parents had wanted him to be Schmuhl after someone special, and that my parents could not abide and so maybe they considered Moishe but also no, not that one, and so Joshua seemed like a compromise of a kind. But with me, about whom they were surprised—I was in grammar school when I first heard Mom say she'd been on the pill still—they didn't have a name.

There was also a maternal illness. "I weighed the same the day I delivered you as I did the day I got pregnant with you," my mother told me when I was tiny. "A kidney infection."

And maybe symptoms of the dawning of a mental illness. "Your father was in the woods with another woman the night you were born," my mother told me when I was not much bigger. "She became covered in a rash from poison ivy."

So the nurses wrote "Wolk Child" on the card in my crib and sent me home from the hospital, and the pictures from those days are of Mom, skinny as a sack, hair in a kerchief, cigarette between fingers, nursing or rocking or putting me in my big sister's lap.

"Child," they called me for some weeks.

"Alexandra!" my mother came home one day and suggested.

No.

"Stephanie," someone else thought.

Not that.

"Child," they called me for weeks.

Until one day it was time for *Sesame Street* and turning the knob with a heavy click and after the gray-blue flash and everything settling up and down and then arranging itself on the screen, there was that lady with the funny voice standing in her pegboard kitchen but also on TV in our living room.

"Mom!" called my brother as though she were far. "Let's name Wolk Child after that nice lady on TV! They already have the same last name."

JULIUS, WHO WAS named for Sekuru, loved my obstetrician so much he named one of his lions after her, as though he already understood the power of naming and was leading by example. Early this morning, Sydna the doctor, not Sydna the lion, pulled this second child out and there he was, a boy. I'd been certain this one was a girl for my whole pregnancy, much of which transpired on the outskirts of the Kalahari Desert in Gaborone, Botswana. And I'd been certain this one was a girl in the suburbs of my own hometown, where we'd moved in September because it was quiet and Ngoni would be able to finish his dissertation and I would be able to lean on my mom for help. I'd been certain this one was a girl for a hundred reasons, but I'd been certain this one was a girl because then I could wiggle out of Ngoni's plans to name him after my dad. I could dodge it and forget my father like I had forever been trying to forget my father.

But there in that hospital where I, too, had been born, Sydna the doctor pulled him out and placed him on the scale by my head instead of showing me his face first, and I turned to look and saw his toes and heard the nurses calling out the number of pounds he weighed, but all I could say was, "Scrotum?"

"This is George," Ngoni said after the nurses swaddled him up and tucked him to my side and wheeled me into my room.

"George Morgan," I corrected. "I'm going to call him Morgan." My mother's mother's maiden name.

Ngoni nodded and stepped out of the room to get me a cup of broth. The nurse walked in to check on us and asked if we'd decided on a name, and I forgot my grand plans and said in a creaky voice quiet with uncertainty, "He's George."

"Oh, you named him after the president!" she shrieked.

"No!" I was horrified. I hadn't thought of that and now there was a whole new George I wished weren't in the room. "No," I said, trying to get the words out because I had to protect my son from this idea. I wanted to tell her we're Democrats, I wanted to tell her she can't ever say that again, I wanted to tell her that no one must ever think that. "No," I said. "We named him after my father," but my voice cracked against the unfamiliar word and his ghost came into the room with the incantation.

◆　◆　◆

I AM TINY, a toddler, just two this week, with two parents and two siblings and a life about to begin. My mother hands me to my father over a wide swath of swaying, slippery waves. I go from the edge of a solid, unmovable dock into the shifting movement of a boat held briefly here by fingertips. The water laps below me, catches the light, sparkles. I pull my legs up and curl my toes against the fall I feel coming. Then I'm in his arms, and there's laughter loud in my ear and the sudden sensation of speed. Do I cling to his shoulder to stay safe? Does he whisper my name to soothe me?

◆　◆　◆

WET CHEEKS WHEN Ngoni returned to the hospital room with my broth. His hand on my hair, he looked at the baby's face and smiled. "It's time to reclaim your father's legacy," he said. "Time to make something positive out of it."

There was a pause before I could agree. I was negotiating with ghosts. I was weighing what I kept hidden in my closet and what I kept hidden in my heart, these mental illnesses coming at my sons from all directions and this legacy we were now asking a brand-new boy to shoulder.

"Your father was more than his illness," Ngoni said. "He was also your father."

ANOTHER LEAP AND George is one, Julius four. We've just moved into an old New England colonial, owned by the college where Ngoni will start teaching in the fall. I sit among a chaos of boxes of books, taking out old treasures and nearly new hardbacks that had been waiting for me in a storage unit these last many months of itinerant living. I place each one carefully onto the freshly painted, built-in bookcases, already regretting my grand plans to alphabetize them upon our arrival. It's too much. The kids are running circles around me, the summer sun is setting, and I don't know where the bedsheets are or who is sleeping where. Ngoni's in the kitchen putting pizza on plates and I am about to get up to help, leave this task for morning, when I look down and see Dad's books at the bottom of a box.

My body tenses and I move to block my sons from seeing them. But when they wander into the empty dining room to test the echo, I pull the books out and hold them up to the light. Maybe here in a new town, starting a new life, I can consider what these books mean to me. To my legacy, to my children. Maybe if I set them on the bookshelf alongside Faulkner and Gordimer and Achebe, my father's memory will stop causing me so much shame. Maybe here I can slide them in alongside Dad's other books, the ones with his real name on the spine, and finally face who he was.

"My father was a writer," I will tell the new friends I hope to make here. "He wrote softcore porn to make a living, but always wanted to do something bigger." But the conversation stops there because no matter who I'm speaking to, I don't have the guts—even in my imagination—to explain his pseudonyms or why I've never read any of his books or what happened after he stopped writing. I don't have the guts to talk about how it's not love I feel when I think of my father, but something closer to dread.

So I find a small box for these four tattered, pulpy pieces of trash, fold the flaps down, and carry it upstairs. Julius is fast at my side.

"Which bedroom do you guys want?" I ask.

He is confident and quick. "This one," he says, choosing the room farthest from the stairs. I step into the other, tuck the box as far back on the closet shelf as it will go, and close the closet door.

PART II

BLINDERS

15

WHEN I FIRST pulled *Chane* out of the closet the winter our kids were nine and twelve, it was with some vague idea that I'd find the source of my father's racism. The winter after the police gunned down a child the same age as Julius, my father's racism seemed like something I needed to understand. But faced with what his career actually was, I found I had to break it down into soluble parts to try to understand the elements from which it was made. And so it has been some weeks since I held this book open on the couch. I do so this time armed with a pen. I will analyze this book. Investigate my father's authorial toolkit. Read like a writer, not a daughter.

So it is that I begin to ask why my dad—no, I stop myself—why *the author* chose slavery as his trope, pornography as his vehicle. Did he want to write historical fiction about the brutality of slavery and feel that he had to include sex scenes in order to be true to the history? Or did he write porn because he enjoyed writing porn and thought slavery might be an interesting structure to hang it on? Or was it just what the publishers wanted—did they call him up and say, "We need the next *Mandingo,* you have a month"?

But even if it was just that, I have to ask myself what my father had access to inside of his mind and inside of his soul to be able to write this shit. I can't maintain the artifice that these books don't tell a deeply personal story—a deeply American story. So I pick it apart, like any personal story—like any novel I need to analyze to understand my country, my history, myself.

I start as basic as I can and trace how my father did physical description in his work, how he indicated the differences between the races of his characters. It doesn't take long to see that every character in *Chane* is described first by the nose. White characters have "thin" noses, "heavy" noses, "long" noses, and noses that "shine like polished white fruit." Too long a horse ride across the African desert can "take the hook out of your nose," if you're white. But Dad's black characters have only one nose, and it is "wide."

His white characters have "shining white skin" or skin that has turned "walnut from the sun." One of them is a "small wiry almost albino white," another "piebald." But black characters are just "black." They are sometimes "black as coke" or "coal black," but most often no adjective is put in front of the word, which my father seems to think is enough to describe all of the many slaves in the novel.

My dad doesn't use the N word until page 43, and by the time I get to it, I have almost relaxed my vigil, have almost let myself imagine that Dad is making a statement by choosing not to use it at all. Once it's out, though, it stays in use. At first, only in dialogue, and a girl can dream that its role is to make the characters sound authentic. But in time, it creeps more directly into the narrative and hopes are lost. There is now a door I have to close in order to keep reading, a hope I have to walk away from if I'm going to continue. My eyes skip over the word now that I see it so often, and I remind myself that I'm here for business, not love. I'm reading like a writer—trying to learn about how my father understood his craft. I remind myself to categorize this pain so it's a thought, not a feeling.

But as I scribble down notes and questions, I see that I *am* angry. Every question in my notebook is also an accusation. Did Dad do any research on African religions before describing the details of the rituals he imagines, or did he just make it all up? Did he know anything about African languages when he wrote that the interpreter was invaluable because he spoke Swahili? Most of the slaves in his story are from Western Sudan—present-day Senegal, Mali, Gambia, Guinea, Guinea

Bissau, Sierra Leone, and Liberia—where the languages spoken were Wolof and Maninka then, as now, and not Swahili.

In time I start to soften. Maybe because I have to if I'm going to continue, or maybe because this is my dad, and he's dead, and I didn't know him well enough to judge him. Didn't know him well enough to love him. In time I give my questions a different purpose, to trace where Dad got lost. Maybe pulp fiction wasn't ever going to be research based, maybe he churned these books out as fast as possible so he could get back to his "real writing," maybe he tried to add nuance where he could, but who has time for libraries when there are contracts to fulfill?

But that road is short, and soon enough I come upon another made-up religious ritual—this one with a black woman writhing on the ground naked and in a trance until a snake enters her, couples having sex all around her as the woman is imbued with the powers of a goddess through the snake now inside her. Maybe my father thought this was a ritual brought over from Africa, but I can't even stop to wonder where he came up with it or if he made it up entirely or what he possibly could have read to help him craft it. I'm just pissed. I don't want to fact-check anymore. I don't want to read anymore. I don't want to know who this man was anymore. Because, of course, as a fiction writer he had license to make things up to advance his plot. But I can't separate that license from what I see as lying, as taking liberties with someone else's history for his own gains. And that feels linked to the white American license my dad seems to embrace in his writing, a license to warp histories to suit our needs. So no, I can't separate fact from fiction, and I want to know why he could.

I also want to know why *this* is the legacy I have to wrestle in my living room when my kids are about to come home from school. Why I don't just have a dad to walk me down the aisle or protect me from the school bully or look out for how my own grandmother treated me when I was falling in love. I do want to know that.

"HE WROTE THOSE books under contract, Jules," my mom assures me when I call her one day, to try to start asking some of these questions. The kids are at school, Ngoni's at work. My current freelance project sits ignored on my desk. "They were just a paycheck."

"Okay," I say, wanting it to be true. "But something else must have been going on. Why was he so preoccupied with race?"

There's a pause before Mom speaks. "It was the sixties, honey. Everyone was preoccupied with race."

On my end of the phone line, I nod, but her answer doesn't feel like enough. I want her to tell me what made my father a racist.

"It wasn't a comfortable living," she says with a sigh. "But the fact remains that he bought us a house the year you were born."

A house that became the sole source of stability in the childhood that followed, I don't need to add. A house without which we really would have been lost. What does it mean that even now—from this distance—I am still so grateful for that house on State Street? What does it mean that my father wrote slavery porn to buy it?

16

ONE AFTERNOON a few weeks into reading my father, I sit in my spot on the green couch, spread the yellow quilt across my knees, and find my place in *Chane*. I don't want to keep reading this book, but I can't do the job halfway. I have to finish my dad's first book if I'm ever going to understand who he was.

When the dog barks, I look up to see Ngoni, home for a surprise lunch. On a typical day I read during breaks from my freelance work, taking the book out of the closet in the morning after walking the kids to the bus stop and then returning it to its hiding spot in the afternoon before anyone comes home. Today I'm in the den with it in my hands when Ngoni walks in, and it's ridiculous to try to hide.

So I hold the book up and say, "I'm looking into my father's books."

I say *looking into* and not *reading* because who could possibly read this schlock? I don't want Ngoni to think that I want to read it. I keep telling myself that I don't have to read all of it. I've been hiding this book in my closet for so many years now that reading it seems absurd.

"It's about time," he says before walking to the back of the house to put his things away.

Despite the fact that this is the first conversation about my father's career I can remember between us, despite the fact that I want to protect my husband from this book in my hands, despite the fact that part of me feels caught in the act when he comes home early, Dad's books don't feel like a secret. I haven't been *not* telling Ngoni about this. I've been keeping it from the kids, sure, but with Ngoni it seems like something we don't really need to talk about. Is this what happens in a long marriage—you question if there's anything you know that your spouse doesn't? Because it feels now as though Ngoni already knows everything. I don't say, "Can you believe my father wrote interracial pornography?" because it's clear that he did. Clear because I hold the book up for Ngoni to see? Or clear because he has known about these books as long as I have, and I just don't remember talking about them before? These aren't questions I ask because I'm too busy noticing that this is the moment the narrative shifts. This is the moment I stop hiding my father's legacy in a closet, the moment I admit I'm trying to understand who I am.

BY THE TIME I get a third of the way through the three-inch-thick tome called *The Wrath of Chane,* the first book ends and I realize with surprise that this is a trilogy. It shouldn't be a surprise that my father's first three books are bound together under this title—it says as much on the cover. But the cover had made me so uncomfortable that I hadn't looked at it for long, so now I'm just relieved to have finished one whole book. I'm so much closer to the end than I thought. I flip through to the title pages and teaser copy of the other two novels bound here and realize that all three books will follow a curse that was handed down to baby Chane on the slave ship, early in book 1. Chane grows up in that book, and he and his mother—a slave on a neighboring plantation—are both killed in the novel's violent conclusion. Books 2 and 3 will follow his sons, and the story will take us into the Civil War and its aftermath. I wonder how many of Chane's descendants I'll meet, and I think how weird it is that in representing an institution infamous for destroying families my dad enforced such filial ties in his fiction. But I don't imagine that's what his readers bought his books for. I think they mainly bought them for scenes like this:

> She grasped the steel blackness of his thighs with hers, her pure
> white thick thighs and screamed with despair and joy and fright
> and hope and obstinacy and faith as he found her vagina with his
> massive sex, the sex she knew, the sex she had slavered over, and
> although it was not the first time, there was a great pain in her
> cry, too, a real, almost physical pain that this might be their last

time, that their youth would end with the end of that throbbing, spiritual, innocent, shattering act of love.

I cringe when I read this scene. Cringe to think that even when the sex my dad writes isn't rape, it's still so structured by assumed racial categories. The difference in skin color is front and center. Chane's "steel blackness" leads the reader to the stereotype of the strong black man. His lover's "white thick thighs" are a symbol of her purity. The contrast is immediate, and the image of these colliding colors photographic. Her compliant yet eager body welcomes his with "slavering." Why not "drooling"? Why not "salivating"? This word seems an intentional reminder of what Chane is, a slave. It does a little extra work, that word, reminding the reader about the real power dynamic at play underneath what might otherwise seem like what my father calls it—an innocent act of love. I cringe because none of this is innocent.

James Baldwin writes about white men "hiding behind the color curtain" in this country. In addition to the immeasurable costs to black hearts and minds, to the souls of black folks, he talks about the damage racism has done also to the white man. The trap in which the white man finds himself ensnared. "And for a moment," Baldwin writes, the white man "seemed nearly to be pleading with the [black] people facing him not to force him to commit yet another crime and not to make yet deeper that ocean of blood in which his conscience was drenched."

I do not suggest my father's work was intended to pull the color curtain back and reveal the moral bankruptcy of whiteness. But when I can read like a writer and not like a daughter, when I can stop cringing at the contents of Dad's book and look at it with academic eyes, I see that the *Chane* series does address some aspects of the barbarism of slavery, such as breeding slaves like animals and forcing them to perform acts of sexual entertainment for their masters. I do not suggest that my father's career was an articulation of his understanding of Baldwin's trap. But when I compare *The Wrath of Chane* to its nauseating model, *Mandingo*, I see that it was different. Kyle Onstott's most famous book—the one that established a subgenre of pulp fiction my mother calls "slavers"—is nearly 700 pages of simple-minded black characters who can't see beyond their love for their white masters, pages and endless pages of violence and shame meted out on black people. It was first published in 1958, and by the time of the used 1964 edition I bought for the purposes of understanding my father's literary context, it could boast on its cover that two million copies had sold. Two million. What was happening in America between 1958 and 1964 that allowed two million people to go out to the five and dime and buy that garbage? Was it the dawning of the Civil Rights Movement, the increasing pitch of black voices posing a threat to white supremacy? Did the purchase of this book and others like it soothe the white imagination into believing that it would always reign? Did the dead black man at the end of *Mandingo* help the white man through his frightened day? And if so, are the consequences of that what we're living through now?

At least, I tell myself about the end of *Chane,* book 1 in the series, the title character has killed the plantation owner and burned the place to the ground. At least in my dad's book, unlike Onstott's, no slaves were boiled and poured onto the graves of the white women they'd slept with. Maybe my dad was intentionally doing something different.

"Be careful," Ngoni says to me as we walk through the woods behind our house one afternoon. "It sounds like you're apologizing for your father's career."

I want to tell him that of course I'm not doing that, that of course I see the injustices in his books. But I also want to tell him that my father's books aren't like the other slavers I've read. When I open my mouth to speak, though, I stop and close it instead. Pick up a stick and start climbing up the hill. I can't make up for what my father did, and I don't get to pretend I can.

White privilege swallows us whole, and we swim around in it unaware that it's the air we breathe. Hiding from those books all those years was a part of that privilege. Reading them now, if I'm not careful, could become part of it, too. White people get to hide from their legacies all the time, and no one asks us to answer to it. But if I decide I'm ready to answer to mine, and then I hold it up and say *but no no no, mine is different,* I'm not looking at anything, not honestly. I'm not investigating if I'm too busy apologizing. I'm not working to understand how my legacy contributed to where we are in this country today if I spend the whole time arguing that really my father was pulling back Baldwin's curtain. So no, I do not mean to suggest that. What I mean to say is, my dad was trapped in this world just like the rest of us, right up until the moment he chose to leave it. I've got to figure out why his answer to that trap was to write slavers. I've got to figure out how it affected him.

17

GEORGE MCNEILL, friend of both my parents before they knew each other, also a writer, was the person who got them all to Rome in 1967. He knew the city, said he could help them find a place to live. I don't know how long he stayed after they got settled, but his name comes up in many stories my mother has told me about that city. He's a white man from the South, raised in Mississippi, and might have been the only southerner my father knew. As I build my narrative about what preoccupied my dad enough to set these novels in the South during slavery, McNeill as source becomes one possible answer. So one morning I pick up the phone and dial. As I do, I realize that yesterday I was a girl without a dad who had learned to live as though that didn't matter. Today I'm a grown woman who calls her father's old friends to ask questions and find out who he was. Today I'm someone who admits this hurts.

"Your dad was stubborn to a fault," McNeill tells me in his thick accent, ten minutes into our call. "He was ambitious, he was hardworking. But what sent your father around the bend was that he'd set a goal of making a million dollars before he turned thirty. It was impossible, considering the pittance each book sold for."

I think about that phrase *around the bend,* and wonder if my dad's old friend really chalks up his mental illness and suicide to a missed financial

goal. If he really thinks it could be that simple. If McNeill thinks my
father is to blame for setting such a stupid goal in the first place.

But before I can ask him any of that, he starts reiterating what my
mother has already told me. That my dad wanted to do something
bigger with his books, didn't want to write slavers forever, but that he
had a mortgage to pay. "He just wrote what was selling," he says. "The
black-white thing was selling, and there were people who couldn't
write that, but your father could write it, so he did."

McNeill doesn't want me to ascribe too much meaning to this and
won't entertain my questions about why exactly he could do it. He
reminds me of my dad's editing position at Tower Books, about how
he knew what the publishing industry was like, what it wanted. "We
cranked books out, production-line style. It didn't have anything to do
with what we were interested in."

As McNeill keeps talking, I think that the more people assure me
Dad's books were just the particular brand of brick he laid, the less I
believe it. But this man on the other end of the line is being sweet to
me, he's telling me about the father I never knew, so I don't want to
get confrontational. I would never get confrontational with Dad's old
friend. I just listen and smile at his memories and try to picture the life
he's outlining for me.

"What was that book he did about the West?" McNeill asks toward
the end of our call, and I supply its title, *Jeremiah Painter*. My old copy
of this book sits on my shelf now, but I haven't read it yet. It's published
under Dad's real name, and on the cover is a black cowboy, but I've
decided to read his books in the order they were published. I'll get to
Jeremiah Painter in time.

"I don't think he'd had any experience in the West, but that's a good
book," McNeill says. He goes on for a minute, describing the first scene
and how movie-like it was, complimenting my father, saying that if
he'd just lived long enough to write more books like that, he could have
been great. I love this thought and am eager to keep McNeill talking.
When he drops a crumb that I pick up without thinking, I don't yet
know how much I will later regret this entire phone call.

"All of these old novels can be sold as e-books now, you know," he
says. "I've sold some of mine, and now I get a certain amount of money

deposited into my checking account each month. It's just free money, I didn't have to do anything for it. The books are already written."

He suggests I tell my mother about this, says *Jeremiah Painter* is the kind of book with shelf life, the kind of book that could do well today. "I've gotten as little as $17 a month, and as much as seven and half thousand dollars," he says, telling me about his "break-out book," *Plantation.* It's set in Louisiana—like the Chane books—and was first published in 1975. McNeill says this book doesn't do "the black-white thing"; the sex here stays within race. I'll find out later, when I order a copy of it, that that's because it's often between siblings.

"But a book like *Jeremiah Painter*, it's so different. It could do really well. I'll e-mail you the publisher's contact information, you share it with your mother," he says just before we hang up. "I bet she's not in a position to turn away free money."

I don't tell McNeill that ever since my mom retired, she's been living on Social Security and a dwindling savings account that was modest to begin with. I don't tell him that I stay up some nights wondering how she'll pay her rent. But as he talks, I do think about what seven and a half thousand dollars could do for her. I do think about how it would feel if my father reached out from the other side to help her today. Maybe he wasn't great when he was alive, but could he be considered great today? Is it possible McNeill is right, and *Jeremiah Painter* is great?

That night when my mom comes to dinner and I tell her about the call with McNeill and the possibility of republishing Dad's old books now, when I tell her about McNeill's seven and half thousand dollars, none of it feels dangerous. That realization won't come until later, because the fact is that my girlhood dreams of a famous father are founded on lies and in reality he wrote slavery porn, not fiction I can stand behind. I know enough by now—or I should have known enough—to see that this is all very dangerous. To see that this is the moment I become complicit in my father's legacy.

But I don't see it yet. I'm still looking for my dad.

18

A COLD SPRING rain beats on my office window as I tab through a used bookseller's Amazon site, a hot cup of tea at hand. This isn't my first internet search for my father, but today I'm not looking for his pseudonyms. Today I'm looking for the real man, the man McNeill told me he thought could have been great. So I type "George Wolk" into the search field and am happy to see them there, the four books he published without a mask, lined up like a cartoon of my childhood bookshelf, proof that he really was once alive. *The Leopold Contract, 400 Brattle Street, The Man Who Dealt in Blood, Jeremiah Painter.*

"*Jeremiah Painter* would've made a great movie," I remember my mom saying one afternoon to her friend Patty soon after Dad's death. They sat across from each other at the long kitchen counter, coffee cooling in the blue hourglass-shaped mugs between them. Mom's voice seemed far away so I looked up at her from the floor where I was coloring Winnie the Pooh outside the lines. But she looked like the same mom as always—her face firm, her laughter loud, her eyes round and blue—so I went back to my task, ignoring the words I didn't understand. Words like *Western* and *Civil War* and *black cowboy.* When I looked at the cover of that book—which I didn't tell anyone I liked to do, but it was my favorite one to hold because it fit right into my hand like it wanted to tell me a story—I thought the image on the cover sort of looked like Dad. They were both so tall, they both had big fancy mustaches and a serious look in their eyes. "God help the man who called him boy!" it announced above my dad's name, but I didn't know what that meant so I just kept looking at Jeremiah's face with its mustache so much like Dad's mustache.

I click "Add to Cart" on an Amazon used bookseller's copy of *Jeremiah Painter.* Goodwill Books is only asking a penny plus shipping, and even though I have a copy of it already—the same one I used to hold those cold afternoons in the back hallway of the house on State Street—I'm feeling sentimental and don't want to leave the things Dad made stranded in some Goodwill warehouse. But as soon as I do it, I forget it, and hardly think twice when, several weeks later, I walk down to the mailbox with my dog and find a small brown book-shaped package waiting for me. This is nothing unusual. Dad's books have been arriving thick and fast these days—slavers as well as the hardcore porn he wrote under other names. It's not until I'm standing in my dim kitchen waiting for the dog that I rip the top off the package and pull out that copy of *Jeremiah Painter* and see the same brown face with the thick black mustache and those same mint-green lapels I studied as a child.

The dog is ready to come in now, so I walk to the mudroom with Jeremiah in my hand, hold open the door for him, and turn the book to the first page. There's a giant black X that looks like it was done in sharpie or a fading black marker, and I'm pissed. "Who the hell wrote in my book?" I ask the dog now at my feet. It takes me a moment to see that the X is crossing out teaser copy, teaser copy that says at the top "I don't like niggers," and I say, "Okay, at least the censor is political." Then I see there's something written below the X in messy handwriting.

"Don't read the goddamn copy," it says. It takes me a minute to make it out.

I turn the page. There on the blank page across from the title it says, in that same messy handwriting, in that same fading black marker, "Read the book. Love George."

The things in this world that I touch that my father has touched are very rare. And, I realize, standing there, I have never seen his handwriting before.

I turn another page, and below the printed dedication, *For Janet and David,* Dad has written, clearer than on the previous pages, "& for John

& U." Underneath that he's signed just his first name, underlined it. *George.* But he's written no surname, so these must have been friends.

Friends who later donated the book to the Goodwill. But friends.

Friends I can't trace. Friends my mom can't help me name.

"Would he have used the letter U to mean the first letter in some-one's first name, or to mean 'you,' like the kids do today?" I ask my mom when I call her to tell her about Dad walking into my kitchen this afternoon.

"He might have done either," she says. She pauses for a long mo-ment, and I can see her lips mouthing the names "John and U" as though she's standing next to me. "I have no idea," she says again.

After we hang up, I bring the book to my desk, put it on top of *Chane,* thankful that it can protect me from *Chane.* It sits there while I make my freelance deadline, but every now and then I open it and look at those words from my dad for a minute. *Love George.* I think about the probability of a book from an Amazon used bookseller having my father's signature in it and making its way to my door.

It seems like a message, so that afternoon I start reading.

JEREMIAH PAINTER is barely one hundred pages long. It's set in the small fictional town of Divide, Wyoming, on the edge of the western frontier, just after the Civil War. Train tracks run along its main street, splitting the town in half. The laundry, hardware store, saloon, and gun shop are on one side. The jail, run by a man named Pierce, and the freight office, operated by a man named Terl, are on the other. Up the road, on Bank Street, is the bank. Down the road, on Woman Street, is the brothel. The men in Divide are hard white men who have all seen tragedy and are trying to make a life in the new country. Some owned slaves before the war, all fought on one side or the other. The women in this book are few, establishing early on that this isn't porn—it's a west-ern. There's a white woman called Mrs., who runs the brothel; a pros-titute who works for her—a black woman named Suzanne who tries to get Jeremiah to leave town before he's killed; and two Native American women. One never gets a name—she's just called Terl's Squaw, and I have to set aside the anger I feel boiling if I'm going to continue. Have to shut down the rage I feel to know my father thought this racial slur

enough to name a woman. The other Native American woman is her
sister, named Fawn because of her big eyes, and I know this is another
kind of reductivism but at least she has a name, I think, as I realize, too,
that she has a name because she and Jeremiah will end up together by
the end. So there is a racial taboo in this book, there is a crossing of
boundaries, but it's neither central to the plot nor Dad's typical taboo.
Still, it's where I find my attention landing.

At one point—just after Jeremiah has saved the life of the same
sheriff who jailed him when he arrived in town—he comes upon Fawn
in the woods. "She had known he was coming," my father writes, "that
someone was coming, because she was looking at him before he saw
her and there was no surprise on her face." Ah, I think, the native person at one with nature. Thanks, Dad.

But then, on the next page, this:

> Fawn looked away and stood up, brushing her hide dress and
> shaking her head just once as if to clear it. "No one knows I
> come up here when my sister takes Terl's courage and makes
> him a white man."

Makes him a white man? Here, through the voice of a Native American
woman, my father acknowledges that a white man who sleeps with an
indigenous woman, a woman whose people he and his people have directly held down and oppressed and killed, is made by that act to feel
more powerful, more important, more *white.* This acknowledgment
does something to me, the reader of my father's slavers. It helps me see
that although he screwed up, that although his path was crooked and
his motivations unsettling, my father knew that race was a complicated
beast. That white power and white privilege depend on the oppression of
black and brown people. And if he knew that, might he also have known
that his books added to the morass? Might he have been trying, in some
weird backward way, to apologize for that with this particular book?

> Jeremiah said nothing. He stood quietly, trying to understand
> what the woman had said. Finally, he said, "Try to make me a
> white man and maybe I'll keep your secret, but you won't make
> it woman, my skin's too black."

"Black-White man," she said. She hissed her words. "You
would be the same as any of them."

"Worse," Jeremiah said.

DID I WONDER if there was a power dynamic that Ngoni and I were
recreating—explicitly or not—when we got married? Of course I
thought about it. But there's no easy answer here. What I can say is
that when I met Ngoni, when we talked late into the night about our
fathers, about the people who raised us, about the illnesses we each
carried in our backgrounds and our genes, I felt for the first time that I
was speaking to someone in my mother tongue.

Ngoni isn't an American, he didn't grow up as a racial minority.
That fact affects what I mean when I say we spoke the same language.
Ngoni grew up in a middle-class family in a country that had just won
its independence from white settlers, a country that believed the worst
was behind them. It wasn't. But my husband grew up in a time of hope,
he was handed a dream and, despite the impediments in his history,
told to try to fly.

I grew up in a middle-class family that had just won independence
from the grip of my father's mental illness. I grew up believing that
the worst was behind me. I was handed a dream and told, despite the
impediments in my history, to try to fly. There are ways in which Ngoni
and I come from the same place. Of course I was protected by white
privilege, and that saved me from so much. Of course I can't compare
the brutality of colonialism to how it felt to live at 98 State Street when
my dad was sick. And, of course, Ngoni also lived with a sick father—
for many more years than I did. My comparisons here are metaphoric,
and I'm not so naïve as to suggest that I can ever fully understand his
childhood experiences. But I do believe that if race structures the power
dynamics within our relationship—and it must some of the time—it
does not take them over because we speak the same language. We can
communicate about all of this, and we do. We are not the characters in
my father's books, we don't even come from their lands.

19

IN MY FAMILY'S lore, there are two stories we tell about my father's illness. One is more of a joke than a story. He used to sit on the front porch of the house on State Street and get the people walking by to scratch their asses.

"I never thought he was serious," my mother always says when she tells it. "But looking back now, I think he really thought he could control other people with his mind."

The other is that Dad's first breakdown happened when he was at Cornell. He woke up one morning and believed the atomic bomb had dropped in the night. He didn't leave his room for two days. Eventually, his friend Bruce convinced him it was safe to come out. This story helps me categorize my father—if he had a breakdown in college, his life followed a certain textbook trajectory. Most schizophrenics show signs of the illness in their late teens or early twenties. Dad was sick a long time, I can tell myself. This calms me for reasons I can't fully explain. Maybe because it means there is a deadline to the disease—if the people I love are still sane in their thirties, they will stay sane forever. I need some kind of marker. Some kind of assurance that what happened to our fathers won't happen to us, that what happened to my mother—to Rose—won't happen to me.

But many people in my family deny the Cornell story. They point to his breakdown at the *sesshin*—the one from which he never recovered—as his first. So one morning that spring, when my kids are at school, I call Bruce on the phone to see if he can trace that tale. He somehow doesn't sound surprised to hear from me, despite never having heard from me before. And when I ask him about Dad, he uses new words like "brash" and "aggressive," instead of the *handsome, charming,* and *funny* I'm used to.

"When your father got to Cornell—remember how young he was, only sixteen—he wanted to look more sophisticated than he was," Bruce says. "And he was pretty sophisticated—he read a lot, stuff I hadn't ever read. He was obviously smart."

But Bruce doesn't remember rescuing him from the dorm room. Has no frame of reference for my story. "Maybe I rescued him without knowing it," he says.

I'm quiet on the other end of the phone, hoping that something will come to the surface if I'm patient. Something to help me piece the puzzle together.

"It never struck me—during that period, or for that matter later—that he was depressive," he says after a minute. Bruce and my dad stayed friends after college. They lived near each other in New York for years, and both men eventually moved to western Massachusetts after they got married. I've driven by the sign for Bruce's medical practice my whole life, though, for reasons I don't know, he and my mother never spoke after the funeral, so we've never really met.

"There was a woman he was attracted to in New York," Bruce says in a tone that makes it sound as though he's changing the subject. His voice isn't tender, he's not protecting me from anything, and I assume he's about to tell me about how my father was a womanizer. It's a story I've heard before. "He was already with Susan, but that didn't stop him from being with other women."

Yes, yes, I want to say. *I know.* Then I smile, because Bruce can't tell me anything new. I'm solid. I can't be taken down so easily. Nothing surprises me. Now I just want this conversation to end, because he hasn't confirmed my story and so I'd like to pretend we never spoke. But I can't hang up yet because he's still talking.

"I visited them in the country when Nan and Josh were little—I don't think you were born yet. Your dad showed me advertisements"— Bruce pronounces the word the old-fashioned way, with the emphasis on 'vert'—"which he believed were messages from her."

"Wait," I say. "From the woman in New York?" I stop myself from adding *That's crazy!* I find my journalist voice and ask a clarifying question. "Were they personal ads? A sort of *Desperately Seeking Susan* kind of thing?"

"God, no!" Bruce laughs at the idea. "He kept finding adverts in the paper, people selling their old refrigerators, people looking to buy a tractor. He thought they were messages from her to him."

There are whole entire worlds I can't see now. My eyes feel like they're spinning backward in my head. I want to hang up the phone. I want to lie down on the floor. "It went on for a long time."

When I don't say anything, Bruce keeps talking. "He showed them to me, he said, 'This is from her, and this is what it means.' It always seemed pretty bizarre to me, but I just said, 'Oh well, okay.'"

This is a whole new origin story, one that may not confirm my father first fell ill in college, but one that seems to indicate he was sick well before he went off to the *sesshin* when I was three. This new story from Bruce tells about a time before I was born.

What would have happened if someone had done something sooner?

20

ON A HUMID summer day in 2015, I sit down at the glass table that takes up most of my aunt Rachel's suburban patio and thank her for letting me come. Rachel's husband Paul brings me a glass of white wine and crinkles his eyes in a smile through his round wire-framed glasses. I thank him and take a sip, hoping it might settle something inside me, and look across at my aunt, who isn't smiling. Her skin is pink and I wonder if she's been in the sun. Her graying hair is cut short. Her nose is longer and more pointed than mine, but clearly from the same mold. I don't come here a lot, but when I called and asked if I could visit, said that I wanted to talk about my dad, she didn't hesitate. Set up a room for me to sleep in.

"I've been reading Dad's books," I tell her now, because the look on her face says it's time to get down to business. My voice is less steady than I like. "I'm trying to find out more about him."

Paul hands me a plate of crackers and cheese, and when I turn to smile at him again, his face seems to be saying, *finally.*

"I'll tell you whatever you want to know," Rachel says, and I realize that with such a wide opening, I'm not sure where to start. I don't have a list of questions.

"Maybe could you tell me about your childhood? Really, anything you feel I should know about him."

Rachel tells me first about the fights they had as children in the Brooklyn apartment where they grew up. In one story, her friend came over to play and my dad went into a rage over something. "Maybe the new TV and what program we were going to watch," she says. "We were scared, so we ran into the bathroom and locked the door. Then we climbed out of the window and down the fire escape and ran down the street to her apartment."

Rachel has to pause here, either to remember it better or to get up her nerve, I can't tell.

"When we got there, this friend said she'd had no idea. 'My brother is mean to me,' she said. 'But he's nothing like that.'" In Rachel's voice is the vindication she must have felt as a little girl, finally being seen as the victim. "My parents blamed me for everything," she says.

But Rachel is clear that she's not tracing Dad's illness, she's not saying it started way back then. She's just saying that he was mean to her when they were little. Really mean. But I don't know what exactly he'd done to scare them so much, and I can't ask because of the look on her face. Because of the fear still present in her eyes. I stay quiet, nod sympathetically.

"You know why I studied psychology in college?" she asks me after a while, and I shake my head. "Because I thought I was crazy. I was the only person of the four of us in the house who thought the way I thought. All three of them had their way of thinking, and it was different from mine, so I thought I must be crazy."

I nod again and smile at her like I understand, but I don't really and I wish she would tell me something I could hold onto. There's a long pause then, and it takes all my energy not to fill it. I want to change the subject or tell her a story about my kids or make a joke to stir up the energy in this fenced-in garden, make it brighter.

When she starts talking again, she brings herself up to what seems at first like safer territory. She talks about which cousin married which neighbor and how they wound up. She reminds me of our family history—stories she's told me before. After a while, she says, "George visited me once when I was at college. I was so excited. I thought he really wanted to see me."

She pauses and I nod, eager to know what she knows already.

"But all he could talk about was Anna. Did I know where she was? Had she called me?"

Anna was my dad's first wife. This is the first I've heard that she might have flirted with leaving him. In the only story I know about her, she was lovesick and unstable and threatened to follow my parents to Rome to get her man back. In the only story I know about Anna, she was a blip on my father's screen, disconnected from everything else in his life. And long gone back to Holland, where she came from.

"Anna and I were close," Rachel says. "But I was a kid. She hadn't called me. She wouldn't call me if they were having problems. But George was sure I would know. He was so paranoid."

"It seems like maybe he was sick longer than we knew," I try. So many of the things she's said seem to point there. So many of them suggest even Bruce's origin story isn't exactly where it began.

"No." She's firm. Resolute. "This wasn't his illness, this was just George."

I can do nothing but nod my head. She has left me no space to hypothesize with her, to connect the dots she laid out and add them to the few I carry in my pocket. I think of my sons and the fights they sometimes have, how neither one has ever needed to run from the house in fear of the other. How this doesn't strike me as the normal behavior of an older brother. I think of the paranoia she has told me my father carried later in life, the certainty that his wife was doing something she shouldn't, and I compare that to my own husband, to the trust I don't have to ask for, have never had to ask for. It's a shadow in the corner of my eye, this notion that there were signs of what was to come. This notion that Dad was ill and no one noticed. But it's a shadow I have to blink away. Rachel won't have it here.

"After I got back from visiting your dad when he was a resident at Austen Riggs, your grandfather and I took a walk along the river," she says after a while. "I told him that I'd studied psychology all my adult life, and that people with these symptoms are the people who kill themselves."

"What did he say?" I ask, as though it's a story I'm following and the hero might after all turn out to be my tall gray-haired grandfather who, now that it's been pointed out to him, sees the danger and swoops in to save his son.

"I don't remember."

I sit across from her deflated, aware of each of the questions I couldn't—or didn't—ask. What *did* my dad do that was so scary she had to run out of the house? Why *was* he looking for Anna, and what was their marriage really like? Was there a treatment that could have saved him? I don't know what stops me from asking these questions, if it's really that Rachel blocks any openings or if it's that despite this quest I'm on, I'm still the girl at my father's funeral, too scared to speak. Because every time I talk about my dad, every time I tell the story or learn something new, a part of me believes that I can put the pieces together right this time. This time he won't be dead when we get to the end. Maybe I can't ask these questions because of the pain I'll feel when their answers don't change a thing.

THESE DAYS I drive by Austen Riggs sometimes, on my way to soccer tournaments and travel league games and the new home of an old friend and the summer place of a cousin I didn't know I had until I started this quest. When the kids are in the backseat I try not to crane my neck as we pass, and I wonder how old I'll let them get before I tell them their grandfather died there. Right there an hour down the road from home. Right there in that building that looks more like a museum than a mental institution. Right there with the tall white walls and the great green garden and the old-fashioned architecture that promises safety and recovery and stability and hope.

But it doesn't say that to me.

I once got a letter from my first love, after he'd left, saying he had a summer job in the Berkshires putting up event tents. Saying he'd spent the day at Riggs putting up a tent. Saying he'd been thinking about me, therefore. First I hated him for knowing that place, for peeping in windows and seeing what I never could. For imagining my small self walking up that path to those great wooden doors. For putting me there, for knowing I'd been there all along.

It was only later that I wondered: What do they celebrate under a tent at Riggs? What festivities are these? Where did we send my dad to die?

PAUL SMEARS WHITEFISH salad on a cracker and passes it over to me across the patio table. Rachel rubs her eyes and gazes at the garden. I take a deep breath and wonder how awkward it would be if I got back in my car and drove home instead of spending the night with the ghosts we've called out.

"I'm so glad you're making these inquiries, Jules," Paul says. "Rachel's memories can help you figure out so much about your father, and that is important. But you know who else you should talk to? Anna."

At the mention of her name again, I hear my mother's voice asking, "Can you imagine if she'd shown up in Rome?" The only possible answer was a loyal *No*, and I've never before thought to ask another thing about her. It has never occurred to me that she was an important person in my father's life. But here in this garden I'm starting to imagine a lot of things I hadn't before. I don't know if Anna did show up in Rome, though I do think Dad flew to Mexico at some point for a quick divorce. But why does Paul mention her now, casually, as though she isn't just someone Dad and Rachel knew fifty years ago? I look at him across the table, his garden gleaming in the background. Rachel's eyes are red and round as saucers when I turn to her for confirmation. She gives a brief smile and nods. I realize they know her now.

"Actually, she was meant to visit us this summer," Paul says, confirming my thought. "But she took a fall and is recuperating in the hospital. If she's well enough, she will come in September."

I look from aunt to uncle, back and forth across a table I've sat at only a handful of times. Rachel was barely in touch with me when I was growing up, never speaks to my mother now, but here they are explaining an active relationship with the woman my father was married to for ten minutes.

I look down at my hands and try to figure out how to get out of this. The prospect of meeting Anna is a step beyond anything I think I'm doing. I don't see yet that I'm only at the beginning of the story, that there are more people to talk to, more doors to walk through. I don't want there to be more people to talk to. I don't want to open myself up to all that this means. I was brave enough to come here to ask my father's sister about his childhood, brave enough to call a few of his old friends, but that is it. There's no more brave left in my bones.

"She doesn't e-mail, Jules," Paul says. "She's very old-fashioned. Let me ask her next time we speak if I can give you her address."

It's that idea—of writing her a letter—that opens me up. Now I'm a journalist and Anna is a source. I smile and thank him for the offer, plan to ask them some more questions over dinner, excuse myself to get a grip.

I GET HOME from Rachel's house on a hot summer night and find Ngoni on the green couch, the windows open to the breeze and the kids in their beds. I pull a book out of my bag and hand it to him, resigned that these things will continue to work their way into our marriage for some time to come.

Rachel had led me down into her basement with the promise of some of Dad's books. I assumed she would have copies of the *Chane* books, or the hardcore porn with white people on the covers—books I was collecting but didn't feel compelled to read to understand my legacy. But she handed me a slaver I didn't have in my stack, *Natchez Kingdom* by Sebastian Watt. As I held it in my hands, a memory started to emerge. I'm a little girl—six or seven years old—standing by the bookcase in the back hallway of the house on the State Street. "Sebastian Watt is George Wolk," I repeat to myself in a whisper. "These names are both Dad's." Do I study the people on the cover or wonder why it says their love is forbidden, their passion savage? Or can I even read those words, can I begin to make sense of this?

Now in our living room, Ngoni glances at it quickly and says, "Oh yeah, that one." He's seen it before.

Wait. He's seen it before? Before that flash in Rachel's basement, I didn't have any memories of Dad's slavers until my cousin brought them into my kitchen. But his memory is so specific—"It was in that glass-fronted bookcase in your mother's bedroom," he says. "You showed them to me the first time I came to meet your mom." And it's impossible to argue. His memory trumps mine because he has it. All I have is an absence.

"I don't remember ever seeing these books before," I say, wanting very much for it to be true. I don't want this to be who I am. I don't want this to be who I have always been.

I sit on the couch with Ngoni, trying to trace when I let myself forget my legacy. After showing him this book, did I push it back onto the shelf, ease shut the glass-fronted bookcase, and let the fact of it slip immediately away? Or was it later, after I became a mother, when I set up a block in my memory? Did I hope to protect myself from who my father was so that I could also protect my family? Ngoni and I face the television, but I don't know if anything plays on it. I'm unsure what to do with the feelings coiling up in my gut and demanding attention. Unsure what it means to be told I've seen something, to be told I've held something in my hands, to be told I showed something to the person I'd brought home to meet my mother, and then to realize that I put that thing away and forgot that it ever even was there. Memory is a slippery thing, indeed.

Ngoni places his hand on top of mine. He doesn't say anything, and neither do I. *Natchez Kingdom* lies on my lap infecting the air around us. I think that, now that I've opened it, the closet door can't be closed. I think about how my legacy allowed me to forget those books, allowed me not to consider their meaning even as I showed them to the man I was falling in love with. Allowed me to wear my blinders, all my life. My legacy is the white supremacy that runs this country, and despite the fact that I'm raising sons in a place that will call them black, in a place that seems hell-bent on destroying the black body, my legacy contributes to what this country is. As Ta-Nehisi Coates tells us, "the police reflect America in all of its will and fear," and isn't it will and fear that kept on my blinders? "The Dream was gilded by novels and adventure stories." And didn't my dad write some of those? My legacy is "the brightly rendered version of [this] country as it has always declared itself" that Coates urges us to look away from. But to understand where

I come from as a white woman and how it contributes to the world in which my mixed-race family is trying to live, I can't look away from the brightly rendered version—I have to look inside it.

THE NEXT DAY I call up my sister and my brother and my mother to ask if they remember Dad's slavers sitting on our shelves. The story comes out in bits and pieces. The glass-fronted bookcase was Dad's. He'd kept copies of his books on the bottom shelf.

"I used to look at them when I was little, to freak myself out," my sister tells me.

"That's where they were until I threw them out," my mom says. "Which I did because I hated them and I didn't want you guys to define your dad in those terms." These are tender words about my father's legacy, about its impact on us. But when did she throw them out? Before or after I brought Ngoni home? She doesn't remember.

Maybe I can't say, after all, that I had no idea how my father made a living when I got married. Maybe, instead, I have to be open to the possibility that I was influenced by ideas of interracial romance from a very young age. I don't remember. But as I work that possibility into my heart, I ask myself how this story would have been different if Dad had survived long enough to meet my husband. Would they have discussed the history of slavery? Would Dad have tried to convince Ngoni that his books were part of an educational enterprise, one in which unsuspecting readers of softcore pornography got lessons in the brutality of that institution? Or would every single thing be different in that world? Would I be married to Ngoni at all in that world? It's not a question I can sit with for long.

22

"I REMEMBER the day Dad got his biggest advance," Nan says, smiling. This is one of the few fun stories we can tell about our dad, and we like to revisit it. We're sitting on the second-story deck of a fish fry above the East River on a warm summer day, a rare sisters' lunch. Nan's brown hair is pulled into a high bun and her sunglasses cover much of her face, but I can see the way her eyes crinkle at the edges when she laughs, as she laughs now. I can see the reason the waiter knew when we sat down that we're sisters. It's in the composite more than a specific trait we share—feature for feature we don't look that much alike, but no one who saw us on the street would guess wrong. "It was meant to be his most literary novel yet."

"When the call came in from his agent, Dad was out on a run, right?" I say. I was only two in this story, Nan's the authority, but I like to pretend I was part of it, like to tell the story, too.

"Right, so Mom piled us all into the old VW with no seatbelts, and we drove in circles until we found him."

I picture the encounter on Elm Street, along the edge of the college campus, just up from the pond and near the chapel where his funeral would be in a few years. I picture Dad wearing a white T-shirt and short green running shorts with white piping. His long legs are hairy and muscular and our black Lab, Shandy, is loyal without a leash at his side. I picture Dad all sweaty, his glasses slipping off his face, his mustache broad when he smiles at seeing us. I picture him so surprised at this gift of his family here on his run, so happy to see us all.

"Mom rolled down the window and shouted at him as we passed," Nan says.

"Forty thousand dollars!" we yell together, making the waiter look over with a question on his face. But Nan and I don't stop.

"He hooted and hollered, but kept on running, pumping his arms above his head like Rocky." I let Nan finish the story. I see Mom at the wheel, her smile wide as she steers us back toward home.

After our food arrives, after we each tell a few stories about our kids, after we catch the waiter's eye so we can order more wine—how often do we have this kind of freedom?—I tell Nan that I'm starting to think Dad was sick longer than we knew. I don't tell her about my phone calls with Dad's friends or much about my visit to Rachel because I don't know how to catalogue the information I'm learning yet. I'm the one who decided to do this, I don't want to inflict it on anyone else—not until I know what it all means, not until I can index it, make sense of it, process it through my own systems so I can help my family process it through theirs when it's time. That is, at least, what I tell myself. It doesn't feel like I'm withholding anything from them—not really. But maybe I do need to keep control of the narrative for now, hold onto it for the time being. Maybe what some might see as emotional reserve—what I might call in my mother emotional reserve—is actually one way to maintain control of a thing that is spinning wild. One way to claim a thing so it can't take everything else over. So instead I ask Nan to remind me of what she knows. And patient and calm like a big sister, even though she's told it to me so many times before, Nan begins where everyone always begins.

"Dad went to a Zen monastery somewhere in upstate New York or western Massachusetts when you were three," she says. "He hoped to become enlightened."

Our father had found Buddhism around the time he and my mom started practicing aikido every night at a dojo across town. Mom would go on to run that dojo, but Nan tells me now that it was Dad's idea to join. "I think he hoped aikido and Buddhism and meditation would hold answers for him," she says. "So he went off to the *sesshin* when he thought he was ready."

About the *sesshin* there are other stories, these from my mother. The call she got from the teacher's disciple announcing that Dad had elected not to sleep for the entire ten-day retreat. Announcing that Dad had stolen the teacher's soup bowl in a misunderstood interpretation of the passage from regular man to enlightened. Announcing the frantic look in his eyes when he left, headed for home. And when he got home, something was different about the way he carried himself, and he spent his days in the small guest room at the front of the house. "He's working," Mom told us. "He's writing."

But the things that came out weren't, either of them, that literary novel he'd gotten the big advance for. I know now that one was *Natchez Kingdom*, published in 1980. Dad died on January 5 of that year, so he probably never saw it in print. When I tell Nan about Rachel giving me that book, I pull up the Goodreads review on my phone and hand it to her, watch her face as she reads it, written by a reader named Karla, who gave it two stars in 2011. "The action up to [a point] was interesting and had some degree of focus, but after that, the writing became very disjointed and, I thought, schizophrenic."

Nan hands me back my phone, a distant look in her eye as she replaces her sunglasses. I want to tell her I can't believe someone read that book in 2011. I want to tell her I'm scared about the impact these books have on the world. I want to ask her why she thinks our father wrote them. Why she thinks Karla wrote in her review that she'd wanted to find "a steamy little plantation tale with voodoo and illicit sex," or if she's as relieved as I am to read that this Goodreads reviewer was disappointed to find the novel "more of a straightforward historical-ish tale." But I can't ask her any of those things because if I did I would have to admit that I've recently suggested our mother republish Dad's old books as e-books, and I'd have to connect the dots right here in this lovely outdoor restaurant on this sunshiny day between our father's racist legacy and my own complicity in it. I'd have to admit to my sister—I'd have to admit to myself—that Karla doesn't only shop at tag sales with old pulpy novels in piles and then post about them on Goodreads. That Karla and others like her will soon be able to find these books on Amazon, thanks to me. And anyway, our second glass of wine has arrived and the curtain has come down across Nan's face and now my job is to make her laugh, bring her back to today. So I change the subject.

THE OTHER THING Dad produced in that small front room upstairs in the house on State Street in the months after his return from the *sesshin* was a long treatise that he told my mother about when she asked.

"They're stealing my money!" he stormed.

When she asked who "they" were, he shouted back something about the shah of Iran and his publisher at *Playboy*, whom he believed to be in cahoots. When she found his notebooks after his death, the writing they contained was composed entirely in numeric code.

23

THESE HOT SUMMER DAYS, reading my father's slavers while my kids are at camp, these days of trying to trace my legacy, I find it easier to talk to people about my father's work than about his illness. I don't want to walk down a path where I discover his final thoughts, the details of his depression, the reasons he broke. These days I change the subject when all that comes up, and I ask more questions about the racism he revealed in the pages of his slavers. Find as many reasons to pile up about why I should hate him for writing that racist smut as I can. It helps it hurt less that he was gone my whole life.

So when I get to my mom's house one afternoon, I don't bring up my father's belief that some woman from New York was communicating with him through personal ads for refrigerators or tell her about my visit to my aunt Rachel. I want to forget those conversations ever happened, so I ask her to tell me about their trip to Rome—the one during which he wrote his first published books.

She starts with the story about the freight ship ride across the Atlantic, and I think about the timing—the summer of 1967, the summer the *Loving v. Virginia* decision abolished the remaining anti-miscegenation laws in the U.S. A summer hot with the Civil Rights Movement. I wonder what it was like to cross the Atlantic on a ship at that time, what ideas might have been sparked traveling the opposite route of the slave ships my dad would write about when they arrived.

Then Mom tells about a pulley system my parents used to get food and wine from the restaurant below. They installed it with the help of the restaurateur's eldest son, Bruno. When they were ready, they simply had to whistle, and Bruno would send up a basket.

"Have I told you before about the outdoor shower?" Mom asks me, and I shake my head. "It was on the rooftop, and there was a baroness or someone who lived across the way. Your dad would always make a big to-do when he was getting ready to take a shower, calling out across the rooftops to get her attention, in case she wanted to watch. As far as I know, she was unimpressed."

I laugh, because this is the old kind of story about my dad. About his giant ego and his tender heart—one that, like a child's, might believe that if he wanted it badly enough, he could have the baroness *and* my mother. And why not? I get the sense from my mom that everything felt possible in Rome. I laugh with my mother because, after all, my dad was funny. He was egocentric and maniacal and possibly a total prick, but he called across the rooftops to a woman he believed to be royalty and hoped she might want to watch him shower. It's funny.

"Jules?" Mom says when I get up to put away our dishes. It's almost time to pick up the kids. "I thought these might be useful to you." She hands me a pile of onionskin papers I hadn't noticed were tucked in the corner of her new red couch. The letters he wrote to her from Rome after she left.

I smile to discover that there is something on this planet my father gave my mother that she saved. In a world full of missing manuscripts and diaries and trinkets he kept on his desk and baronesses who will never remember him, here is one actual thing he left behind. She hands them to me now.

"I tried to read them last night, to make sure there wasn't anything too racy in there, but I can't read his handwriting anymore," she says.

In a world full of questions I don't even know how to ask, my mother has just provided a possible answer. But I know even as I accept the letters that this is an answer I'm not yet brave enough to look inside. I know as I drive home that bright afternoon that they will sit unopened on my desk for some time.

It's not only his handwriting I don't think I'll be able to read.

24

"THE FIRST BOOK is on Amazon," Mom calls me one day late that summer to report. I've largely put the e-books, like so many things I don't like to think about, out of my mind, categorized them as not really about me, not really about my journey to understand my dad. But my mom has spent the summer proofing the scans the publisher made of the old paperbacks, and so reading some of the same books I've been reading. Sometimes when she comes for dinner, I try to get her to talk about their plotlines, about the racism and misogyny I see in every sentence. But she doesn't want to talk about that. She talks instead about how it could be possible that she missed some of these typos the last time she read the books—in manuscript form as he wrote them, when she was his first editor. She is tired of my argument that my father was racist, she wants to change the subject when I bring it up. I don't let myself consider how this might link her to him, how she is complicit in this story, too. It's so much better to think of my mom as the hero who raised three children on her own after her husband's suicide. I'd just like to keep her there.

When she calls me about the first e-book, though, I'm driving back from a research trip, deep in the woods of Maine, and I just hope our call doesn't drop. She's excited and hopeful, and I can hear McNeill's seven and half thousand dollars clattering around on the inside of her head like a beam of light.

"Oh!" I say. "Which one did they publish first?" Of course I want it to be *The Leopold Contract* or *The Man Who Dealt in Blood*. Even *Jeremiah Painter* would be better, but I'm not so naïve anymore. These last months have stripped most of that away, and the deeper into my father's career I've gotten the more I just get it that the e-book folks will start with a slaver. So I'm not surprised when Mom says it's *Chane*.

"How does it look?" I ask, because now my worry shifts to the "cover" of the *Chane* e-books, to what these publishers will decide to use to represent a slaver in the current climate.

"Good!" she says. She means she hopes they'll sell like hotcakes.

I pull over after we hang up, hope for service in these woods, and do a search on Amazon for George Wolk. The editor had told Mom he'd publish them all under the original pseudonym Dad used, but that they would have a banner reading "From the George Wolk Collection," so folks would know one man wrote them all. Nothing comes up but the old used softcovers I've found before, so I type in "Norman Gant" and there it is and I have to blink to refocus.

The cover of the e-book version of *Chane* is a photograph of an actual human being. A model, an actor, someone who came into a studio and was paid to take off his shirt and put a thick chain around his neck and hold it up like a noose and reveal his actual, alive muscles and actual present-day six-pack. A real man who stared into a camera and let the photographer take his picture. Did he know what he was posing for? Does he know he's representing the hero in a racist book based on stereotypes of blackness?

Superimposed in the background is a large plantation house, but I hardly see it here in the woods because I'm shaking with fury. I type in "George McNeill" to get that picture off my screen and to see if his books are represented the same way, with photographs of actual people. Why hadn't I thought to expect photographs of actual people? The covers of Dad's paperbacks—paintings based on the artist's imagination—are bad enough. But photographs of actual human beings? This different level of exploitation makes real for me what I've done, releasing these books into the world. It makes real for me how complicit I have become in my father's legacy. Why did it take this photograph for me to see it?

As Amazon loads the George McNeill list, it occurs to me that I still might have the contact information for the publisher in my phone. I look out the window into the sunshine and take some deep breaths and look back at my screen to see the e-book version of *Plantation*. The cover shows a white plantation house a lot like the one on the cover of *Chane*. But there's no person, no actor, no main character in chains in front of it.

"David, it's Julia Munemo, Susan Wolk's daughter," I say in as steady a voice as I can find. I want this to start off right. I want to be polite and not angry. I want to convince him that it's not too late to make a change. I want to throttle him for thinking this cover is acceptable. I want to introduce him to my sons and ask him what will happen to them when they Google their grandfather and this image comes up. Ask him what will happen when they realize it's my fault. "I just got a call from my mom that you put *Chane* up. I'm wondering if we can talk about the cover?" I'm pacing in circles around my Subaru.

His voice is immediately defensive. "I know what you're thinking," he says. But he doesn't. Not at all. If he'd known what I was thinking, he wouldn't have approved that cover in the first place.

"I guess what I'm thinking is, why can't we commission paintings like the ones on the paperback covers?" I'm trying to keep my voice calm. "At least then, no one would actually have to put chains around their neck for a photographer—the artist could work from the originals."

"There's no way we could afford that. With 40 percent of the profits going to your mom"—he is a chess player moving his queen—"we have no budget for real artists."

So whatever you paid this guy to stand in the studio is less than you'd pay an artist for a portrait? I don't say it out loud. I want to hold onto the possibility that this is a stock photo, that they bought the photo but didn't take the photo. That this guy is paid well each time someone else uses it. That his copyright protects him from the racist eyes reading these books. I'm building myself an illusion, putting on my blinders to protect myself from the truth.

"Plus," David says, "when we just put up a picture of a plantation house for your mom's friend McNeill, we got slaughtered. Readers got the sense that it was just a historical novel, and we have to prepare them for what your dad's books actually are. *Chane* is historical fiction," he tells me, putting emphasis on the *is* because he wants me to know he gives my father credit for not just writing smut, "but it's not only historical fiction."

"So there's nothing I can do to convince you to change the cover?"

"There's nothing to do," he says. "But this is why we decided not to include the George Wolk Collection banner on this series."

Like that will make it better, if no one knows it was my dad who wrote them? I hang up.

When I pull into our driveway the next day, home from my research trip, I call up Amazon on my phone before I turn off my car. I climb out as Ngoni walks over to greet me. He's warm from the sun and the gift the garden gives him, and his smile is broad and not yet aware of what he'll see in my eyes when he gets close. The kids are in the background, taking turns shooting on goal. He hollers to them when he hears a ball sail over his fence and crash into his corn, "Watch it!" and they laugh because they know it happens all the time. They are ten and thirteen and the late summer air stirs them up and they wave at me because they're glad to see me but they don't need to come running to greet me anymore. They're used to my days away now, used to my return. It's a loss I can't abide, but in this moment I'm glad for the space because I need just Ngoni right now. I need to tell him how angry I am, how powerless. I need to ask him if he sees a way I haven't thought of to fix this mess.

Having presented my mother with a potential income from these books, I now can't ask her to take them down. I can make the argument in my head that I have realized these books are damaging, that they can't be out in the world, that we have to protect the world from my dad. But every time I start thinking that way, how it feels instead is that I am a burden on my family and that none of them want to deal with me. That if I ask my mother to do something, it will annoy her and she will get mad at me for causing needless trouble. I am a little girl who has to shut down her own desires so that they don't get in the way of the people with more important things to do, more important things to worry about. The deeper down this hole I go, the less these e-books become about my own complicity with my father's career or my own adult understanding of what these books are. The deeper down this hole I go, the more I am just a child trying to take up less space. Trying not to be a burden on anyone. So I can't ask my mother to take the books down, because asking my mother to take the books down would reveal that I have needs she hasn't met.

I can't say any of this to Ngoni—I am hardly aware of it myself—so when he approaches, I just hand him my phone and hope he can connect the dots. After he's looked at it for a bit, I tell him about my conversation with the editor. Ngoni looks down at me there in our driveway and it's sadness I see in his eyes. I think it's worry.

"It's Pandora's box, honey," he says. "You opened it. Now you have to deal with the consequences."

I WAS SO quick to discount that my dad wrote those books for money. Obviously he was doing something else, obviously he was preoccupied with race for reasons I'm only beginning to understand, obviously he was a racist hack and a fool to exploit stereotypes as he did. Obviously I'm nothing like him and our motivations in this world couldn't be more different. Obviously.

Yet here I am, encouraging the release of his books back into the world for the money. Here I am, asking you to put yourself in my shoes, not to think it was my racism that allowed me to act without considering who my actions would harm. Asking you to consider my worries about my fixed-income, strapped-for-cash mother. Asking you to get it that there are reasons beyond race that make me unable to pull those books off the e-shelves even now that I see so clearly what they are. Asking you not to hate me for acting without even thinking first of my own children.

White folks so often do shit we shouldn't do, we think about it too late, and by then it's just too fucking late. The damage is done, and if we're even aware we did it we can move on, go about our lives, not ever be affected by the shit that we set in motion. I don't know what the consequences of the e-books will be, can't imagine if or how they'll influence the current conversation about race in this country. Can't begin to imagine how it will feel to my sons when they Google their grandfather and see these pictures. How it feels to Ngoni to have me bring this bullshit home to him. The best I can hope for is that the books will be ignored, that they'll be sent into a void. That no one wants to read this crap anymore. I don't let myself think about Karla from Goodreads in 2011. I don't let myself consider what this world really is.

Racism is a virus none of us can escape, and I am no exception. I didn't stop and ask myself how it was possible for me to tell my mom about the e-book publisher, I just told her about it. I didn't wait until I had thoroughly analyzed my father's slavers so I could consider what it would mean for them to reemerge in today's fraught racial times. And I haven't looked in the mirror when I ask about the roots of my father's racism. How badly I want to be vaccinated against this blight. Since I'm not, I do what I've always done and shut it down. I put these feelings in a box in my heart and keep moving, keep pretending that as long as I'm chasing my father's ghost, I don't have to look for my own.

25

ONE WARM SEPTEMBER morning, I leave the kids at the bus stop and point the car toward Vermont, a box of chocolates on the seat beside me, my fancy high-heeled boots zipped up my calves for strength. My father's cousin Chuck has invited me to his house to meet Anna, visiting from Holland as promised after her hip healed. As I drive, I don't think about the e-books or my own complicity in my father's career, just about my hope to find the key that unlocks why he could do "the black-white thing" on the page, the moment that reveals he was a racist fool. The moment that proves to me that I can stop mourning him and move on like he never existed. The moment that proves that I am nothing like him.

When I arrive, my father's first wife sits on the deck in a black party dress in the middle of the morning. She is tan and skinny and wrinkled and keeps her brown hair cut short. She wears green plastic flip-flops on her feet and holds a cigarette to her lips. When she sees me coming, she stabs it out and stands up, and I walk over wondering if I should offer a hug or a handshake.

Chuck is seated at the table, not looking in my direction, talking on his cell phone. His pasty white skin, his balding head, the family nose should all be familiar, but I don't think I've ever seen this man before so I don't wait for him to hang up. I hand Anna the chocolates and say I'm very glad to meet her, and her crystal-blue eyes pierce me a little before she smiles and says the same. Then I ask where the bathroom is because I need a moment to get myself together. While this meeting has been scheduled for several weeks, nothing, really, can prepare me for what it means to look at the face of my father's first wife. I lock the door and turn on the taps, sit on the toilet seat, stand up and look in the mirror, take deep breaths, splash water on my face. When I get back to the table and pull out the chair Anna motions to, the box of chocolates is open and untouched in the sun, well out of my reach. I want a chocolate very much, but instead I repeat what I've already said.

"It's so good to meet you."

After a short silence, Anna says what we're both thinking. "It's a bit awkward, no?" Chuck hangs up the phone and reaches across the table to shake my hand, but he can't quite reach, so I stand up and lean over the rough wood and grasp his hand as much for balance as in greeting. Everything here feels awkward.

WHAT COMES OUT first is how Anna stayed connected to the family all these years. Chuck's parents, my great-aunt and great-uncle, were close to my dad and Anna. They accepted her from the first, didn't care that she wasn't Jewish. "We always stayed in touch," she tells me. "We wrote letters, we talked on the phone." First I think what a betrayal this will be for my mother, who also loved them. Then I think about how they must have been the ones who called Anna that sad January day in 1980 to tell her that Dad was dead. Then I think about how they never called my mom after the funeral, never visited again.

For a while, we don't talk about my grandmother Rose, but I start to think she might be a key that would help Anna open up to me. Maybe Anna doesn't know that I've seen how Rose treated outsiders— that she refused to look my husband in the eye or learn his name or shake his hand, and that I imagine it was similar with her, a Christian from Europe come to take her son away. So in a quiet moment I say, "You know Rose and I had a complicated relationship."

"No one had a simple relationship with Aunt Rose," Chuck says, a little laughter on his lips.

"Indeed, but I think I'm the only grandchild she cut out of her life," I say. "Which she did when I got married." I don't tell Anna and

Chuck that Rose eventually accepted my phone calls and letters, in part because my motivations for reaching out are unclear even to me. I don't tell them that I visited her a few times in her final years or that I attended her funeral. Whatever bond we'd once had was broken that day in her kitchen, and our gestures at reunion felt false to me. I believe they felt false to her. What I've just said to Anna and Chuck is the clearest truth I hold about my grandmother.

And immediately I see I was right. Anna is open now, ready to talk. "We'd go over to the house for supper, and Rose would ask me to set the table," she leans toward me in conspiracy and says. "Of course you know she kept a kosher home, but she wouldn't tell me what was for supper. So I'd go into the kitchen, lift up the lids, and then I'd set the table." She smiles at the memory of her own cleverness. "I never made a mistake, I put the right dishes and the right cutlery out. She'd be so upset!" During the war, Anna's family had taken in several Jewish refugees, she tells me. "Yiddish was the first language I heard. I knew what I was doing."

Chuck and I laugh at this story, are pleased at Anna's ability to avoid Rose's traps, but her face grows serious.

"As soon as George was within a few miles of Rose," Anna says, "he would get covered, just covered, in eczema." She moves her hands up and down her body to show how it was everywhere, just like my mom moved her hands up and down her body when she told me about Dad's return from Rome. I think about the evil white woman in each of the books in the *Chane* series and how she always meets her violent end, and I wonder, not for the first time, if this was how my father processed whatever pain there was in his childhood. If the hatred of women my father expressed in his books started as a hatred of his mother, and how that could happen in a family. I wonder what she might have done to him, and when. I wonder if Anna can blame his skin condition on his mother, what else Rose might have been responsible for. But these aren't questions I can ask Anna. They are hardly questions I can admit to myself that I have.

ANNA HELPS ME fit in missing puzzle pieces on the deck that sunny morning. I learn dates and specifics, like that Dad graduated from

Cornell in 1961—when he was twenty. Like that he went, as all self-respecting budding authors with enough cash did back then, to Europe to write books. Like that he met Anna on the French coast and followed her home to Holland and married her there. Like that they moved to New York and Anna worked at the World's Fair while Dad held odd jobs like parking and simonizing cars in city lots.

"George got a kick out of that job because it was close to the New School," Anna laughs. "He liked being watched by the young women walking to and from class."

Something in the stories I grew up hearing—spare though they were—always communicated this fact. That my dad thought he was sexy, that he wanted women to notice him. But this is the first time it's been revealed in such tender words. Anna found charming a trait my mother saw as distasteful.

After a silence during which I do the math and realize this woman was married to my father for far longer than I knew—six years, not ten minutes—I ask, "Was Dad writing when you lived in New York?"

"Oh yes," Anna says. "Always writing. And you know, I never thought he was sick. I just thought he was sad, when rejection letters would arrive in the mailbox." I want to tell Anna that she's swiftly changed the subject from Dad's work to his illness, and I want to ask her not to do that. I want to tell her that everyone I call to talk about Dad's work starts talking instead about his illness, and that I don't want to learn more about his illness. Just tell me about his writing, I want to say. But I don't. Instead, I watch as her face quickly turns back into a smile.

"He eventually got a job as an editor at Tower Books," she says. "And he said to me once, about the books he was editing, 'If you take one chapter from each of ten books and staple them together, you have an eleventh.'"

"That sounds like the formula he might have used for the slavers I'm reading," I tell her.

I try to relax a little, to listen as Anna tells stories about my dad and his family, to watch nostalgia and love and sadness mix in her eyes and come across the table to me as warmth. I think, *Thank God he left you.* Because it saved her life. She didn't have to get broken like the rest of us. And I think how strange it is to meet the woman whose life, had it gone as she'd hoped it would, would have meant the obliteration of the possibility of my own.

WHEN THE KIDS were very little, they met my first love, though I didn't tell them who he'd once been to me. A couple of years later, my friend Stef and I drove up a snowy mountain road in Vermont, our children all giggling in the back. After Stef told me a long story about her first heartbreak, Julius called out, "Who was that guy?"

"What guy?" I asked, looking out the window to see who we'd passed.

"That weird guy with yellow hair who made us play Frisbee and asked a lot of questions."

"Oh, him," I said, turning to look at my son. "We dated in college." I tried to make my voice constant as I looked across to Stef with eyes wide in a question about a little boy making such an associative leap. I tried to make my voice unwavering as I asserted that there'd been a life before his father.

"Thank God that guy isn't my dad!" he shouted, and laughed for a long moment.

Indeed. But doesn't it beg an interesting question? Julius was convinced that no matter what happened in my life, I would be his mother. He would exist as he is, the only variable was the father.

Not so for me. I'd had no doubt, growing up, that if my parents had stayed married to their first people, I would not exist. That I was a very careful and possibly accidental result of them, those two, for better or for worse. I was very small when I began to measure the narrow distance between what I am and a world without me.

I STEER MY Subaru west across Vermont, coming home now to meet the bus after my morning with Anna and Chuck. I wish I felt answers swirling in my gut, but instead I struggle against disappointment. Against the sadness that although she was warm and open and kind, Anna didn't, in the end, give me very much. Some facts to fill in blanks, some sense of a life before. But she wasn't the holder of the truth, the one who could make it all line up and fall into place and organize my soul. She was just a woman who loved my father fifty years ago, and who survived.

I drive along an edge of road that follows a pipeline through twists and over mountaintops and into the distance. In front of me is a flatbed truck with an enormous piece of piping strapped to its bed. It's made of black plastic, and its thin edging makes it only just visible to me from my angle behind it. It looks like a giant O, a void, a big black hole. I think, looking at it, that if I drive into it I will disappear.

PART III

THE BONE CLOCK

ONE EARLY FALL afternoon, I hear the kids laughing as they walk up the driveway from the bus. The windows are open to the warm air, and their laughter—and the dog's bark it inspires—is my signal to get up and put *The Wrath of Chane* in the closet. I'm almost done with this trilogy, finally. It takes eons to read it because I stop for weeks at a time to protect myself a little, give myself breaks from the violence and the shame and the hatred my father put down on these pages. But I'm in the last chapter of the final book now, and when I hear the kids, I just don't move. I just let them walk in the den and see me sitting on the couch with that thing in my lap.

They're loud and hungry and their scent is sour and sharp and warm and it quiets my anxiety just to have them in my sight line again. I haven't smiled since they left this morning. They report on the lockdown drill at school and their homework assignments and the playdates they want me to arrange for the weekend. I know their buzzing is about to launch them into the other room and their own activities, so before they leave I say, "Boys, sit down a minute. There's something I need to show you."

Sometimes, when I have to do the hardest things with them, I find I can do it better if I don't plan it. If I just start talking it's as though some other person takes over and the words that come out are either right or they're wrong—they will either help or they will damage—but the words come out. If I'd tried to script it, the words would never come out. It's equal measures exhilarating and terrifying.

What I say this time is, "I've been reading the books your grandfather wrote. You'll see them lying around and I want to warn you that the covers are gross." I pick up the book from my lap and lift it so they can see. "They are yucky and sexual and racialized and they might make you feel weird to look at." I watch their faces to see if the book makes them feel weird to look at, but neither of my children seems surprised, or particularly interested. For them, a black man and a white woman standing arm in arm looks a little bit like the sidelines of a soccer game, or our kitchen when one of them is telling a long story. Maybe they don't see the chains on Chane's wrists, maybe they don't notice the look in his lover's eye, or see the nuance in their different postures. Or maybe they are more able than I am to file that under a category that doesn't matter, to accept that these books have nothing to do with them. "I'm reading these books because they might help me understand who my father was," I continue, though I can see they're getting bored. "And I just want you to know that if you have questions about any of this, you can ask me anything."

My kids are accustomed to my lengthy explanations of things they didn't ask to know, so when they think I'm done talking they just look glad this one didn't last so long. A part of me hopes that one of them will come over and hug me and tell me it's going to be okay, but I know that isn't their job. A part of me—one I'll never let them see—wishes they would stay here with me. I'm braver when they're around.

"Okay, Mom," they say in unison, getting up.

"Can I have a snack?" Julius asks as George heads out the kitchen door with his cleats in hand. And that's it. They don't ask any questions or show any signs of damage. They just want a snack and a soccer ball, so I set *Chane* aside and get up, too, to get them those things.

A FEW WEEKS LATER, George comes home from school and reports that today was the annual book sale.

"They had a whole room of used books! We could just take them—for free!" he says.

I smile and ask if he got anything.

"No," he says, disappointed. "I looked through all the used books for you, Mom, but I couldn't find any by Norman Gant."

A laugh bursts out of my mouth and I hug him and plan to tell Ngoni this story tonight because I know we'll laugh together about this child who is so sweet and caring and warm and open to this world. And because it's funny that our ten-year-old went to school today and looked for my father's porn in those piles.

But after we laugh about it, I can't sleep thinking about the damage I've done. I have normalized slavery porn to the extent that my son thinks he might find it at a children's book sale. I have normalized slavery porn that my father wrote, not conveyed my disgust in the racism and misogyny he expressed in those pages or my fears about where I come from or my scorn about what his work says about the country we live in. In my attempts to help the kids not see what I'm doing as scary, scarring, to help them think of it as something any mom might do, I've made it unremarkable. But if it's unremarkable, how will they contextualize the harm my legacy has done? How will they understand that books like these prey on stereotypes about bodies like theirs, and that those stereotypes need to be destroyed? Because of course I want them to question this world. I want to teach them that it's our job to question this world, to try like hell to fix this world. I want to show them that what I'm doing isn't as simple as reading the books my father wrote so I can understand who he was, that what I'm doing is shining a light on a taboo that tarnished my childhood, that has tarnished this country, in order to make what's underneath it fallible. Because if we don't talk about it, it holds so much power. If we don't talk about it, it becomes just another American monument to slavery, and I can't have that in my house. So I normalized slavery porn because it isn't unique at all. But that doesn't make it safe. Perhaps the realization that something can be both unremarkable and harmful—the cop on the side of the road I don't blink at but who carries a murder weapon in his holster—is what I should most fear. So no, it's not as simple as I made it sound to them, but I've made it sound simple to protect them. I'm their mom. All I ever want is to protect them.

I'm not just reading their grandfather's books to understand who he was. I'm examining my complicity in this treasonous history we call America, and it's excruciating.

27

BLACK SCARAB, a slaver my father set in Congo, opens, "The Wara Sura were torturing the dwarf beneath the liana near the edge of the plantain grove," and as soon as I read those words I'm in a fury. Who are the Wara Sura and how did a man who had never traveled to sub-Saharan Africa know anything about them? What right did he have to suggest these people—if there are such a people—ever tortured anyone? And a dwarf? Are you kidding me? I don't know much about the populations of the Congolese forests, but I know they are not inhabited by people with a medical condition that results in short stature, but rather by ethnic groups most commonly described as 'pygmy' in the scholarly literature of my father's time. That word, used to describe a people who average no more than four and a half feet in height, is itself problematic today. But I don't believe that word was considered problematic when my dad was writing. So while I think Dad just wanted his readers to understand that the man he was describing was very short, as I read that opening sentence all I can think is that we're not calling a character in a book by anyone but Tolkien a dwarf. Not in my family.

In the second paragraph I read about the giant root of an acacia tree and I know for sure now that this man knew nothing about Africa. Baobab trees have giant roots that stick out of the ground, not tidy acacias. Acacias are what Gogo calls "umbrella trees," and they spot the countryside and the mall parking lot, offering much-needed shade in both locations. I've stood close to them and touched the thorns scattered thick on their branches and trunk.

I pull out my pen to underline every word or phrase I'll fact-check. I will prove my father wrong, prove that he didn't know anything about Congo or sub-Saharan Africa and shouldn't ever have tried to write about a place he'd never even visited. By the bottom of the first page— three and a half paragraphs of setting and character introduction—I've scrawled fifteen question marks, each indicating a detail I plan to disprove. I meet the hero, Objuga, a prince of the Mazamboni tribe, and pull out my notebook to start a list of questions: Is the name *Objuga* authentic or invented? Who were the Mazamboni? I read on and meet Objuga's sidekick—my dad's heroes always have a sidekick. This one is a "Wambutti pigmie," or just "the dwarf," whom the hero names "Doo" because it's a noise the man makes and these two fellows don't speak the same language. Later, when they've come to depend on one another and can communicate quite well, "Doo" never tells Objuga his real name. Objuga never asks.

I have access to sources my father didn't. Access, maybe, to a more enlightened time. I can do internet searches and speak with librarians and historians and read thoughtful critiques of how Westerners have represented Africans as less than human for centuries. What did my dad have as he wrote his only book set entirely in Africa? He didn't have Chinua Achebe's "An Image of Africa," but did he have *The Forest People* by Colin Turnbull, first published in 1961? My hunch is that if he had, he wouldn't have called Doo *Doo,* or a dwarf. Did Dad do any research, or did he speak in stereotypes in order to give his readers what they wanted? Or did he speak in stereotypes because stereotypes helped him maintain his perception of the world?

Early on in the book I come to a scene with a female prisoner, a Wara Sura woman whom my father describes as looking "like her brethren [with a] thick nose and a large mouth and a low brow. But," he assures his reader, "she was not unpleasant to look at." This is his signal that we're coming to a promised sex scene, only fifteen pages in. Not his typical template, but nothing about this book feels typical. Like how the sex in this scene won't be between races, but it will be between tribes. The differences noted in her appearance and language show the reader that we're crossing a taboo, just like in all of Dad's books. So don't worry, things will get steamy, right? But wait—she's a *prisoner.*

> Objuga had expected her to shake with fear, but strangely, she did just the opposite. She smiled broadly and her eyes told them that she was happy to see them. [As her] eyes fell on [Objuga's lieutenant] Onto, she smiled and her fear evaporated. The woman cocked her thigh revealing herself to Onto.

bell hooks told us all the way back in 1981 that "black women have always been seen by the white public as sexually permissive, as available and eager." And here is my dad, sketching out the contours of a black woman as available and eager, even when she's a prisoner. And here is my dad, fantasizing on the page about raping her, so that his readers can fantasize about raping this "savage" black woman who will love what's coming. She asking for it, right? Look how available and eager she is.

Dad stays at a remove in this scene, occupying the mind of Objuga, not Onto the lieutenant or those of his soldiers who will take their turn during the long night. It isn't until the morning that Objuga finally shouts, "Onto! Enough! It is time to go! Onto, you swine!"

> At last Onto appeared from behind the palm, naked and breathing hard. Objuga watched while behind him the Wara Sura woman appeared as well, also naked, also breathing hard, and reaching up for Onto's shoulders, caused the Mazamboni to fall back to the ground with her again.

It's the Jezebel stereotype coming at me from my dad. My father apparently believed that African women were oversexed, that they would not feel raped even when what was happening to them was very much rape. bell hooks also told us that "the designation of all black women as sexually depraved, immoral, and loose had its roots in the slave system," and while this book isn't yet revealing how, exactly, its characters are related to the slave system, I know that's a system my dad studied. I know where he got his ideas. "From such thinking emerged the stereotype of black women as sexual savages, and in sexist terms a sexual savage, a non-human, an animal cannot be raped," bell hooks told us all the way back in 1981. *Black Scarab* could have been her case study. At the end of the chapter, Objuga's soldiers bring the prisoner back to her people, but they don't take the risk of walking her all the way home— they know they'll be killed if they do.

It's terrible to sit on my couch and read a scene that shows my father's thinking to be so simplistic, terrible to consider what parts of himself this scene supported. Did he see himself as Objuga, the slightly reserved, slightly superior man in the shadows, or was he imagining himself as one of the Mazamboni warriors, taking their turn?

FOR A WHILE, I'd held onto the possibility that my dad didn't write all of these books. Maybe the publishing house owned the name "Norman Gant" and hired a bunch of people to write slavers using it. I would scour the books I'd found under this name, I decided at the outset. Look for places that indicated someone else wrote them. It was easy to develop a checklist from the *Chane* series: The powerful, sexy black man, always the hero. His sidekick, often a considerably shorter man who lacks intelligence but not humor. The white woman who both detests and desires the black man, and whose evil ways are always punished in the end. The word "home" used to describe sexual climax, as in "and then he thrust home hard." The sadistic slavemaster who ritualizes sex, makes a performance out of it.

But those, I realize, might be the trademarks of all slavers. It wasn't a big genre, but I've found enough of these books written by other people to know these weren't entirely original ideas. I'd need to dig deeper, find something unique about my father's voice, his tastes. Like the fact that his characters are always described first by their noses. Or the cave somewhere in the plotline that only the hero knows about, and in which he and his lover can be safe. More ominously, a hanging, a suicide, the question of whether the hero will maintain his sanity in the face of all he's forced to suffer.

As I trace those features and more in *Black Scarab*, I have to accept that my dad wrote them all.

28

AT MY DESK one morning, I Google the word "Mazamboni," the name
my father gave to Objuga's tribe, and come upon a book called *In
Darkest Africa*. Published in 1890 by the explorer Henry Morton Stanley,
it's an account of his rescue mission across the continent. I order it, to
see what my dad might have seen. To read what he might have read.

The copy that arrives was published in 2001, but reading it I feel like
I'm in a conversation with my father. Where did you find this book,
Dad? Did you think Stanley was a trustworthy source? Did you notice
how simplistically he represented the Africans he came across? What
did you think about his "plucky natives" or how they were juxtaposed
with the "hospitable Belgians"? Of his search for "that ideal Governor
in the midst of his garrisons" facing "the Mahdist hordes advancing
with frantic cries." Did you, as I do, find his paternalism just too much
to bear? Or did it sit tight inside you, a brother to your own?

The deeper in I follow Stanley on his journey, the more features I
recognize. There's the Ituri River, whose brown waters I can see thanks
to Dad's descriptions. There are groves of plantains—the only food
Doo and Objuga found on their own journey. There are abandoned
"pigmie" villages and sightings of "Dwarfs," believed (according to the
characters in my dad's book) unable to survive outside of the rain forest. Did Stanley give you that idea, too, Dad? On page 267, I read about

"a people called the Wara Sura, armed with guns like ours, who simply killed people," and I realize here is where Dad found his antagonist.

But Mazamboni isn't mentioned until page 319, and he's a man, not a tribe. A strong man who is part of what Stanley calls "a proud, high-caste race." But his tribe has another name. Did Dad even read this book, or just glance through it?

And then I turn the page and see a drawing of one of Mazamboni's warriors, and it's Objuga to the teeth. Dad must have studied this picture for some minutes before arriving at his description of our hero. "Objuga wore the white dress of the Mazamboni officer. Around his ankles were six rings of flat iron." I count them in the picture. Six. "There were four around his upper arm," my father writes. Four in the picture. "On his head he wore the palm cluster that showed he was of the highest rank. He carried a long spear, a bow and six arrows." I only count three arrows, and it's the only detail Dad amended. "Over his left shoulder he wore the rectangular shield of the Mazamboni." So he did. I hadn't seen it when I first looked.

But there's something still gnawing at me about *Black Scarab*, and I can't answer it with Stanley. Chapter 2 of my dad's only slaver set entirely in Africa is called "The Avatiko Cannibals," and they are, according to my father, neighbors of the Mazamboni. And when a Mazamboni commits a crime, he's brought to them. To be eaten.

My father's Africa is like no Africa I have visited. I can check all of his facts, I can accept that he was writing about a long-ago time, but his willingness to include this detail says something about my dad that I don't know how to swallow. Did he really believe Africans were cannibals? Or did he just find this idea sexy, saleable, stereotypically alluring?

"It's like finding out your father was Joseph Conrad," I say to Ngoni when he comes home. "This one is set in Congo in the late nineteenth century. There are pygmies and cannibals and barkcloth loin coverings."

Ngoni tilts his head to one side and frowns, his lower lip sticking out a little. The look in his eyes is sad, and stops me from saying more. As he walks through the den to put his bag away, I realize this might be a line he can't cross with me. Realize I can't ask him to help me carry the contents of a book my father set in "Darkest Africa."

My husband has spent his life fighting stereotypes about that myth-
ical place and what it holds for the American imagination. He does this
quietly, as he does everything. He doesn't show his anger or his frustration in the face of these stereotypes and assumptions, just puts on his
teacher voice and explains his truth patiently to the liberal white folks
desperate to hold tight to their own. He doesn't need to do it in his own
house, and I won't ask him to again.

I BRING *Black Scarab* to the barbershop on the small main street of my little New England town one rainy, late fall afternoon. Duane takes his time cutting my sons' hair, and I'll need something to do. But I also bring along Achebe's *Hopes and Impediments*. The first essay in there is about *Heart of Darkness*, and I want to think about Conrad, I want to think about what he did in his book about Congo and about if what my father did in his was similar. I've read the essay before, but not since I started reading Dad's books, and I'll need it again, I'll need the armor it gives me.

I've also brought Achebe along because he gives me cover. His book hides me and my quest from those around me. It's a bit bigger than *Scarab,* and if I slide Dad's book inside it, it protects the other folks at the barbershop—two white boys who go to school with mine, their gentle mother, a couple of college students, and Duane, the first black barber to open up shop in our town in its long history—from seeing Dad's book. Achebe gives cover to Gant. Protects me from my dad.

I open to book 2 of *Black Scarab* and find Objuga on a dhow. He's been captured, tied to the mast on the deck of this ship headed north. There's something special about this guy, and he isn't below decks with all of the other people captured on the slave-trader's trip. The reader already knows Objuga can navigate through the desert at night by reading the stars, so we're not surprised to learn that he spends nights on the ship staring at the heavens "so that he would know where he had been, where he was, and where he was being taken." I long for such a guiding star, for the knowledge of how to follow it. I wonder if Dad did, too.

But it's the next line I underline, sitting there in the barbershop: "He fought to keep his mind empty . . . so that his sanity would not leave him." I don't think much about it, just notice that maybe by this point in Dad's life, sanity—and its potential for leaving—was on his mind. This book was published the year I turned two.

Some pages later, after his captors begin to teach Objuga Arabic, because they have plans for him we don't yet understand, I read that our hero "used the lessons . . . as therapy and a preventative against loneliness and madness." Huh, I think. Was Dad lonely? Did he need a preventative against it? And why did his preventative against madness stop working?

But I keep reading because I'm at the barbershop with my sons and I can't get too deep into this here. A few pages on Objuga hears a chant rising up from below decks and has to "make a great effort of will to combat the overwhelming feeling of loneliness that rose in him as he listened to that stark, pitiful rhythm of his homeland. He looked to the [guard] to bring his mind back to what was real, to what was happening to him." I underline that part, too, with two lines under the bit about bringing his mind back to what was real.

◆   ◆   ◆

ONE DAY WHEN I was sixteen and Mom was at aikido practice and Josh was in California and Nan was at college, one day when I was meant to be studying, I stood in front of my mother's big oak desk, looking for secrets. That desk took up the entire wall on one side of her bedroom. Before my hands found the slim center drawer, I looked up at the pictures on the wall of each of us when we were little. Sunny smiling photographs of children who didn't know what was coming. Then I looked down and pulled the drawer open as though my only purpose was to hear the sharp squeak that warned of the invasion. Inside, an envelope. A letter in my mom's confident cursive, written but never mailed. The words blur in my memory.

"My husband went off to a sesshin," I read in her handwriting. I remembered all the times I'd heard that word. I knew it as the place Dad went to and came back from changed. I knew it as the place we blamed everything on.

"When he returned, he believed he and I and our two eldest children were reincarnated Zen Buddhist masters," my mother wrote to someone. "He believed we were powerful, that we knew secrets, that we should be honored," my mother wrote to a nameless friend. "He also believed we needed to be protected from our youngest daughter, whom he thought was a witch come to take our powers away," my mother did not mean to write to me.

I couldn't decode this idea at sixteen, I still don't know where to file it. If my father thought I was a witch, was I a witch? People had told me all my life that he was ill, people told me that he had delusions, but is every thought an invention of a disordered mind, or are some things real? Who could I ask for absolution?

I folded the letter back up along its lines and slid it into its envelope. I picked up and put down each of the items in my mother's desk drawer. A heavy black fountain pen, a pile of paperclips, a snake carved from ivory, a stamp she had made with the signature of her boss, a stamp she had made with the address of her business, a nail file, a quarter-inch-long golden articulated fish. I tried to place each item back where it went, first proving and then hiding that I was there. I tried to push the drawer closed smooth, but it stuck and I couldn't set it straight. I pulled it back out to try again, this time sending the thing home with my hips. The contents shifted and scrambled and the items rolled over on top of each other. When I opened the drawer to try again, I saw there was no way to set things right.

WHEN JULIUS CLIMBS out of Duane's chair with his short Afro trimmed and tidy, George climbs in and shows Duane the picture he's drawn of the haircut he'd like this time. Duane looks at me for confirmation.

"Mommy," he says, "is it okay for me to shave two waves in the side of little man's head?"

I nod my agreement and smile at my sons, each so different from one another, each so exactly his own self. Then I turn back to my dad's book and underline four more references to sanity, and how Objuga keeps his, in the next twenty pages. He keeps firm hold of his faculties by studying Arabic, he keeps firm hold by reading the stars at night, he keeps firm hold by making love to the women he meets, he keeps firm hold by remembering the one he truly loves back home.

I think back to the plot points of the *Chane* series and realize that at every turn there was a man pushed to his limit and almost broken, but in each case he prevailed. In each case he held firm to his sanity, or was killed before the test could come to its end.

There in the barbershop with my sons looking sharp, my paper cup of tea grown cold in my fist, it hits me hard. Maybe Dad didn't write so many books about slavery because he was preoccupied by race during the Civil Rights Movement. Maybe Dad wrote so many books about slavery because the people captured and born into that institution were pushed to limits no human being should ever be pushed to, and in astonishingly large numbers they held firm to their sanity. Maybe he was studying how to do it. Maybe he was using the enslavement of the body as an object lesson in maintaining sovereignty over the mind. Because everything I'm learning about my father points to the idea that sanity was much on his mind. Something had happened in his mind or to his body that made it clear he'd need to be able to hold firm to his if he was going to survive. And he wasn't sure he'd have the strength or the will or the sovereignty or whatever he thought it might require.

I take a breath and lean back into the deep leather couch in Duane's waiting area and consider what it means to think that my father compared his experience of mental illness to mass enslavement. Do I mean I think that he—a privileged white man making a living off his chosen craft—truly understood the trauma of slavery, or even the fact of modern-day racism? Fuck, no. Do I mean I think that he—a man whose traumas were all located inside his mind and not at the hands of society—was legitimate in making such a comparison? Fuck, no. His ability to use his fiction for this end, if this is indeed what he intended, strikes me as further evidence of his bias, his denial or ignorance of his own privilege, his power in the racist world he wandered.

But though different, I come away from reading this book with a sense that he *was* traumatized. That the trauma he experienced pushed him to a limit. That he used his chosen craft to explore a different limit to see what he could learn. This suddenly seems not very far from what I'm doing now. I accept that my father was naïve to explore his own limitations on the backs of those already burdened—and so I must question whether my own goals are equally naïve.

But the possibility that I might have hit on something true to my father's experience provides me with a window into his soul, and these are rare indeed. If I open the window, will it lead to another one, into myself? Am I, as his friend at the funeral promised me, sure to become just like him? Or can the books he left behind point me toward a better path?

30

SOME WEEKS AFTER watching *13th* on Netflix in our living room, Ngoni and I take the kids out to see *I Am Not Your Negro*. I sit between them and alternate resting my head on Julius's shoulder so he knows I know this is hard and that I'm here, and squeezing George's hand, which stays pressed deep in mine. Sometimes I look over George's head at Ngoni, but he doesn't turn from the screen to meet my eyes. I shouldn't look away either.

When the film ends, I resist the urge to wipe my tears away because I see all the other white liberals in my town wiping their tears away and I want to be different from them. I want not to feel the liberty to cry like this when the people in my family don't feel the liberty to cry like this in public. But the fact is, I'm crying.

Julius pushes past us and leaves the theater and storms to the car, parked on our quiet main street. When we catch up and unlock the doors, he slams his shut behind him and I climb into the driver's seat and turn to face him. I'm ready to apologize for the terrifying history of the world we brought him into, I'm ready to apologize that this is the life we made for him and thought it was fair to ask him to handle. He doesn't give me the chance.

"I'm never watching another fucking documentary in my life," says my fourteen-year-old son.

"Fair enough," Ngoni says, and we ride home in silence. When I look in the rearview mirror at George, he meets my eyes and smiles. But his face looks different than it did two hours ago, more guarded. His smile in the mirror looks like a mask. I wonder if it was wise to ask him to try to understand all of that.

After we watched *13th* earlier this winter, I had tried to get the kids to stay in the living room and talk to us, but neither one did. "Let them go," Ngoni said. "They'll talk to us when they're ready. That's a lot to process."

"I know," I said. "Which is why I want them to talk to us, not disappear into their own worlds right away."

"Let them go," Ngoni said again, and I had no choice. By then they had gone, and Ngoni and I were left on the couch staring at each other. Maybe we all needed time to process.

A WEEK AFTER seeing the Baldwin film, Julius comes home from school and in the time we have alone in the house before George's bus arrives, I make him a smoothie and listen as he tells me about his day. He mentions a project he's doing about slavery for eighth-grade social studies. I ask him to describe it.

"It's a clock face," he says. "But the clock isn't hours, it's history."

He can see I'm not following, so he backs up.

"My project is a drawing. I decided to draw history. At twelve o'clock it says the year 1815, and I drew a skull there. At three o'clock it's 1865, six o'clock it's 1965, and nine o'clock it's 2015. And instead of hands for the seconds, minutes, and hours, there are people. One is a lynched slave, one is Martin Luther King Jr., and one is Trayvon Martin. But he's not only Trayvon Martin, he could be Michael Brown or Tamir Rice, too."

I ask him to bring it home when he's ready, tell him how much I want to see it. I expect he'll forget, I expect I'll have to wait until the end of the year when he cleans out his locker. But he brings the drawing home the next day. Unrolls it and lays it flat on the counter where we eat breakfast. Holds its curling edges down so I can look.

Julius has drawn the clock face in pencil, a tall oval outlined in long bones. As he runs his finger along the bones he drew, he explains that they're broken. "The only thing I'm bummed about is that I didn't think about making the intervals regular, like on a clock," he says. "Each year ends in five, but I didn't do the math before drawing it."

It's all very lightly penciled, and I have to look closely to see the detail. Each of the figures' heads is set at the center of the clock, their bodies extending out and pointing to the numbers, to the dates. The slave is hanging from a rope, and I glance quickly to see his ribs and his scrubby shorts, but I can't look at him for long because I always avert my eyes when I see someone hanging. His feet point to the place the two would be, between 1815 and 1865.

Martin Luther King Jr. is flat on his back, his tie partially covering his face. His feet point a little left of 1965. "How is it that you can make it so clearly Martin Luther King when you're drawing is so small?" I ask, and pride spreads across his cheeks.

Then he tells me about how he'd been thinking of erasing the face he drew on Trayvon Martin, whose feet point just south of 2015. It takes me a moment to notice that the 5 in that date looks like it's falling down, as though Martin's feet have knocked it off its axis.

"If his hoodie covers his face, he can represent all of them," he says.

The Martin figure looks like he's lying in the street. His hands are behind his back and there's blood dripping out of a wound in his side. I nod and tell him I think that would be a very potent message. There are tears at the backs of my eyes as I realize that I don't know how to make this child know that I would die if it meant he could live in a safe world. I don't know how to make this child safe. I don't even know if he would have felt safe with my own father. I put my arms around his muscular frame and squeeze him and he lets me for a second before saying, "I decided not to color anything in except the blood." Each figure has a little blood somewhere, as does the giant skull on the top.

As I trace the circle of broken bones around the clock face, I send up silent gratitude that George won't be home for a bit. That this drawing is something we'll be able to keep from him for a while. That how his brother understands this history is something we can wait for him to catch up on. George will get to this place in his own time. He's still so little. I still want to protect him from the parts I can. I still don't know what damage was done by those documentaries, what damage has been done by this world he witnesses every day from our small New England corner. I walk a balance beam between what we owe to him to discuss and what he's too young to comprehend. What a privilege it is to be able to walk that beam.

What I say to this son here with me in the kitchen, the one who came home to show me that he's ready to talk, is, "It's so powerful how it suggests that time isn't making linear progress, but that it goes in circles, years repeating themselves if we don't learn our lesson." I think he'll be proud of himself for conveying the message he meant to convey.

But when I look up at his face, it's not pride I see. It's fear.

MY ANXIETY is a virus that stops my body from moving. Some days I feel like I can't get out of bed for the fear of what has happened overnight, what I'll learn when I go downstairs and turn on NPR. I fantasize about not letting my children go to college, not letting them out of the house in the morning, not letting them get in the car with their father, not letting them get driver's licenses when they're old enough. I dream about moving to Canada, Europe, Zimbabwe, fucking Syria, because any place would be safer than this place and maybe we should just leave.

But the fact is I do get out of bed. Every single day. I don't have a choice. And the police are not the only people I fear in this world. Back when both my kids were at the elementary school, I dropped them off the Monday after the Sandy Hook shooting, rather than putting them on the bus. I needed to be with them a little bit longer, I needed to see the school for myself, needed to stay close in case I noticed a bad guy lurking in the bushes. As I drove out of the parking lot, the sound that came out of my mouth wasn't crying, it was closer to keening. I had to tell myself to breathe. I had to tell myself that their school was the same school it had been the week before. That one madman in one small New England town didn't madmen in small towns all over the country make. By the time I got home and climbed the stairs to my office, I was breathing automatically again. I had a deadline that day, and I made it. The next day was a little bit easier.

There's been a cop in the elementary school parking lot every morning since, and when I drop George off there these days, I wave at her. She waves back. Every time I wonder if she's noticed the Black Lives Matter bumper sticker on my car. If she thinks we're on opposite sides. I don't think we're on opposite sides. I think she's a nice woman who makes a living in a small New England town doing a job someone needs to do. Do I wish she did it with a nightstick instead of a gun? Yes. Do I wonder if her training was the same militarized police trainings I've been reading about these last fifteen years? Yes. Do I think she might pull her gun out at a traffic stop when my kids learn to drive? On my good days that's a question I can answer.

Today isn't a good day.

31

WHEN I STARTED reading my dad's slavers, what I wanted more than anything was to find out that he was different from other writers of slavers. I wanted the books to redeem him, I wanted to prove that he did it differently, that he did it better than the other writers of this bullshit genre. That he was politically radical, that he used *his* slavers to teach his stupid white male readership what was so diseased about their small-minded thinking.

I wanted my father to be great.

But that's not how it works. That's not what legacy is. I don't get to re-envision my father's goals or contextualize him within today's political climate. I don't get to pretend my father was anything but what he was. But I realize that what I do have to do—what I am compelled to do by asking that question—is understand the ramifications of my own life. To investigate the consequences of being a white woman in this country founded on white supremacy. To understand the dynamics inside of and in reaction to my marriage. To try to understand what might happen to my children on these American streets. And to do all of that, I have to understand who I am, where I come from, what I present to a room, what I carry behind me into a room, what I carry on my shoulders, what I trip on, how I mess up, whom I hurt.

So throughout this journey, I keep coming back to Dad's slavers, because if I don't know where I come from and what my legacy is, I can't figure any of the rest of it out. When I was reading the books in the *Chane* series, the question of what it means to write from the perspective of an other nagged at me. My father didn't write in the first person in that trilogy, but he inhabited each of his characters—the Moroccan slave trader, the Dutch captain, the pregnant African queen, the plantation's Scottish overseer. I was preoccupied with what he thought gave him the right to do that, since none of those characters were anything like him. My father was raised in an orthodox Jewish household in Brooklyn in the forties and fifties, a place so divided by race and religion, what could he have learned about this world but to define people by category?

But I grew up hearing that he'd renounced Judaism by the time he met my mom, that it was no skin off his teeth when his parents disapproved of my mom because she wouldn't convert. That he laughed along with her at their expectation that she would claim a religion she didn't believe in just so the kids would inherit it through her. For all these reasons, and because Judaism is a whole world I don't know how to access, I never thought to look for him behind that door. But one day I picked up a book he published the year I was born, *The Man Who Dealt in Blood*, and realized Judaism did indeed hold an important place in his heart, in his imagination. It's written all over the cover. "He was the Chairman of the Board, the Kingpin of Crime, the Jew who became the Capo of Capos!" Various Mafia-movie images form a collage on the cover—a dead man in a barber's chair, blue-uniformed cops on the chase, white male hands counting money, and at the bottom, a tank flying the Israeli flag.

"Your dad removed our listing from the phone book when that book came out," my mother told me when she saw it on my coffee table. "He was sure the Jewish mafia would try to find him."

We laughed a little, as families with a history of mental illness often have to laugh, and I decided it was another sign I could add to my list. He *was* sick longer than we knew. When would we start to say it out loud?

"Oh," she said, picking it up. "I didn't realize he published it under his own name. Maybe his paranoia wasn't so unfounded."

Maybe this book contains secrets, Mom seemed to be saying. Jewish secrets about Israel and its place on the world stage. I don't know anything about any mafia, Jewish or otherwise, so it wasn't a question I could help her answer. And when I finished the book that weekend, it only raised more questions about who my father was. Did he have a personal stake in the history of imperial Russia or the Polish shtetl where his characters came from? Did he care about Palestine's transformation—the issue that drives the plot forward—any more than as a topic of conversation at a dinner party? Did he know what the tenements on the Lower East Side—where much of the book takes place—were really like to live in? Did he feel vulnerable as a Jew in America? What research did he have to do to enter the characters he created, or did it come as a natural outcrop of his upbringing? I realized I was asking questions a lot like the ones I had asked about *Chane,* even though in this book Dad's ethnic and cultural identity matched that of his characters.

"LIKE MANY CHILDREN of Jews who lived through the Holocaust, who lived through that time, even if they weren't in it, it affected everything they did," one of my dad's friends told me over the phone early that first summer I started looking for him. Unlike Dad's other friends I spoke to, I still know this one a little bit. Tracy and his wife stayed in my mother's life after Dad died. Their kids went to the same school we did. I hadn't spoken to him in a couple of years, but a phone call from me wasn't so out of the ordinary. Still, I shivered in the sun on my deck as I listened to his voice. This wasn't our typical topic, and it was hard to ask him these questions. "The message was *be careful, you're always in danger.* So, yes, it was a subject of great, real, and genuine interest to your dad."

This shouldn't have come as a surprise, but it did. "How can you be sure?" I asked.

"Here's a story that might help you see it," Tracy said. I could hear his breath as he spoke. I thought I could hear a load lightening. "Your dad was quite taken with our neighbor, a Dutch man who studied Judaism and had been through the Second World War. He told this neighbor about a book he was planning to write, and it sounded as if your father was planning to make pornography out of the Holocaust."

Many of my father's friends laughed when they remembered him—they told me about how charming he was, how funny, and I laughed with them as we conjured up the kind of man he must have been. This phone call wasn't like that. Tracy and I weren't laughing.

"Well, the distaste with which my neighbor received this was palpable, and your dad was quite upset afterward. It was as if he'd been asking for absolution, and when he didn't get it, he worried about it. He was very upset."

My father had not before been painted as a man who would ask anyone for permission to do anything. He had not before been shown to be vulnerable, affected by the opinions of others. And this new view of him helped me see something I hadn't before. Because of course it matters that he didn't want to offend the Jewish people by representing the Holocaust through porn. It matters because it shows that he cared about representation, about how his books would land. But did he have similar concerns about how he was received by other people he represented? No one told me a story of him asking a black friend for absolution about his representations of slavery through porn. Anna was the only person who suggested he knew any black people, and the relationship she told me about with their neighbor was hardly intimate—a few trips to the beach some summers. Was there no time on those trips to ask what this man thought of Dad's idea for the *Chane* series, or had he not yet come up with that one? Or worse, did he not see this topic as requiring anyone's absolution, anyone's permission?

"This work was to make a living, sure," Tracy said over the phone. "But it was also a refuge."

Tracy and I talked for a while longer, but after we hung up it was the idea that Dad sought refuge in his work that stayed with me. I e-mailed Tracy later, asking what kind of refuge he thought my father sought—one from his disordered thinking? I was now seeking out the connection so many of his friends had made for me, between his work and his mental health.

"That's not how I saw it then, no," Tracy replied. "Announcing that he was writing trash protected him from failure. No doubt he dreamed that he was writing something good, but admitting that would have left him open to criticism and worse. I always thought he was scared and vulnerable under that big exterior. I guess he was looking for refuge from a lot of things."

As I read those words, I wondered if my dad needed a safe place in which to play out his fantasy life. A fantasy life where he got to play the part of the strong black slave, of the strong Jewish mobster, one where he compensated for his own shame about who he was by making himself big and strong—and sane—on the page.

32

AFTER THAT EXCHANGE with Tracy, I found myself thinking about the letter in my mother's desk, the one I read when I was sixteen. I'm not sure what brought it back to me in those days—maybe Tracy's insistence that Dad sought refuge from more than one thing. Maybe the sense that I would never understand who he was. Or maybe that old childhood fear, sparked by talking to someone I knew when I was a child.

If my father called me a witch, was I a witch? Did my dad need refuge from me?

So one Saturday morning I picked up another book he wrote early in his career, *The Revenge of Increase Sewall,* published under the pseudonym Heinrich Graat. According to the teaser copy on the cover, "The evil shadow of witchcraft hung over the town and unspeakable rites were performed in secret." Maybe this book would help me understand what my father thought about witches, what he thought about me.

It didn't take me long to recognize Dad as the main character, a history professor named Ben Camden who moves from New York City to a small, sleepy town in the hills of western Massachusetts. The opening scene is set at the Riviera, the bar where my parents met. The next scenes are set in a house much like the one in which my parents lived for the first year of my life, in Cummington, Massachusetts. Mrs.

Camden is clearly modeled on my mother, and despite Ben's love and attraction to her, he can't resist the mysterious woman who lives across the street. She is, just like the love interest in *Chane*, of Dutch ancestry, and as she and Camden begin their affair, I wonder, not for the first time, what hold his Dutch ex-wife held on Dad's heart long after he'd left her.

Though there are hints at witchcraft throughout the early pages of this book, it takes until the final pages to get to those promised "unspeakable rites," which aren't actually so unspeakable. I found this book easier to read than his slavers. It took me a morning, not a month. Maybe, despite the letter I found in Mom's desk drawer, this subject matter isn't as fraught for me as the interracial sex and violence in the slavers. Even if my dad thought I was a witch, his pulpy plot about the unlikely hero who saves the town from "The Powers of Darkness" just doesn't pinch at my heart.

Like *Chane*, this book is also the first in a trilogy, and Dad also wrote several other books about witchcraft under the name Heinrich Graat after completing it. So a pattern emerges about how he wrote, how he conceived of topics and their development, how he made a living. I've learned enough about the pulp fiction industry by now to understand that readers of novels like my dad's expected a few climactic sex scenes per book, places they could return to, but which their children likely wouldn't encounter should the book be left on the side table and flipped through. So Dad was expected to create context, story, plot for each of his books. I imagine him studying slavery in order to do that, getting interested enough in it to write a trilogy and hoping to make a name in the genre, then publishing two or three other books as branches on that same idea. So why not also study witchcraft, write another trilogy, make another name, and publish a couple more books about it, too. Mortgage paid, family safe. But what about the effects of this study on his heart, on his mind?

In the days after reading the first Ben Camden book, that's the question I walked around with. If I can accept that Dad studied slavery in hopes of finding a way to secure his own mental health, why did he study witchcraft? His witches and warlocks are evil, they're controlled by the powers of darkness, they're magically immortal and, even if killed, can come back to seek revenge after hundreds of years. They walk around in small, sleepy New England towns, fooling all but their most observant neighbors. One might notice that their group numbers thirteen and make the connection that a coven needs thirteen participants. Another might spot a cat in the most unusual places, or a blooming cyclamen in an otherwise uninhabited house, and make connections to the dark arts that the reader only half understands. But it takes the bumbling—but handsome—Ben Camden to put all the pieces together and to finally kill the ancient warlock and free the beautiful Dutch girl.

To inhabit Ben Camden, as I believe my father inhabited all of his characters, I think he had to go to the library and learn about witchcraft. He must have had to. Even if he could imagine the "unspeakable rites" just as I believe he imagined and made up the rituals in his slavers, there are details about witches and their powers that he must have read about in books. Where else would a nice Jewish boy from Brooklyn learn about this shit?

So after all that study, what happened when he finally broke? Sometimes I sketch it like this: A happy urban couple tires of the city and moves to a sleepy Massachusetts town. Soon they have two children, eighteen months apart. The mother cooks stew on the old-fashioned gas stove, bakes bread in the oven, sews curtains and clothing from patterns she buys at the general store. The father sits upstairs in his office and writes books. He comes down at cocktail hour and pours himself a martini from the pitcher his wife has mixed up, or sometimes just a scotch on the rocks. The toddlers toddle at their feet. There are neighbors and dinner parties and swimming pool visits in the summers. There are poker groups and long jogs along winding country roads. There are stops at the gas station where everyone knows their names, long drives into town where the kids go to school. When it's the father's turn to drive the carpool, he continues his serial story, told in thirty-minute car-ride segments. The story is about many things, but the detail that will be remembered so many years later is that the main character was a member of the Farter Police. The children think the father is the funniest, best father in the world. At night, the mother quiets the dread in her belly with a drink.

Until one day, despite the other thing she swallows daily that maybe isn't working because of the antibiotics her doctor has prescribed to treat a nasty infection, she's over the toilet just as she was over the toilet the first two times. And when she tells the handsome, funny father the news, his first reaction—does he stop himself?—is a slap across the face. "Another thing to take your attention away from me," he says to her. Not so funny anymore.

Was the woman who got poison ivy in the woods the July night I was born also of Dutch ancestry?

And then everything is changed. The family must move into town because the mother is tired of the long carpool to school, of the difficulty of shopping with three children in tow, of the isolation she now finds everywhere in the sleepy old town. Of the mysterious cats? Of the blooming cyclamen? No, don't be silly—those are just details from a stupid book the father wrote, not facts about the life of the family. They were not outrunning the witch. Not yet.

So they buy a house—a wonderful, wonderful house in town! It's next door to the children's school, it's down the street from the shops, the children can walk downtown when they're older, they can walk to school now. How lucky the father is that his books have been selling, he can buy the wife this house, he can quiet the voices in his head by making her happy. But what is that sound he can't quiet? Who now is making this fuss, what baby is this, come to take his wife's attention away? Wasn't everything perfect before? When will she quiet down so that he can have his woman back?

Who is this demon child now at her breast, what life is she sucking from the mother?

WHEN I TELL it this way, it's not such a long leap to think that the contents of his books affected the contents of his mind, and that when he broke it was easy enough to get confused. Of course I know I'm not a witch. But my father thought I was a witch.

Which is just another way of saying that some people in my family think I caused my father's death.

Which is just another way of saying that sometimes I think so, too.

33

IT'S A COLD morning and the train to New York is full, the conductor tells us over the loudspeaker to make room, to clear off extra seats. I have my usual spot in the quiet car by the window on the river side, though I won't look at the water very much on this trip, I think as I settle my bag under my feet and make room for the woman—white, in her fifties, frosted hair, perfume—just on from Hudson. The black man seated across from me, by the window on the land side, is still sitting alone, and I wonder if it pisses him off that none of these white folks will sit with him on his way to the city, or if he's quietly relieved for the space.

I'm just coming back to *Black Scarab* after some weeks away. It's on my lap in its protective Achebe sheath, and while the woman settles herself next to me, I take it out and start where I'd left off on page 111 and then 112 and turn the page and find myself backward in plot, rereading phrases I've already seen, and I glance down and it says page 97. I worry the rest of the book will be reprinted pages from earlier in the story, just to make it look longer, just to give the illusion of resolution when there never will be any at all. If you can't depend on pulp fiction to get you to the end of a simple story, what the hell is there in this world worth asking?

But I find the second page 112, and when I turn it I land on 113 and pick back up with Objuga, and I breathe an audible sigh. The woman in the seat next to me fidgets and shifts around, and I think about looking up and smiling and telling her everything is going to be okay because I'll find out what happens to Objuga, but she would never understand. She's too busy putting on eyeliner and blush and lipstick, but regardless, she couldn't see my protective sheath even if she looked over at me now. She doesn't know from sitting next to me on a train that just as Achebe covers Gant, Ngoni covers Julia. It's an uncomfortable question rising up, if my marriage gives me permission to go on this quest, credibility when maybe I deserve none. How fair is it of me to ask Achebe to carry the burden I bury behind his cover? How fair to ask my husband to carry me? If the woman next to me could see the salacious cover of the book I'm actually reading, she would think I was another Karla from Goodreads, another white woman looking for a steamy little plantation tale with voodoo and illicit sex. I couldn't handle that assumption, and alone on the train I have no way to tell her who I really am. Why I'm really here.

But why am I here and who do I think I am to dig into this history? What right do I have to pull my husband and our children along on this journey? What damage do I do when I unpack where I came from and uncover its essential ugliness? Was this whole enterprise a mistake founded, like so much, in my white-girl naïveté? Or is it my duty to figure out where I came from, can I move the needle forward if I try?

These are questions I can't answer today, so, as I have become accustomed to doing, I put them away and turn back to my father's words. As the Hudson passes by out my window, I find Objuga hiding out in a house in the suburbs of Tangier with a loyal servant named Mustaphah, trusty old Doo, and two beautiful women. One is black, and she's been with Objuga as they traveled north up the coast on the dhow. The other is white, and has green eyes that astound Objuga when he sees them—"Green eyes! Green eyes!"—and I think about my own hazel greens in a family of blue-eyed women and what they looked like to Dad in 1976 when this book was published and I was two.

The reader still doesn't know why Objuga is getting this special treatment. Why he wasn't sold with the other Africans as a slave. Why he's been taught Arabic or brought to this house in Tangier or given a servant and two women to please him. It's a lot to ask your reader to believe, even if the book is less than two hundred pages long and filled with the sex scenes you bought it for. My mother told me recently that before he'd sit down to write, Dad used to speak aloud that old yarn about the suspension of disbelief, and right now I think he's taken it too far. But the fact remains that this book doesn't follow the formula he'd established in the Chane series, and I love Objuga now. I love his bravery and his fear and his respect for traditions—even if they're entirely the inventions of my father's racial imagination—and I need to know what happens to him. I've suspended disbelief at least for this train ride to the city, but I'd kind of like my dad to get on with it.

Rhinecliff out the window and I don't even look. "Listen to me," Objuga's protector says to him. "Twenty odd years before you met your fate as a captive . . . your father met the same fate." Objuga's dad had been king, but Objuga had never known him. He was rumored to have died on an expedition far from the village when the prince was small. So this is news. "The Sultan was forming his elite bodyguard of black slaves . . . and your father was tested to see if he could become one of El Bokhari." I circle "Sultan" and "El Bokhari" because I want to come back to these ideas, find out if they're founded in fact. "Your father was admitted into the bodyguard of our most high protector of the faith."

"And my father lives?" Objuga asks. I underline this part. Write "my dreams," in the margin. "Yes, yes. He is the high commander of El Bokhari." And now it's a race to get to him. The last thirty pages of the book are filled with tension and narrow escapes and the trademark cave hideout as the group makes its way from the lovely small house in the suburbs to the Sultan's palace in Marrakesh, and I think about how important that trip had been to my dad, how his experiences in North Africa populate all of his stories. The boat ride, the weeks in Tangier, a journey they took to Marrakesh that my mother describes—even all these years later—as astonishing.

I read next about a disquieting sexual ritual performance for the Sultan in his palace and a hair-raising capture and a good deal more torture for our hero. The pages left in the book are few now, and I wonder if Dad will let the end be sad, if Objuga might die in his cell. But no, there's a quick rescue and in the darkness a voice comes to him from what feels like a great distance. He barely recognizes the language, which he hears as if after "years spent in utter silence." The voice asks for his name and the name of his mother.

"I am Objuga-Ka-Oto. I am a Prince of the Mazamboni. They say my mother's name was Ommah. I have never seen my father."

And the voice replies, "Then look up and see him now."

If I wipe away the tears on my cheeks, the frosty-haired white woman to my left will know what's happening to me on this seat on the Amtrak train to New York. She'll know that my father is dead and that I don't want him to be, she'll know that he's just spoken to me about reunions anyway, she'll know that his suicide has defined me and that the shame I carry works its way into every decision I make. The fear. It's why my coat isn't folded up in the storage compartment above my head—I need its protection around my shoulders. She'll know why I'm wearing my black Frye boots—so I'm strong and make a loud noise on the concrete sidewalks and the wooden hallways in New York. She'll know why I'm wearing lipstick already and not putting it on here, in public like she did, on the train where anyone could see. She'll know why Achebe covers Gant, what it means that I let Ngoni give cover to me, why I'm worried the black man across the aisle has hurt feelings, why I can't yell at my husband when I'm mad or why I tell the kids I love them six hundred times a day so there's no possibility of forgetting. If I reach up and wipe away the tears on my cheeks, the frosty-haired white woman will know that I dream sometimes that my father is really alive and he's just been hiding from me. She'll know that when I go to bed at night I hope to have the dream again because when I have the dream it feels like I have a father and like if I'm very, very careful I could still have him when I wake up. She'll know that I want to look up and see him now.

34

THE OFFICE OF Kensington Books is in midtown Manhattan, and I have an appointment with Steve Zacharius, who runs the place. His father was my father's publisher. As I follow the receptionist to his office, I notice a sculpture of a zebra dominating the waiting area and bookcase-lined walls jammed with romance novels featuring black people in lingerie. Inside Steve's office, I see several more zebras—a stuffed animal, a bookend, a painting on the wall. I don't think I'll get a straight answer if I ask Steve, but I'm pretty sure that the house that published most of my dad's slavers, Lancer Books, became Zebra Books after Walter Zacharius died. It's now called Kensington Books, and though I don't know why they decided to change the name again, as I look around at all those zebras I think it was wise not to let a black-and-white-striped animal represent the books you publish unless you plan to be explicit about "doing the black-white thing" and can live with the messed-up symbolism.

Or maybe I'm reading too much into it. Steve told me over e-mail that his publishing house is not the same house as his father's, that I shouldn't have expectations about finding any old Lancer materials when I come, and that he had no idea what this genre I call "slavers" was all about.

Steve is a large white man with several chins and a big belly, and he sits behind a big desk. When he asks me how he can help and I remind him what I said in my e-mail, he laughs loudly and I feel immediately uncomfortable across the desk from him, just a small girl asking stupid small unanswerable questions. His laugh seems to tell me I should go home now to play with my dolls. Instead, I dig in my bag and pull out several of Dad's slavers and place them on his desk. It isn't exactly a challenge, but I notice that I feel bolder now with those books in front of me. With his books on the desk in front of me, I think that Dad knew I'd be the one to come for him. He's here with me now, eager to lead me to the end of this road.

"I guess I'm hoping you can tell me something about the industry around books like these," I say.

Steve picks up *Chane* and looks at the cover for a minute before saying, "I'm not sure I can help you. The business is so different now than it was in my dad's day, and though I worked at Lancer during the summers, I didn't really know how the machine operated."

I want facts, data points about who was buying my dad's books, or where they were sold, or to whom they were marketed, or how well they did, or why publishers like Lancer asked for them from writers-for-hire like my dad, but it seems as though Steve is going to sweep this whole history under the carpet. Before I had contacted him, I Googled Lancer Books, and while I found out about some of what they'd published, I didn't find a single slaver. They published a Conan series, some comic books, and a whole lot of porn. But Google Images only shows Lancer publications with white folks on the covers. Most of the other slavers on my shelf—by other writers—are also published by Lancer, but I found out about them from ads in the back of Dad's books. So I wonder if Lancer decided at some point to hide their slavers from the public, if this subgenre became a disgrace, or if there just wasn't as much of it as I've come to believe. I'm here because this is the only house that published my dad's slavers that still exists in some form—albeit under a new name and different management. I'm here because I hope Steve Zacharius might stop laughing at me long enough to answer some of my questions.

"Is there anyone working here now who was around in the sixties and seventies?" I ask after he gives another reason for not knowing anything about this industry in which he was raised.

"The one guy who was is out today with kidney stones," Steve tells me, disarming me with the too-personal detail. He then makes small talk for a couple of minutes before ushering me out the door.

Which is why I'm so surprised to see an e-mail from him in my inbox a couple of days later. "Disregard Gary's crass humor," it starts. "But see what he remembers about your dad," and he forwards an e-mail from a man named Goldstein, who first updates Steve on his health and then writes:

> I remember those Gant epics, and seeing them on the spinning racks at drugstores in the late 1960s. Chane is this massive strong black guy who knocked up the daughters of plantation owners, raped white women (who loved it), all kinds of black/white perversions. The Gants were clearly inspired by Kyle Onstott's massive bestseller MANDINGO, so it's clear where Gant and your father got their inspiration from. They were not alone. There were tons of knockoffs from all the paperback houses.

Before I reply to Steve to thank him for this contact, before I can set aside my frustration that he wasn't willing to look at this racist legacy head-on with me, I note that this e-mail is wrong on one important point. Chane doesn't get any of his white lovers pregnant. His children are all born to black women. I have to quiet the question this raises—if my dad was scared to represent interracial children in his fiction, what might that reveal about how he would feel about my sons? I put the question away and e-mail Goldstein. The response that comes back in minutes is a welcome distraction.

"When your father wrote those books in the '60s and '70s, it was possible to actually make a decent living if one was prolific enough to churn out a new one every couple of months," he writes. Goldstein seems like that unusual mix of a man who gets it that I'm on a quest to know my father, but who isn't particularly concerned about tarnishing anyone's image. I find it refreshing. "Some smaller houses, like New English Library or Lancer, paid anywhere from $500–$2,000 a pop." I get up to look at my bookcase and scan the publishers, spot the New English label on a couple of Dad's later slavers. Maybe he went there when things slowed down at Lancer. "It was not unusual for a paperback to sell 100,000 copies (especially the sexy ones) or more. I don't remember much advertising being done for paperback originals; with the lurid covers and titillating titles, people knew what they were getting for their 75 cents. They were pretty much dumped onto the racks to fend for themselves."

I want to know who read these books and how they were marketed, how different the sixties and seventies were from today. I know I can see sexy covers in the grocery store book aisle now, though I don't know how they compare to Dad's except that everyone on those covers is white. Maybe the books in Kensington's hallways are shipped to grocery stores in the black cities and neighborhoods of our divided nation.

So I ask Goldstein if he knows how I might find sales information, anything that would tell me if my dad made a good living off these books. Not because that would justify them to me, but because it would help me understand his motivations.

"Getting ahold of any kind of sales information after all these years would be quite a formidable task," he types back. "Most of the paperback houses are long gone and with them went the bookkeeping ledgers and canceled checks. No computers then, so everything was done by hand."

The further I get from really understanding the market for Dad's books, the more I realize that's not really what this is about for me. Would knowing he made a good living help me sleep better, or would it make my nightmares worse? Maybe it's safer here, in a world where I can imagine that no one much read Norman Gant, where I can pretend none of his books sold a hundred thousand copies, where I can imagine his damage was limited. I don't let myself think about the recently released e-books or consider that it is again possible for a hundred thousand copies of my father's damaging novels to sell. Instead, I send one more question over to Goldstein.

"Why do you think there was such a market for these books?" I ask.

Goldstein is quick as ever with his reply. "Enterprising publishers like Walter Zacharius, and a host of others, exploited the new sexual freedom in literature."

I appreciate that someone in this industry will say it to me so plain: publishers exploited the sexual freedom of the sixties and seventies to sell books. Some of them depended on stereotypes about power dynamics when the racial boundary was crossed. Books sold. It was business.

It's not theirs to understand why, to ask about the consequences of their choices. To investigate all the tentacles of this particular beast. It should be, but if my conversation with Steve Zacharius is anything to go by, they don't take it. I'm the one who came here to understand how this industry's legacy might affect my children, might have contributed to the white supremacy that rules this country, might play a part in the world we'll send our kids off into in a couple of years. I'm the one with skin in the game.

Even when others are implicated, it will always, for me, come back to my dad and the only source I have about who he was. His books. I can't figure out who read them, I can't determine how well they sold or if they were largely ignored on the racks. I can say that I think these books contributed to the normalization of slavery, and that contribution to this racist world is hard to bear. There are days the weight pulls me under. But I return to them because they are the only thing I have of my father's, and I need to know where I come from.

35

AS I TAKE a long drink of water from the fountain in the hallway outside my first-grade classroom I realize that now that Reagan is president, the red phone will be a problem. Josh had told me about the red phone, and I know it sits on the president's desk, know it has only one button. If the president decides it's time, all he has to do is push the button, and I know Reagan is the guy to push it. I stand up and wipe the water off my lips with the back of my hand and look at the kid behind me and say, "Not long now."

"Until what?" he asks.

"War," I say.

There's a power to being the only person in my class to know about the dangers in this world.

AUSTEN RIGGS HAS a red phone, too. I've known about it always. It's the phone that rings at Riggs when I call. Anyone else who calls gets their regular line, but if I call them, their red phone will ring and they'll know it's me. "Nope, we don't have any files for you, Ms. Wolk." And that will be the end of a world in which I ever get any answers.

Only it's years later now. Reagan never dialed in a nuclear war and the world is still spinning and I'm married and a mother and my name isn't Ms. Wolk. But I'm still certain that if I call and ask for Dad's records, they'll have their answer waiting. I look them up anyway, one bright cold day in February, a year after I first picked up Dad's books. Find their website and click on Contact Us and see a listing for a Medical Records Administrator. The next day, I dial.

"I'm wondering if it would be possible," I start. But I have to start over. "My father was a patient there in 1980." But that's wrong, too. It was only a few days into 1980 when he died. That date might trigger the red phone. "I'm sorry," I say. "This is difficult." I'm looking for my journalist voice, but I can't find it. "My dad was a patient there. I'm wondering if I could come and get a copy of his medical records. I don't live far away."

"I'm so sorry to have to ask this," says the sweet voice on the other end of the line, and I'm certain it's the big fat No I've been expecting, certain it was the red phone that rang. "But is your father still living?"

"Oh! God. No. No, of course not!" relief tight in my chest. She doesn't know it's me yet. "That's why I need his records!" Maybe I'm yelling.

"Okay. There's a chance I can help you, but I'll need to ask you a couple of questions first." And the kind woman on the other end of the phone, who has talked to people like me before, starts listing the possibilities.

"Is there a surviving spouse?"

"Yes! And she's even willing to come in and sign for the records for me! It's my mother!"

"Well, it's more complicated than that. Does she have his will?"

"Will?" I don't think there was a will.

"Or his power of attorney?"

"He died thirty-six years ago."

"I know, but there are forms we need to fill out, paperwork we have to set straight. It sounds strange, but we have an obligation to protect our patients even in death."

I stand in the middle of my living room with the phone to my ear. Breathing.

"I have to look this up every time, so hang on and let me look it up," she says.

I wait for her to look it up. I don't know what "it" is, but I feel a possibility in the waiting.

"Here it is," she says after some time. "Can I e-mail this to you? What's your e-mail address?"

I am a childhood drawing of a gleeful girl. I've gotten all this way in the conversation without once saying my dad's name out loud, and she still won't know it's me now, because my name is so different! I can give her my e-mail address and the red phone will stay quiet on her desk. I spell it the way I always spell it for people who are not ready to hear this name. M like mary. U. N like nancy. E. M like mary. O.

"1980," she says in her secretary voice on the other end. "I'm pretty sure the files from 1980 are on microfilm, so when you come in for them it shouldn't take me long to get you the copies."

We hang up and I want to kiss her, I want to send her flowers, I want to thank her for not once asking me who I was calling about. We're still safe, Dad. They don't know I'm looking for you yet.

When the "it" she'd found comes into my e-mail account, it tells me all the things I will need to do to get the paperwork straight to come in and request that Riggs copy his files for me. The paperwork will protect me from the red phone. I'll have the paperwork and they'll have to give me the files. But it's all in legalese and I can't read it right so I e-mail the lawyer who helped us buy our house and set up an appointment.

"I'll get all the ducks in a row," he tells me over the wide expanse of a wooden desk some days later. "There are a couple things I'll need from you. The death certificate, for sure, and a form designating you as his executor, signed by all of his survivors, which I'll draw up for you. Do you know if there is a police report?"

I smile and nod because I don't know anything, but of course I will find out because he is protecting me from the red phone. He will arm me with what I need to get my father's medical records. I will get him anything he asks for because I love him for protecting me from Riggs.

When I get up and walk out of his office onto the small main street in my town, the sun reflects off the snow-covered cars and I feel victorious and so close to the end. But then I wonder, have I considered what I might find?

36

"HI, I'M JULIA," I say to the pretty white Stockbridge town clerk in my journalist voice a couple of weeks later. "Are you Terri? We spoke on the phone." I'm here for Dad's death certificate.

"Oh yes," she says, getting up from her chair. She reaches for the papers on her desk and takes the sheet on top without confirming any facts, without confirming she knows why I'm here. The one she picks up is light blue with a dark-blue border, and I can see it's official and stamped and certified. Underneath is another sheet printed on the same paper, and I wonder how many death certificates Terri has to process on any given day. I also wonder how she can be sure without asking for confirmation that she's grabbed the right one for me.

So when she slides it over to me and says, "This is the one?" I look and see handwriting in the center portion of the page, and my eyes go there first. I expect to see his name, and I start to say, "Oh this isn't his." This one, I almost say out loud, is for someone named Staunton, Hank Staunton. See? It says it right here. It says it right here because just like in my dream, Dad isn't dead. There's been a mistake and I'm just here to confirm that, thanks.

But then I look closer and it doesn't say Hank Staunton in old-fashioned handwriting in the center of the page. What it says in old-fashioned handwriting on the center of the page is Strangulation. And it also says Hanging. Without checking the name on the top or what fields these are or why they're filled in with handwriting and not typed, I look up at Terri the town clerk and smile. "Yes, thank you," I say, and she folds the paper in thirds and puts it in an envelope while I write her a check for five dollars.

"Thank you for making this so easy," I say as I tear the check out of the book and hand it to her. I say that because I can't say, "Thank you for not making me feel like a freak, thank you for not judging me for having a suicide for a father." I walk out of her office and think about how good I've become at wearing this mask. My hands are not shaking, my legs are solid on the steps.

I climb into my car and, despite my certainty that Terri has X-ray vision and can see through the walls of the offices around her to me in the parking lot, I sit in the driver's seat and turn the car on so the seat warmer can comfort me. I open the envelope, right in the parking lot, like it's normal to idle a car in Stockbridge and read a death certificate. I sit there and read every line from top to bottom.

Name, gender, date of death. Place of death, race, age. Date of birth, place of birth, marriage status, spouse name. Occupation, social security number. Oh! I think. Now I have his social security number—as though this might come in handy. It says he was not a veteran of any U.S. wars. It lists his residence. The name of his father, the place of his father's birth. Which is on his death certificate, why? I wonder. But then just as fast I think, Cecil was born in Ohio? Who knew! A slight smile on my lips at the new nugget, the potential new angle. Name of mother, place of her birth. Name and address of informant—my mom, my house. The last line of this top typed section lists the date of the burial, confirming my memory that it was quick.

Then the handwriting section. Filled out by what I can see crisp as mist was an old MD with a shaking hand. Was he recovering from what he saw, or was he palsied with age? His handwriting is old-fashioned all caps. This is the Cause of Death section, and it states it like this: due to a consequence of STRANGULATION; due to a consequence of HANGING; other significant conditions MANIC DEPRESSIVE PSYCHOSIS. Autopsy? NO. Referred to medical examiner? YES. Then in a smaller hand, because the boxes here are tighter: SUICIDE, JAN. 5, 1980, SELF INFLICTED. Right, I think. Is there any other kind?

The next box asks, Place of injury? HOSPITAL ROOM. Two boxes at the top of this section each say "15 MIN," and I have to squint now to see what this is about. Tears starting in the backs of my eyes. "Interval between onset and death" after each Due to a consequence of. After STRANGULATION. After HANGING.

The interval between onset and death calls up memories of when my mom told me his method some years after his death. She'd said it was quick. She'd said that sometimes a hanging is slow but not to worry, Dad's was fast. He hadn't suffered. His neck had snapped in a flash. And now details from the trial, when my mom sued Austen Riggs for negligence or wrongful death or abandonment of duty, swirl into focus. "They were meant to check on him every hour," I remember her saying over and over into the phone, shaking her head at the injustice. "They hadn't checked on him in four." She lost.

I try to deduce from the few facts I know how he must have planned it. Been clean and ready with everything in its hiding spot under the bed at the noontime check-in. Thought he only had an hour before the next check-in. But was hanging long since when a nurse finally returned. I think about those fifteen minutes the doctor recorded and how he could have determined them based on whatever sources doctors use. He was confident enough, this Donald Campbell, MD, to write those hours down. To write down those minutes. Pronounced dead at 4:30. I picture the nurse walking into the room for the check-in. I picture her scream-ing. I picture her reaction as the pronouncement of death. But if the interval was fifteen minutes, did he suffer? Did his neck snap in a flash?

My eyes skim back to the top of the page as I fold this paper up and plan to pull out of the parking lot. I'm leaving this place now with my facts. But then I see it, just next to the date of death, over by the name of the Hospital or Other Institution. A very small box in the corner. One I hadn't thought to look at before. It's not very big because its label is an acronym, one we've become so accustomed to hearing on crime TV that it's almost a joke. And the answer is also so small. DOA (yes or no) it says in the tiniest font in the world.

Typed in answer to the question: No.

37

"MOM TOLD BELLA how Dad died," my brother said to me over the phone once, back when Julius was a baby. His voice was hot with anger.

"What? Why?" was all I could think to ask.

"Because she asked."

Josh's daughter Bella was three and curious about our dad. Her questions foreshadowed ones my own sons would ask one day, but I didn't know that yet. Didn't understand what captured her wonder. Josh had, up to then, used only the vaguest language, *he was sick,* so Bella went to the source.

"What happened?" I asked, the long phone cord twisting around my body as I set Julius in his bouncy seat on the counter of our small New York City kitchen.

Josh said Mom picked Bella up from preschool that day and when she climbed into her booster seat, the first thing she said was, "How did my dad's dad die?"

"Mom didn't skip a beat," Josh said. "'He killed himself,' she said, just as she said to us all those years ago."

Josh's voice changed when he played the part of his daughter, and I could see her thick blonde hair coming out from her head in a messy halo, her round brown eyes wide in alarm, I could hear her voice high with fear when he mimicked, "Did he shoot himself in the head with a gun?"

"What did Mom say to that?" I asked.

"She said, 'No. He hanged himself from the ceiling of the loony bin with his belt strap,'" and Josh was still talking, telling me what happened next, but I couldn't hear him anymore because the sound in my ears was too loud and I was losing my balance there in my kitchen and I suddenly needed to sit down because when I was a little older than Bella I learned this story in real time.

Except Mom never told me it was a belt strap.

And in the absence of that knowledge, I had created my own stories. I spent my life picturing bedsheets knotted together out a window, picturing his body flapping in the wind, picturing a rope tied into a noose like in TV Westerns, but where in the world would he get that in the loony bin? I pictured everything imaginable, but I never pictured a belt. I'd been unable to imagine that they would admit him to the hospital carrying his own murder weapon.

WHEN I SET out on this journey to find my father, I didn't want to uncover more details like the belt strap. I wanted to find out about his career, I wanted to understand his creative mind, not his troubled mind. When I set out on this journey to find my father, I just planned to read his books and figure out what made him write slavery porn. Nothing more. But a week after my visit to the Stockbridge Town Offices, I sit on the long wooden bench with the blue cushion under the kitchen window while Ngoni stir-fries pork and vegetables and tells me about his day on campus and some of the details of a deanship he's about to take over. When the phone rings, I jump up to answer it even though we never answer the landline. Caller ID says Stockbridge, so I know who's returning my call. Police Chief Bob Eaton, in a voice lowered in respect and soft with kindness, says, "I found that report you asked about."

"Wow," I say. Because I really am surprised. It's thirty-six years old, that report. I wasn't even sure I wanted to call the police station to see if they still had it, but there's something about this journey I can't stop now. It's no longer about what I want to hide from. It's about understanding everything I can. "Thank you so much," I say. Because this man knows me now, if he has that report. I understand the kindness in his voice and want to return it.

"I'm going to need you to fill out a request for public records," he says.

"Of course. Could you e-mail it to me?" I'd driven to Stockbridge last week—it's only an hour away, but I have deadlines I can't continue to ignore. Now that I know the report exists, I can wait.

But still I check e-mail every few minutes after we hang up. When one comes in half an hour later, it isn't the request for information form, it's the report itself. "No need for the form," Bob Eaton the police chief writes.

"People are really nice to me," I say to Ngoni at the stove. "When I call these places and ask for these documents, they find them and they know what I'm doing and they know what this is and they treat me really nicely." Because that is what I want to talk about right now. People being nice to me. I don't think about my white privilege in this moment or how my race might have influenced Bob Eaton's treatment of me. I just let him be nice to me because it makes a hard thing a little less hard.

But my husband is familiar with the masks I wear, knows how to cut through them. "Are you going to read it?" he asks.

"Not right here just before dinner." A pause. I tap on the screen in my hand. "But it's right here on my phone." I stand up and turn so he can see it. He wipes his hand on a dish towel, reaches out and scrolls. Shows me there's only one page. "Oh," I say. "Maybe I'll read it." I sit back down.

At 4:07 in the afternoon of Saturday, January 5, 1980, officer Karl G. Cooper Jr. got a call from Audrey LaFontana, a nurse at Austen Riggs. Officer Cooper wrote, some hours later, that the call "stated that someone had just hung themself." I stumble on the grammar and decide that's maybe all I can do today, all I can do while the kids crash into the kitchen laughing, stand at the sink to wash their hands. All I can do when Ngoni wants to tell me about his job and I'm supposed to be listening. But the phone is alive on the bench beside me. I can't let it rest.

When I pick it back up, I learn that Dad's room was on the second floor. I learn the names of the nurses in room #26 when officer Cooper arrives. He types, "Nurse Jane Boyle had gone to the victims room to inform him there was a party at Riggs." *What do they celebrate under a tent at Riggs?* "When she entered the room she found the victim hanging from a sprinkler pipe located on the south wall almost centered with his bed. Mr. Wolk had hung himself with his belt from the pipe." *Did he shoot himself in the head with a gun?* "Jane Boyle tried to take the body down but was unable to." *DOA (yes or no)?*

I want to find nurse Jane Boyle and hug her. I want to sit on the couch with her and tell her I love her. I want her to know that she did the best she could. I want to smooth her hair and hold onto her shaking hand. I want her not to be broken by this death like the rest of us.

But I also have some questions for nurse Jane Boyle: Why did my mother say it had been four hours since anyone had checked on him? And why did the death certificate say, No, not dead on arrival? Was he alive when she knocked? Did she hear his last breaths? Was there screaming, or struggling? If someone had checked earlier, could they have saved him? If she'd been faster to collect nurse Audrey LaFontana, could they have saved him together?

Because once nurse Audrey LaFontana got there, they lifted all six feet three inches of him, all however many pounds he weighed by then, all that thick black wavy hair and mustache, all those long legs now gone limp—and got him on the floor. "Once they had Mr. Wolk on the floor they tried to revive him by using oxygen & C.P.R. but there attempts were unsuccessful," Officer Cooper typed. Was Officer Cooper shaking at his desk? He next lists the names of the people he summoned and the times they arrived. I see him in the corner of room #26, watching the door and the clock and writing notes in his small hand each time the people who know what to do come into the room.

4:25 p.m. Chief Obanhein arrived.

5:16 p.m. Dr. Campbell who is the Medical Examiner.

5:21 p.m. Stevens Funeral Home which is located in Great Barrington.

Which one of them called my mom? What time did she find out? Did she cry?

"Mr. Wolk was last seen alive around 2:00 p.m. this same day," Cooper sums up, and I wonder if that's accurate. "It was stated to me by nurse June Pederson that Mr. Wolk had been very depressed. Mr. Wolk had been a patient at the Austen Riggs Foundation since approximately December 3, 1979."

Ngoni knows me well enough not to ask about the report just yet, and while the kids put plates and forks on the table and pull the jug of milk out of the fridge and fold napkins under knives, he goes back to reporting on his day. I can't hear what he's saying, but he knows that.

38

MORE THAN A YEAR after my mother gave me the letters my father wrote to her from Rome, I take them out into the sunshine of a spring afternoon and sit on my deck, willing myself to read. I don't know why I haven't tried to read them yet, except maybe because it's impossible to face the fact that my father was really once alive. That he'd had dreams and hopes he wrote down on a page not for a publisher, but for my mom. It'd been hard enough to decide to finally read his books, and they were just pulpy pieces of trash he didn't really care about. But his letters? They sat for a long time on my desk, and later I moved them into a filing cabinet so they wouldn't distract me from deadlines I had to stop missing, or the real work of reading his books. They'd been there now for months.

When I finally open each onionskin envelope, I see that several are typewritten and that for those that aren't, there might be no way to decode my father's words. There's some solace in that—I know now where I got my terrible handwriting, and also, I can set some of these aside. I don't have to read them all. I can't possibly read them all. I start where I can, with a letter typed up and tidy and marked in the right corner simply as being written on Monday. Since I have no way of ordering his world, I decide Monday is a good place to start.

"It seems I've gone quite mad," he sits at his typewriter and types. He then describes, in one extraordinary run-on sentence, his eczema, a walk along the Tiber, a visit to a place he spells—his spelling is legendarily atrocious—the Castle of the Holy Angle. "Somehow between then and now the falcon has lost the voice of the falconer," he types.

"The last two nights have been lunatic," he sits at his typewriter and types in 1967. Then another run-on about a lack of sleep for fear my mother doesn't love him. "I tossed all night with these psychogenic tricks," he types.

"When the itch has settled behind my ears, somehow liquid there as if it were the place where my brain seeps out, it makes me think I know how it was with Vincent and I can't bear it and I don't want to live without it," he types, and it takes me a moment to realize he's comparing himself to Vincent van Gogh. To the desire to cut off his own ear, somehow liquid there.

The "it" is so large it fills my big backyard, and I draw the blanket around my shoulders to protect me from the cold I feel creeping in. I listen to the tissue-paper words rustle in the wind and imagine letting them blow away.

"And what sort of madness is it for a woman to become a wife to all or any of this?" he types. "Because the longer it stays checked the worse it's going to be later," he types eleven years before his breakdown at the *sesshin*. "But how can I support it without a wife. And how will I ever support it with a wife." There are no question marks to these questions, but the falcon is coming back, he assures her.

"As if suicide were a sine curve," he types thirteen years before his own. "It is as tempting to leap from the top as to drown at the bottom."

I think of my mother reading these words in her childhood bedroom in Albany, New York, her parents downstairs with their drinks. Did she think he could escape it through her? Did she think he was her escape? How did she not see what he was showing her?

Then I put myself in her shoes. If Ngoni's letters from Zimbabwe had exposed such disordered thinking, would I have run away? Or would I have held fast to that word *wife*, and prayed that it could bring magic? Prayed that it could keep him sane, keep him with us? I have no doubt that even if Ngoni had revealed he heard voices in his letters to me from across the world, even if he had started to disappear after our wedding, I would have held on tight and tried to help him return to me.

My mother saw what he was showing her, and hoped for what we all hope for.

39

IT'S A MONDAY in summer when I walk into the building where he died. I step onto the carpet—it is no longer red, but an industrial gray, recently installed, clean and with a tall, quieting pile—and my silent footprints radiate through the rooms as I used to imagine my steps radiated when I was little. My school was a very short walk across a lawn and through a parking lot and up a paved path hill, and as I walked there in the mornings, I imagined my steps rippling out from the spot on which my foot touched the earth, an echo of emotion rounding out in all directions. *If I have been here, I have also been over there,* I used to think. *Someday I will have been everywhere. Someday I will find you.* So it is that I imagine my feet climbing the stairs I stood behind all those years ago, all the way into room #26, where I wonder if there is still a strong pipe across the ceiling. And finally my footprints meet his, which cannot be removed with the old carpet. They meet in the middle where we can never see.

I stand at the desk and look, but there is no red phone. Just a computer screen with a box around the edges so no matter how far a person might lean over, he cannot read it from this side. Just a slippery glass top across the expanse of wood so that no matter how hard a person might try, he can never scratch the surface with his fingernails. Just a white girl at the desk, looking up at me from her chair. She is only tiny,

only small. Are you sixteen? I want to ask. Can you really be old enough
to work?

Instead I say, "I'm looking for the medical records office," and she
gives me directions and I make my way down the hall and try not to peek
in open doorways or read the names spelled across closed ones. I try to
keep my eyes on the great gray carpet and the directions from the girl at
the desk.

"Are you Julia," says Corinne, the medical records keeper. It's not
a question, and who else could I be? I stand with my bracelets jangling
on my arm, my lipstick strong on my lip, my eyes on her desk, on the
filing cabinets, on the little basement windows along the top of the
back wall. Then I reach out and shake her hand. I grasp it firmly. See, I
want to say, I am not like him. I am solid. I cannot be moved. Look how
I dressed up to come see you today. See, I want to say, this file cannot
harm me. I am solid, I cannot be moved. Look.

"I didn't seal it," she says, inviting me to open the envelope in this
room. Handing me the envelope she thinks I could open in this room.
"In case you . . ." But she doesn't finish.

"I'm sure you included everything," I say, and I smile. I am not like
him. Look. "Thank you very much." And I am out the door and up the
stairs and past the desk and I don't look back at the staircase once carpeted
in red because I am not here anymore. I never need to be here again.

SOME OF THE facts I learn. He wasn't six foot three. He was six foot
one and a half. Why does this matter? Why does this shatter the dream
I've carried all my life? My father was larger than life, too big to be contained by life, my father was six foot three and a giant and I loved the
hero that meant he was even when I knew everything else said he was
no hero at all. My dad was six foot three and his long legs folded into
a square just for me. But this file says my dad was less than that. This
file says my facts were wrong. And now that I have this file there are
new facts I can't not know. Like that he didn't remember how old I was
when his doctor asked.

He weighed 187 pounds the day he was admitted. His heart beat 72
times each minute. His temperature was 100 degrees Fahrenheit, but
don't worry, it had gone down by the next day. His first memory was

of being held by his mother. A babe in arms. And his mother repeating, over and over and over and over, you are killing me.

You are killing me.

His IQ was one hundred and twenty-three.

SOME OF THE facts I once knew, some of the facts I have unlearned. Some of the facts in the file are reminders. His admission to the hospital was a condition of his continued marriage to my mother. "Mrs. Wolk came across as a smart, rather tough, level-headed woman," wrote the director of admissions. "Mr. Wolk presented as somewhat dazed, highly occupied with his obsessions, and as a sad, depressed, older-than-his-age looking man," wrote the director of admissions. "Mr. Wolk is probably capable of being highly charming and seductive," wrote the director of admissions. "Mrs. Wolk has taken a definite position regarding the continued presence of her husband in the family home," wrote the director of admissions.

SOME OF THE facts are foils. He told his doctor he'd written forty novels in ten years. Told his doctor it was all the more impressive when one considered that he'd been unable to write for the last year. "So that's really forty novels in nine," his doctor wrote in his file. Unless there are names I never found, I poke holes in his story so many years later. Unless there are names I never found, I think he was fooling. Himself. His caregiver. Himself.

I found seven pseudonyms. I found twenty-one books.

A WORD I don't know and must learn. Decompensate. As in, "The patient experienced a gross psychotic decompensation approximately one year ago when he attended a Zen Buddhist retreat." As in, "Mr. Wolk's difficulties first began a year ago when he decompensated following an intensive week of involvement with a Zen Buddhist master."

"I believe that Mr. Wolk has lived with this monk in his head for the last year," his doctor wrote in his file. I believe that Mr. Wolk has lived in my head far longer.

SOME OF THE facts are revelations. Some of the facts are Revelations. "He has become sexually estranged from his wife, who is Gentile," says his file at one point. I check the name of the doctor and see it's vaguely Semitic. We still said "Gentile" in 1979? Does this reveal my father's religious preoccupation, or his doctor's?

"He realized when in the presence of the Buddhist master that he was really a Jew from New York City," says his file at one point. Ah ha. He did? And so the life I spent living as a non-Jew—"your father renounced Judaism before we were married," my mother always said. "Your father was not a Jew and neither are you"—this, too, is false? Was it just here in the hospital that he could admit to a yearning, to a wish to return? Or did he try to tell my mother, too? Was it something she could abide?

Some of these facts bring to a boil my lifelong confusions of religion. Some of these facts bring to a boil questions I have always asked about God. Some of these facts bring to a boil parts of myself I can't place because I don't know where I fit. Don't know where he fit. He didn't know where to fit.

A WORD I don't know and must learn. Recompensate. As in, "The patient has been attempting to recompensate for the last thirteen months." As in, Mr. Wolk's attempts at recompensation have thus far failed.

I read in his records that the day before he died he asked a nurse if she thought he should be in a closed hospital. I read that the day before he died he played Boggle but couldn't concentrate. I read that the day before he died he walked in the cemetery and said that his children seemed happier without him. I read that the day before he died he was scared to be alone.

And his doctor gave him his home phone number in case he needed to reach him over the weekend. And the nurse reminded him about the doctor on call. Pointed out that seeking help was the first step in recovery. Told him she was just there, just outside his door, when he asked to be alone. Anyway.

AND. HIS BODY was cold when she unlocked the door because he didn't respond to her knock. His limbs were stiff. The CPR administered was perfunctory, necessary, a requirement of an institution tasked with medical as well as mental care.

After sleepless nights wondering if he'd still been alive when nurse Jane Boyle walked through the door, the answer comes across the distance in her sweet, slanted script. "Pupils dilated and fixed, his body was cold to the touch. It was evident that considerable time had passed before he was discovered." My mother said they hadn't checked on him in hours.

So.

40

ONE MORNING, back at my desk where I find I can best set the emotions aside—set them out—I file my father's medical records in my cabinet and put them out of my mind the way I was taught to put difficult things out of my mind. I take a long sip of tea, adjust myself on my chair, look out the window for the pair of red-tailed hawks I sometimes see circling above the pines outside, and type the words "plantation novel" into Goodreads. I know what I'm doing, I know I'm mimicking the model of emotional reserve I was raised with—I even know by now that such reservation can deepen the damage. But that doesn't mean I know how not to do it. So I'm back with Dad's books, trying to figure out what the slavers he wrote gave rise to. It's the only way I know how to keep going.

"Plantation novel" is the phrase Steve Zacharius at Kensington had used when he talked about Dad's books, and it's also on the cover of one of the later slavers on my shelf, written by someone named Saliee O'Brien and published in 1986. A long list fills my screen in seconds, and for a moment I think I might have a chance at finding out how my father's career is implicated in what America has become. But the trail is hard to follow and clues are few. O'Brien wrote hundreds of novels and short stories—many of them slavers, some of them published a decade after my father invented Norman Gant—but according to her Goodreads biography she was born in 1908, and so following her career

won't tell me how the generations of writers after my father were influenced, or not, by his books.

As I scroll through this odd Goodreads category, it's clear that these
books just aren't slavers. They aren't porn, they're just books about the
antebellum South. Some look literary, others more mass-markety—but
based on their descriptions, they're not novels I can categorize as much
like my dad's.

Those that might be, and were published in the eighties or after,
all have white lovers on their covers. Any racial element within is hidden from view, and only implied in the descriptions. Such as this one,
for a novel called *Come Love a Stranger*: "Then another enters their lives,
threatening to destroy the happiness they have rediscovered in each other's arms—the dark and dangerous Malcolm Sinclair." But it was published as early as 1980, and I find that later books are even harder to
interpret, such as a description of a book published in 1994, one with no
people on the cover at all: "[T]he stunning story of a family that carves
a sensuous and compelling life out of the untamed wilderness of the
Carolinas, from the first settlement on Roanoke Island through the Civil
War." What can I infer about the inhabitants of that "untamed wilderness," and what am I meant to infer? What does it mean about America
that something that started so explicitly, so violently, with the publication of *Mandingo* has become so shrouded and hidden from view?

And that's when I see that my search for what my father's genre
gave rise to is much like my search for understanding his racism, understanding why he could do what he did with his pen. It's also, when
I let myself connect the dots this way, similar to my search for the moment he became ill. The clues are submerged, they're hidden—be they
about the contents of a book or the contents of my father's heart or
the makeup of his mind. Like so many of the things I'm seeking and
trying to catch hold of—racism, mental illness—this search for how
my father's career influenced what came after it is emblematic of how
I learned to survive. If we pretend we can't see it, if we cover it up and
call it something else, maybe it's not really there. Maybe it was never
there in the first place.

Except everyone everywhere knows it's there. Everyone, everywhere is hiding from something.

41

TWO DAYS AFTER the police murdered Alton Sterling in Baton Rouge, one day after the police murdered Philando Castile in Falcon Heights, a black man named Michael George Smith, twenty-two years old, was found hanging from a tree in Piedmont Park, Atlanta, Georgia. The media called it a suicide. Then they moved on.

I hear about it early that July morning, whispered in the rooms of a writing conference, and the fear is electric. The familiar fear for my sons—a fear I grow close to these hot, hateful days of a deadly summer. The familiar fear of a hanging—a fear I've been close to since I was five and they found my father.

I keep asking, silently screaming, was it a lynching or a suicide? How can we live in a world where we wonder, in 2016, if it was a lynching or a suicide? These twin fears are not accustomed to living so close up inside my white body, but lately everything is crashing together. My father's madness and the books he made his living on. My children's safety, my husband's safety, and this country we try to call home. I'm used to only worrying about one fear at a time, but that isn't the way of it anymore.

In my bedroom at the conference I scour the media and read that on the trash can near the tree they found a Chuck Taylor shoeprint that matched the Chuck Taylor shoe Michael George Smith was wearing on his foot. In my bedroom at the conference I scour the media and read that there was pollen on the front of Michael George Smith's shirt. That they thought he climbed up the tree unassisted. But I can't stop asking if he did.

"What are you hearing about the hanging?" I text my oldest friend, a community organizer in Atlanta.

"Everything I'm hearing is BS," she replies. "I'll tell you if I hear anything real."

Are lynchings as far in the past as we white folks want to believe? Perched on the bed in my room at the conference, I want to fly away from this country and this world and find a land where I don't have to worry when my people get in a car to drive to the market. I want to fly away from this country and this world and this land where George can't sleep because I brought him home a book to read and in it the KKK came for the little girl.

I want to fly away.

But there's something else in my mind, in my body, when I think about Michael George Smith found hanging from a tree in Piedmont Park, Atlanta, Georgia. Because I'm someone else, too. I'm the daughter of a suicide. I'm the daughter of someone who chose to end his life. I'm the daughter of a man who made the decision to die. His name was George Michael Wolk.

In a week or two, I will read about Michael George Smith and his Facebook posts that reveal his reasons for this kind of death. In a week or two, I will be reminded that suicide sometimes feels like the only option, felt like the only option for Michael George Smith, felt like the only option for George Michael Wolk. It feels like the only option when there are no more doors to open. Which will be how those Facebook posts will make it seem it looked for Michael George Smith, unaccepted in a homophobic family. Which is how his medical records made it seem it looked for George Michael Wolk, unsure how to peel off the depression and return to his family.

That night in my anxiety all I know is that I'm raising children in a world with no more doors to open. That night all I know is that I can't ever hope to keep them safe. That night all I know is what Ngoni said to me when he set off on the highway last week for a five-hour journey alone. "I am in no more peril today than I was yesterday, *you* are just more aware of it now." That night all I know is the weight of my own naïveté. I am helpless to change anything. Desperate to change any fucking thing.

In my bed at that lonely writer's conference, I wonder if I were Michael George Smith and I wanted to fly away from this country and this world and this city in which I could not survive, would I climb a tree in a park, would I use a trash can to hoist myself up, would I make a statement with my body, would I take my last breath with the hope that this time—*this* death—might finally be the one to get the world's attention? Would I hope that maybe this one—this death—might get people talking about modern-day lynchings? Because how many more do there have to be?

Maybe, if I'm Michael George Smith and I know my name will expire like a last breath, I hope there can be a statement in my suicide. I might accidentally smudge my shirt with pollen before I tie my own noose. I might want folks to wonder what this death was.

◆   ◆   ◆

I'M FOUR AND huddled in the backseat of the VW squareback. My fingers are dusty from the dirt of the community garden. The patched knees of my jeans are caked and brown. The community garden is a city of square plots with a spigot in the middle, it's a sea of green beans and lettuce there's no room to grow at home. It's communism and free choice and the land of the people. It's ideals I don't understand. Home is a left out of the parking lot, and we always turn left out of the parking lot and go home after. But today Dad turns right, and I can hear my heart in my ears when I reach my thumb into my mouth. I have never turned right out of the parking lot, and what is up this hill, what is beyond these gardens, how far does this road go and where will it lead us?

"We are lost!" Dad says, and it's laughter in his voice, and cunning. "Let's get lost!" he shouts, and am I alone in the car and how far do we drive?

Lost! The word throbs through my head like lightning and I can't see out the window but I strain to see something I recognize and my thumb is in my mouth and then I close my eyes but I still see him, wild at the wheel. He drives a cartoon car with television abandon.

We are lost.

PART IV

IL PROFESSORE

MY EYES ARE red and swollen after an overnight flight to Rome I didn't mean to cry through. It takes me a minute to orient myself and find baggage claim, and as soon as I do, I forget to think about my dad. To wonder if he saw similar sights in this airport—white-and-green signs directing traffic, communal-style seating, tourists and locals jostling for space—when he was leaving this city fifty years ago. I just keep wondering what I'm doing here and why I thought I could spend a week alone in a city where I know no one and don't speak the language and whose idea this was anyway.

The Leopold Contract, my dad's spy novel set in Rome, is in my purse, and it and the letters he sent my mother from here in the final months of 1967—which I've still not read in their entirety—will be my guidebook for the week. I read *Leopold* two years ago, when I first started reading Dad's slavers, because an old friend of my parents told me that she could hear his voice in it. "It sounded just like him," she'd said, and I had wanted to know what he sounded like. But I'd had trouble following the plot, and all I remember about it now is that at the end nothing was solved, the hero didn't save the world.

I turn on my phone, test that it really works here as the phone company promised, text Ngoni that I've landed, and see my teal-colored suitcase making its way toward me. I don't know where I learned to look like I know what I'm doing when I don't—maybe watching my mother ward off attacks on the aikido mat night after night—but I grab my bag and square my shoulders and walk in the direction everyone else with a bag is walking, to find a cab.

"Are you here for business or pleasure?" Marco asks from the front seat after I've given him the address of the hotel—a few blocks from my parents' old place. It's a question I got as I was making plans for this trip, so I've said this before, but it feels ridiculous to suggest that I'm visiting *Rome* on business.

"I'm doing research for a book," I say, hoping to make it sound like the truth. Hoping that in my saying it, it will become the truth.

As Marco asks and I try to answer questions, the tenor of his voice shifts. He's in his fifties, I'd guess. Tall, with thick wavy gray hair and a kind smile. His skin is smooth and tan, his nose is big, and—I decide for no sound reason—he feels safe. "So you'll find some of your father's old friends?" he says after digesting my description of my work. "Or his family? And spend time with them?" I have not told Marco about my father's career as a pornographer, just that he lived in Rome in the sixties. His English is good, and I wonder what he thinks about as he drives around this city, who his people are, what he loves.

"No," I say, smiling and trying to hide my own confusion. "He wasn't from Rome. He lived here during an important period of his life, but none of his friends are still here." I want to change the subject, I want not to have told Marco about my dad. I want to have said that I write fiction, I want to hide from this history here in this place where no one knows me. "But it's okay." I make my voice bright. "It'll be an adventure!" I can smile for Marco. Inside I'm quivering.

"It will be dangerous," Marco says.

"Dangerous?" I ask. "I hope not." It takes me a moment to realize he's repeating what he thinks I said. "No, I mean, it will be an *adventure*." I say the word a little slowly this time. He laughs a little too much in response.

When we get to the hotel, Marco gives me his phone number and suggests we have a drink, and I tell myself it's because he's paternal, worried about me, alone in a city I don't know, no one to call, no Italian language skills.

"I think I overtipped my cab driver," I text Stef, who studies this city, knows all of its contours. "And it's possible he asked me out."

"Avoid eye contact," she replies.

This advice keeps me solid in Rome, allows me to retreat into myself. In Rome, I decide that first morning, I don't need to be the eager-to-please white American who wants everyone to like her, who smiles at strangers on the street in case someday they become friends. Avoiding eye contact in Rome adds steel to my armor and frees me to follow my father's footsteps through the city, to see what might be revealed.

Except I have no idea what I'm looking for.

43

JUST BEFORE I left, Ngoni and I went out for a long-overdue date. As I settled the heavy cloth napkin on my lap, I worried I would ruin the romance of the evening with the questions I wanted to ask him, but then I looked around at the tables occupied mainly by people we know—this is a small town—and thought it might be better to build us a cocoon of memory anyway. Maybe no one would stop by our table if they saw the tilt of our heads. After these years of researching my dad's career, I wanted to give Ngoni a chance to tell me what he thinks about it without the pressure of supporting me in my quest. I decided to start at the place our memories diverge, so I asked him to tell me again where he first saw my dad's slavers.

"When we were dating," he said. "You took me up to the room outside your mom's bedroom. You showed them to me very deliberately. They lined the bottom shelf of that glassed-in bookcase."

Ngoni knew I couldn't find my way back to that bookcase, to that moment. Yet this didn't make him question—as it did me—the reliability of the rest of my memories. He just helped me paint the picture, and I nodded and hoped he'd keep talking.

"I'd seen books like your dad's before," he said next. "This was nothing new for me."

"In Zimbabwe?" I asked, surprised.

"Yeah, at flea markets and in garbage piles."

"Books with the same racial element?"

"Ummhmm," Ngoni paused a minute. Sipped his water. "How to put it? The notion that there are folks who had such fantasies is like the sun rising and setting. Policing those relationships was an obsession in southern Africa—and you only police something that happens a lot."

I nodded again, but I wasn't sure I understood. I supposed he meant that there was a time when it happened a lot, because in my—admittedly limited—experience of Zimbabwe, interracial couples were a rarity. I thought back to my readings of Doris Lessing and Nadine Gordimer, tried to imagine what colonial Africa felt like. How it looked. What I thought was that black women were raped so often by white men that a new race was born, a race whose name—Coloured—continues to confuse Americans visiting or studying the region, Americans who thought they had sole propriety over that word even if they know they're not supposed to use it anymore. Even if their grandmothers used that word all the time, as mine did. Ngoni grew up in a world where it made sense to call someone Coloured when both of his parents had skin tones much like their children's. When we first met, I struggled with the idea that this word does not exclusively mean *biracial,* but that way back, something happened between two races and a third was born.

Perhaps, I thought, sitting in that fancy restaurant with my husband, the Coloured people in southern Africa share a history with the Creole people in Louisiana. People I learned about from my father's slavers, though I don't know what I can trust from those tales. I first read the word "quadroon" in one of Dad's books, and it would be okay with me if that were also the last place I read it. But my surprise at that word, when I looked it up, points to a gap in my education, points to my naïveté and the damage it can do. Did I skip school the day we learned about Louisiana's racial history? Or did it enter and exit my mind because with no context for why it mattered, this white girl from the north could just forget it? Lately I think it's more likely we just never learned about it at all in my majority white liberal Massachusetts hometown, because we up north think we're so above all that. What damage is done when people don't know history but are expected to move beyond it?

"I guess when I first saw your dad's books," Ngoni said as our drinks arrived, "my thought was *Yeah, someone has to write those.* You handed me one, I think it was *Natchez Kingdom,* and I thought, okay, this is just like any other place that has the black/white divide—and all the associated dramas and pathologies and fantasies around it. So, no, it didn't stand out. It didn't surprise me."

I pressed him a little. Asked if it was hard for him then—or now—to see those books and know my connection to them. He smiled at me, laughed a minute. Then said, "Emotions are like math. I figure out how to get to the answer, but I don't show my work."

We both laughed, and I clinked my wine glass on his tumbler of scotch. I've lived with this man for a long time, I know that he processes everything more quietly than I do. I've come to admire this skill in some ways, I've come to mimic it in some ways. But I won't lie—I used to sit up nights worrying that he would get cancer and die from repressing his emotions. I used to sit up nights worrying that repressing his emotions would be the thing that takes him from me, that leaves me alone at the end of the story, just as I was alone at the beginning. It took me some long years to realize that my understanding of how to do emotions is—like everything else about me—founded in my own liberal white American upbringing. I can't expect him to do it the way I do it, I can't assume that my way of doing it is right.

But after a minute, I pressed him again anyway. I just had to be sure we were okay. "Take me back there for a second, can you? Did seeing those books make you feel unsafe with my family? In my house?"

He rattled the ice in his scotch glass, he looked at the menu and asked me what I thought he should order. He squeezed my knee under the table to remind me that we were in this together. Then he said, "My grandparents raised me to believe that you are not judged by who your parents are, but by who you are." He looked into the space above the table or at the candle in its votive or backward into memory. "You are you," he said. "Why would what your father did cast a shadow on anybody but your father?"

I smiled at my husband, this complicated man who was put in the care of a traditional healer when he was a child so that his father's illness could be removed before it presented in him. But, he was telling me now, he also learned different lessons, ones with less dramatic story lines. He was also taught that he shouldn't feel that his parents' mistakes or struggles or illnesses would determine his own future. And he can carry both truths, he can hold both things. I thought then about who I was, who I had determined myself to be by bringing the shadow of my father onto my own head when I encouraged the release of the e-books into the world. They may have my father's pseudonyms on their covers, the contract may be in my mother's name, but those e-books are available today because of me. I have to carry that, I have to own that truth.

But I didn't ask Ngoni to talk about the e-books that night. For one thing, the issue is closed for him. I messed up, I feel bad about it, there's not a lot more to say. But I also didn't want to co-opt Ngoni's story with more of my white guilt. I shook out my thoughts and focused again on my husband. But I took solace in his words that night. In his belief that my father's shadow couldn't reach me. I really wanted it to be true.

44

I CAN'T CHECK into my hotel in Rome for several hours, so I drop my luggage in the lobby, listen to the voice of the receptionist as she highlights the major tourist spots on a thin paper map, wash my face in the closet-sized bathroom, and set out into the sunny morning. I follow the map to Campo Dei Fiori, and once there I pull out the directions my mom gave me to the apartment where she and Dad lived in 1967. They were on the fourth floor of Vicolo De Bovari 11, just a block from the Campo. They had the back two rooms, "what were meant to be the servants' quarters, I'm sure," my mother had explained. Two expats from Australia occupied the part of the flat with the kitchen. Mom and Dad got access to that rooftop shower and a window above the Pollarola restaurant at street level.

When I find the building, I'm not sure what to think, what to do. I stand outside its enormous wooden double door set deep into the brick-colored stucco with a grillwork arch at the top. I try to read the graffiti on the wall and determine if it might have been there in 1967. I figure it wasn't. I peer to the top of the building and see plants growing from the terrace and wonder if they kept a garden in 1967. I take some pictures of the building, send an embarrassed-looking selfie with the brass address plate in the background to my mom, so she knows I arrived, and walk around to the restaurant side of the building. It makes up part of a small square occupied mostly by a parking area, a couple other restaurants, and a construction zone cordoned off with orange plastic fencing in the middle. There are two construction work-ers standing around smoking, and I wonder what they're building and if they're from here and if they can tell I don't belong.

This was the wall where, in 1967, my parents' favorite waiter Bruno delivered food and wine to them with the pulley system they'd rigged up together. I crane my neck and look up and try to figure out from this side which window was theirs. I walk around the building a couple more times, hope that I might see someone walking into or out of that giant doorway, and when I don't, I calculate the time until I can check in and decide to eat. I take an outside table at the Pollarola and order a salad from a waiter I briefly dream might be Bruno. But as he turns back to the door of the restaurant, I realize how silly that is. He's not old enough, in his sixties, maybe. His hair is mostly black, his wrinkled skin is tough, not papery like my mom's. But then the only other customers in the place call over to him, "Eh, Bruno!" and a tiny bell rings in my chest.

When he comes with my meal, I sit up straight and tame my fuzzy-from-the-plane hair and ask if he speaks English. Bruno shakes his head and frowns before walking inside, and I'm ashamed that he thinks I'm just like all the Americans who come to Italy without speaking the lan-guage and think they can get along without trying. Of course that's exactly what I've done, but I want to tell Bruno how stupid I feel about it. When a younger man walks out of the dark interior and smiles at me and says "Yes?" I realize my opportunity to meet Bruno might not be lost. This waiter is bald, his white shirt and black waistcoat are tight across his belly, and I think he's probably about my age. I wonder if he's Bruno's son, if Bruno asked him to come talk to me.

"That man inside is Bruno, no?" I say and he nods, narrows his eyes at me a little. "Might I show him a picture and ask you to find out if he knew this man?" I pull out *The Leopold Contract* and hand it to him, pointing to the picture on the back. "He lived here in the sixties," I say.

When Bruno returns to my table with his son, I think I see his tough face soften into a smile as I hand him the book. In the black-and-white portrait, Dad is standing outside in a shearling jacket unbuttoned over a dark sweater and a white button-front shirt, some leafless trees in the background. His hands are in his pockets and he's gazing over the photographer's shoulder, looking dashing and intellectual. His brow is a little furrowed, he's recently run his hands through his thick black hair, and the glasses on his face are similar to the tortoiseshells I wear today. As I watch Bruno look at the picture, I think about what Dad would look like today. It's the first time I've ever tried to imagine what Dad would look like today.

But then Bruno's smile fades and he starts speaking quickly and I can tell from the Spanish I still know from college that it's not right. I hear him say "Il professore" several times as he describes what I think was a group of academics who used to visit Rome every year. I listen hard and watch the younger waiter's face for signs of a story I'm missing, for a sign of hope that Bruno is who I think he is. That he once knew my dad. But when he turns back to me with my book in his hand, he shakes his head and Bruno squints his eyes and walks inside without looking at me again. Without smiling. So I know I was wrong to come here.

"Fifty years is a long time ago," the waiter says as he hands me the book. "You know he maybe can't," and he waves his hands up and down a little, "remember so good that time."

I hide my disappointment. Tell myself it's better to have this out of the way early. When I ask for the bill, he chides me for only eating a salad, but I can't defend myself. Food isn't what I'm hungry for. I walk back to the hotel hoping they'll let me in my room a little early, and by the time I get in the shower I'm crying, though I can't point to a reason. Maybe I'm just exhausted. But when I choke on my breath and wonder if anyone would notice if I fainted under this peeling plaster ceiling in Rome, when I think of my kids at home in their beds and how no one knows exactly where I am right this minute, I realize it's something more.

Missing my father feels different in Rome. It has a shape and a texture and I have to find a way to carry it. What did I want from Bruno? An anecdote about the pulley system, maybe. Or maybe just validation that my father was really once alive.

❖ ❖ ❖

I SIT CROSS-LEGGED on the hardwood floor in the back hallway of the house on State Street, nine, maybe ten years old. The thick black encyclopedias stand sentinel along the bottom shelf of the bookcase my parents built. Just above them sit four novels my father wrote, slid between books by people whose names I don't know, like Wiesel and Woolf.

"They're just spy books," my mother said once when I asked if I could read one. I could hear the derision deep in her tone and knew better than to ask again. My brother calls them "espionage novels" and acts like he's read them all, but I'm not fooled. None of us knows what's inside.

The Leopold Contract looks superior to the rest. It is hardbacked and glossy and calls to me from the shelf. Subtitle: *A Suspense-Mystery.* Yes, I think. Right. I crack the book open just a little—I don't need to read the words deep inside, I just want to see that they are real. I don't need to read the words deep inside, I just want to prove to myself that I can. My eyes land on the dedication page, and now I have a new question in my heart: Am I in this book? What if Dad dedicated a book to me and I never knew it because I never looked in? What if he's been hiding here in this book with a message just for me and I forgot to wonder?

Wait. Did he love me?

I don't see my name on that page, but many, many names running down like a ladder, with thick black lines between each one. *FOR John Le Carré*, it says, and who is that? *Ernest Hemingway* it says next. I've heard of him. But why is this book for him? *Jean-Paul Belmondo, Harry Palmer, Rex Stout.* These are not the people in this house. This is not my family. Why isn't he talking to me? *Humphrey Bogart.* Is this what people mean when they say he was funny? *Dashiell Hammett—AND* he types in all caps. There is hope in that *and. AND Susan. WHO IS ALSO TOUGH.*

Who are these men and how is my mother tough like them? Why is it important that my mother be tough like them? Do I need to be tough like these men?

◆   ◆   ◆

MY HOTEL ROOM is just bigger than its double bed, with enough space to stand by the window and open the shutters to let in the light, but nowhere to put my suitcase, no bureau to unpack into. I climb on the bed from the foot and roll to the end to straighten my legs up the wall, reverse the flow of blood and rest my feet. I trace a crack in the plaster with my eyes, tears sliding past my ears onto the beige blanket under my head. From the window come the evening light and the sounds of sirens and mufflerless motorbikes and shouts I can't understand. It's my second day here and I already want to go home.

I pull out my phone and text Ngoni, "I don't know what I'm doing here."

I walked for nine hours today. I saw things I never thought I'd see except in pictures. In *The Leopold Contract*, my dad wrote that the hero threaded his way through tourists in the Piazza di Spagna, which I did last night before sitting on the steps and pulling out his book to find that place in it. My dad described the view from the Pincio, which I read this morning while looking at it as a street musician sang "Yesterday" in English to the small crowd. My dad wrote that the Piazza Navona is one of the "places where every man ought to be forced to sit and look, the way every man ought to be forced to sit and listen to Beethoven," and although the phrase made me giggle when I read it, I did that today. I did that yesterday. I will keep doing it each day.

My dad wrote that his hero "do[es] like looking at the Pantheon," and when I went there this afternoon, a different street musician sang Leonard Cohen's "Hallelujah" in Italian just outside. I was the only one of the throngs who stopped to listen, and I had to focus on her high-heeled leather boot keeping the beat to stop myself from weeping. This song has haunted me for years—I last heard it at the memorial service for a mentor and mother figure who died unexpectedly and left an empty space that will never refill. Hearing this song in Rome brings her to me, and I realize that I need her here, that she would know how to guide me here. Because I still don't know what I'm looking for. But if her ghost followed me into the Pantheon, she stayed quiet, didn't point out a path.

My phone lights up on the bed beside me. "It will come," Ngoni types to me from across the world. "Walking in the footsteps of your forebears—trust that your dad will reveal something important."

I want to. But I don't see it yet. I don't know if I will see it.

45

ON MY THIRD morning in Rome, I wake up early and spread my father's letters out on the bed in front of me. I hope that maybe without a family coming home at the end of each day—without the need to put on the mask I wear after the hardest days—I'll be able to face my father's words in Rome.

I reread the typed letters first, to get a sense of his letter-writing rhythm. It's different from his novel-writing rhythm, and when I feel I have it down, have his voice in my head, I unfold the first handwritten note in the stack. I find after a moment that though it takes time and concentration, I can decipher his script now. In Rome, I can be patient with who my father was.

"This river lined with trees is not for you and me," he writes to my mother in a letter dated Tuesday, and of course he's talking about the Tiber. He wrote about it in one of his typed letters, too, and I know now how it dominates this city, carves it into shapes. I've walked along it a little bit each day. "What is for you and me is clenched here in this fist, this raw stone of my engraving." I think he's talking about his writing, about making a life with his words, but I can't be sure. It seems he's being intentionally cryptic, almost like he's playing the part of an intellectual. So after an hour spent deciphering this letter set on the banks of the river, after discovering that I will be able to read the rest of these handwritten words, I decide to leave them for a time. I need fresh air. I need to see the river myself. I need to stretch my legs. I need breakfast. I need to step away from this bed with visions of what is and is not clenched there in my dad's fist. If I'm avoiding him and his words isn't something I try to discern. I just pull on my spring jacket, wrap a scarf around my neck, and head out.

I know from his typed letters that Dad walked along the Tiber on Christmas Eve and that he felt something on that walk I would call illness, even though no one in my family thinks he was sick so early. I know from his typed letters that he saw these sycamore trees I'm walking under now, that he stood under the tunnel they create, these trees whose leaves drop into the water on the far side of this stone wall. I lean on the wall now and wonder if he leaned here, too, as he thought that these trees were not for him and my mom. The Castel Sant'Angelo is across from me, quiet in the morning, and there's very little traffic on the street behind me. Words from Dad's letters circle though my head, ones about the itch he felt as he walked along the pathway, the itch behind his ear that felt liquid to him, "as if it were the place where my brain seeps out," and how it made him think of van Gogh. How it made him compare himself to Vincent van Gogh. He was comparing himself to Vincent van Gogh in 1967, ten years before his breakdown. I just think he was sick longer than we knew.

I turn to my right and set out along the sidewalk, similar to the sidewalk that circles Central Park—a wall on one side, a street on the other. There's freedom in having no destination, no one expecting me, but there's also fear in it. I look behind me to see if anyone's following, and when I turn back, secure that I'm alone, three bright green birds fly toward me from across the river. They flutter in my face for a moment—so close I have to stop walking, so close I want to stop walking. They land in the tree above me. One goes into a hole in the thick branch that arcs above the sidewalk, and I can't see it anymore. One perches farther away, on the street side, standing watch. And one sits just above my head and peers at me, unmoving. We have a staring contest, me and this bright green tropical bird in Rome. I want to pull out my camera and record these birds for Ngoni and the kids—and I will do that, in a minute. But right now, this bright green bird—bigger than a blue jay and with a much longer tail and a black ring around its neck, a small red curved beak—is keeping its eye on me, and I won't break the spell.

"Rome is a place to get metaphysical," Stef texted me last week as I sat hunched in a chair by the departure gate at Logan. I had made it that far but when they called us to start boarding, I was stuck in my seat. How did I think I could fly away from my family and spend a week alone in a city I didn't know? I considered walking back to my car, thought I might be developing a fever. Stef said the angel on top of the Castel Sant'Angelo was all about the past and the future, and that he would protect me. When I didn't reply for a while, she added, "You also know your dad's going to be around. So I feel like you're pretty covered." Then she offered to talk to the police in Italian if I got arrested, forcing me to laugh out loud, stand up, and join the line to board.

So as I stare into the eyes of that big green bird along the banks of a river I know my father walked, does it occur to me that this bird is protecting me or telling me something or speaking to me from the beyond? Maybe. Rome is a place to get metaphysical. A place where the past and the future can coexist. Which may be why, after a minute of making eye contact with a bird, of feeling suddenly less alone in Rome, I head back to my hotel.

The pile of letters is still on the bed, and I know now that it's time to finish them. I came here to find my father, and these letters are one of my only windows. So I open the shutters, change into my sweatpants, and sit on the bed to read them all.

"I have just decided not to whore again," Dad writes in a letter dated Wednesday, and I startle to realize he's talking about *Chane*. I've been so wrapped up in *The Leopold Contract* I almost forgot he wrote his first slavers in Rome, too. "I am ashamed—yes though not for the conventional understanding of 'selling out.'"

What is he ashamed of, then? Stereotyping black men's sexuality? Or white women's attraction? Commodifying a love that, in 1967—just months after the *Loving v. Virginia* decision—is still scandalous? Or is he ashamed that it occurred to him to do it in the first place, is he ashamed of his own racialized sexual fantasies? Or am I just grasping, just reading meaning into words he didn't intend for me? Was he just ashamed not to be "confronting his art," as he'd promised my mother he would? There's no way to know. Dad doesn't finish the thought.

In a letter dated Thursday, my dad writes to my mom that he wants to "do one small thing . . . a raw gem of my own force to be hewn by my own craft with something enduring for you." But he can't. He says so himself. "Today I have been comforted with the 'schlock,' the superficial use of my chosen craft." I stumble to think that my father was comforted writing about a black man strangling a white woman who had forced him to carry out sexual favors. I stumble to realize that this work—writing slavers—*was* a refuge for him. Tracy was right. It comforted him to write this shit as he struggled through a lonely Thursday in Rome. It's what comforted him for the rest of his life. He wrote *Natchez Kingdom* from that tiny room at the front of the house on State Street, months before going to Riggs with his belt strap.

What does it mean that my white father took refuge in imagining the lives of black slaves, of building complex sex lives for black men? What does it mean that when he needed to find an escape, the route he chose to take was the creation of characters from a racial other? As these familiar questions spin, I put the letter down and turn on my laptop, pull up the website of the magazine I freelance for, find the excerpt we published of Claudia Rankine and Beth Loffreda's book about the racial imaginary. I need to remind myself of their words, I need their analysis to remind me that I'm not in this alone.

Rankine and Loffreda bring up the common question about whether writers of one race can or should "write from a different racial other's point of view," but they don't answer it. They're not here to absolve. Rather, they point out that this isn't the question to start with. It is "to ask instead why and what for, not just if and how. What is the charisma of what I feel estranged from, and why might I wish to enter and inhabit it?" What was the charisma of what my father felt estranged from? Why did entering and inhabiting the life of an enslaved black man offer him refuge, over and over and over again?

And what, I wonder from my small hotel room in Rome, are the consequences of this racial imaginary serving as the lens through which so many white people still see the world?

46

WHEN I STARTED planning this trip, I decided to visit the Castel Sant'Angelo first. From his letters, I knew it was an important place to my dad, and I wanted to see it right away. But it takes me a while to get up whatever I need—nerve? resolve? strength?—to face whatever Dad faced after he walked along the banks of the Tiber to the Castle thinking about Vincent van Gogh. Each morning this week, I've made it that far before turning in the other direction, exploring all the other places instead. Each morning I let myself get lost. But today when I come up a hill and expect to see something else, I turn a corner and there's the bridge with all those angel statues beckoning me over. It's time to cross, at least look at the building from the outside. I tell myself I don't have to go inside.

"BACK TO WHAT worries me now," my father wrote to my mother a month after she left him in Rome. "Us," he wrote. "Rather me. See a shrink? Want a family, want to walk in streets of my hometown. See a shrink? Perhaps an unbased fear after all. Me, a shrink? After I've come so far myself, let some insignificant professional help me over the finish line? Not likely! Are you on top of all this??? I have your picture here, close."

To enter the Castel Sant'Angelo, first you walk around the outside of the building in a circular courtyard open to the sky above. It seems to be at

street level, but the windowless walls go so far up on either side, it's hard
to tell. The castle is on your right, the city street behind the wall on your
left. In various nooks there are some very old things, doorways, parts of
stones that mean something, though you won't stop to learn what.

You become aware that the bricks seem to have melted together,
that these walls on either side have been standing here melting together
for almost two thousand years, and they do not look like the bricks in
the house where you grew up. You want to touch them. You do touch
them. You wonder if your father touched them.

Soon you walk through a doorway and climb long steps that lead
to a ramp and walk up and up and up a hill. While you climb, you are
aware that there is much more below you than above. Dungeons and
prisons and places where popes were kept safe. You come out onto a
landing and there is a small stone angel with copper wings on his back
and you think he looks nice, but this is not the angel you came to see.
You are not yet at the top.

You walk up another staircase and continue to walk the circumference of the castle, not sure how many levels there are above you. You
stop at the turrets and lookouts where the soldiers stood to protect this
place. The ground is uneven at your feet.

You climb another staircase and walk the circumference again on
this level, pass by a café, think about stopping once you've seen some
more. But you can't find another staircase to climb to the top. You look
into the rooms and windows and libraries and feel a vague sense of
awe, but you're not sure this is what you came for. You're not sure what
you came for, so you linger behind an art history class and its English-
speaking professor. Maybe he'll reveal why you're all here. At the very
least, if you follow them, he might lead you to a staircase. When the
students look at you sideways, you walk away and circle the castle for a
fourth time, tell yourself that if you come to the café again, you'll ask.

But you don't ask. You decide this is something you have to do
alone. On the next pass, or the next, you find a small door and although
there's a sign with a big red circle that means No Entrance, you sneak
up the stairs anyway. By now you're tired and hungry and walking the
circumference of the castle six times, or sixteen, is making you grouchy.
You need to get to the top. You're certain your father has been to the top.

People coming down the stairs give you dirty looks as you go up them, but you pretend you're a stupid foreigner and can't read signs meant for illiterates and smile as you let them pass. There is a joy in being unrecognizable inside a crowd, and you wonder if your father felt the same joy.

Then you finally get to the top and you see the angel with his sword up close. You take pictures of the view for your sons. You stand in the sun and look at the umbrella pines and wonder what your father thought when he looked up at this angel with his sword. If he felt protected. You ask how it feels to feel protected. But up so high, you don't feel protected. You're not sure you have ever felt protected. You don't linger.

"BUT WHY GO back?" my father asked my mother in a letter he was certain she would ignore. "Rome is so fine. So much beauty here. So drab, cold in NY." I wonder if he was trying to convince himself to stay. That maybe my mother wasn't worth it after all. "If it weren't for you I'd never move in that direction again. That's not an accusation," he told her. "I want you to know that you leaving here has upset me. I want you back god damn it. God damn it I want you back."

AS YOU LEAVE the castle, down the ramp you walked up, there is a dark stone passageway cut into the wall off to the right that you vaguely remember passing on your way in. You take that passage now. You go down and down and down. The ramp is steep and a little girl behind you lets go of her father's fingers and starts running and you want to shout to her to be careful, that she could trip on this ancient stone corridor, that if she fell she would roll down and down and down and we don't know where we're going yet and what if she gets lost?

But the little girl is agile and close to the ground and soon she runs past you again, up this time, to tell her father what she saw, to urge her father to hurry. You stall here, let the pair pass, let them walk in front of you so that you can be alone with the tears you didn't know were falling onto your shirt.

Down and down and down you go, and you wonder if this is how deep the subways are in New York. Down and down and down and you wonder if the prisoners on this pathway knew their fate or if they still had hope. You think about the loss of hope and how a person marks that moment. What happens after that moment. Down and down and down and you ask yourself if your father visited this part of the castle and if it made him think about all the same things you are now thinking about. Like how you will get out of this dungeon, or where this circular arcing pathway leads or if it would even be possible to see light should a window crack open in the rooftop.

And then quite quickly, you're at the end. There's a small model in a glass box of what this castle looked like when it was Hadrian's tomb, and you stop and look at it not because you care about the history, but because by now you are dizzy from the circular walking and the uneven ramp and the questions swirling in your head. You stop and look at it long enough to see that the girl and her father have turned left, that there is a short staircase and the sunshine and the blessed, perhaps even the miraculous, exit onto the street.

"I MISSED YOU so badly the first days you were gone I was in insane nervous turmoil," my father wrote in another letter. "I have resigned myself to the remaining separation, a separation which has not so far done a great deal of good, and perhaps it is with a tinge of fear that my self consciousness and morbid seriousness may return as I prepare to journey again to Never Never Land, that resort called Stateside where depression hides in eighty guises in back alleys and behind subway pillars in bars and bathrooms in bedrooms in discoteques and public transports, mile high monuments of white collar madness, parking garages, courtrooms, synagogues, homes of the oppressed, in the stairwells of the Statue of Liberty, in the stock exchange, the public libraries and in all, all of the suburbs. I count on you to keep me out of all but the gayest of places. I am returning to make money with my wit and my pen. I also count on you to correct my spelling. You see we are indispensable to each other."

YOU CLIMB THE metal staircase up to the sun and think how odd it is that this staircase is here at all. It feels just like a fire escape. It's metal and modern. You walk out into the bright afternoon and squint into the sun and find your sunglasses in your purse and wonder if returning to the U.S. is what killed your father. Wonder in what way your father was indispensable to your mother. Wonder if she could have lived without him. Realize that not so very long after he returned to her, she did.

You can't remember where you turn next.

47

"THERE ARE MORE interracial couples in Rome than any other city I've been to," I text Ngoni from the Trevi Fountain the next day. I am elbow to elbow with other tourists, though the water roars above us and if I close my eyes I could pretend I'm alone. I stand against the wall of the building opposite the fountain where the waters are meant to be tamed, yet how it feels here is chaotic and uncontrolled. I've heard that if I stand with my back to the water and throw a coin into the pool over my shoulder, it will guarantee my return to Rome, but I neither have the wherewithal to work my way down to the water nor the certainty that I want to come back.

"Europe is more advanced than the US in many ways," Ngoni texts back. By the time I see his response, it's hours later and I'm back at Piazza Navona, my touchstone place. I try to read *The Leopold Contract* sitting in the café I've visited each day here, but I'm distracted by Ngoni's idea—that progress might be measured in the number of interracial couples in a place. That the concept of crossing boundaries could be considered a sign of advancement. So instead of reading, I sit and watch as Dad would have wanted me to sit and watch, anyway.

What is progress? It can't just be the crossing of boundaries when we know the first mixed-race babies were likely the result of colonizers raping the women in the places they invaded or the result of the kind of encounters described in my father's slavers. Though, I wonder as I sip my cappuccino, did Dad show a kind of progress himself, when—by the end of the last book in the *Chane* series—each of Chane's surviving sons is engaged in a consensual and loving relationship with a white woman? By this point in my father's historical fiction, the war is over and each of these couples is looking for a safe place to settle. A safe place to call home. Would that be a sign of progress—if they were able to find such a place?

I once heard a political theorist friend—a Kenyan woman who studies the concept of progress—discuss her work. She said one possible definition is simply "Get your boot off my neck, thank you." She also explained that some people in her field argue that every societal advancement has led only to deeper pain for those meant to be freed, to more sophisticated means of oppression. I think about that as I try to catalogue my father's career. If his work was an iteration of the national anxiety white people felt during the Civil Rights Movement, doesn't it, by normalizing slavery and making it the topic of a stupid book, push back on the progress made to that point and contribute to new and different means of oppression? Was his interracial happy ending meant to solve for that X? Was it meant to absolve him, teach his readers a lesson, show everyone that after all we *really* are just people underneath our skins? A part of me wants that ending, too, Dad. A pretty big part. But I'm not buying it. That's not the world I live in. It's not the world I think you lived in, either.

As I walk through Piazza Navona toward my hotel, I realize I sent Ngoni that text because I'm just a mother wondering where my family can feel safe. Wondering if we could come to Rome and feel safe. Wondering if, when I get back to the mess America is in right now, we will feel safe on the streets of our little white town, or in our house at the end of the road.

WE TAKE THE boys to New York City a couple of times a year. When our friends ask if we're seeing a show or doing something particularly New York-y, I'm sometimes brave enough to tell the truth. "We're going to remind ourselves that there are other people of color in the world," I say. I don't mean that we look at the city's inhabitants as objects in a museum, I mean we return to the city where Julius was born to walk the streets, see a movie, visit museums, be who we are. I mean that our kids need to remember that they can do all of those things—that they might prefer to do all of those things—among folks who more closely resemble them. I used to justify these trips differently. I used to tell people that no one looked at us in New York, that we weren't remarkable in that city where everyone is remarkable. But that's not how it is, not really. The fact is people turn for a second look in New York just as they do in rural New England. The fact is, we're still a spectacle.

On the subway this spring, on a trip Ngoni couldn't join, I noticed a dark-skinned black kid about Julius's age looking at my kids sideways, out of the corner of his eye. When his gaze landed on me, I thought I saw him trying to figure out how we fit, and I tried to imagine what he was thinking. If my sons—one light-skinned and one dark—were full brothers? What kind of a mother I was? Where their dad was? Was he thinking about what sets him and my kids apart, or was he thinking about how they're similar?

George had a nightmare on that trip. "Something bad had happened and I couldn't find you," he told me in the morning when I'd climbed into his bed to ask how he slept. I nodded and rolled toward him and held him tight as he described a scene of violence, an accident, a calamity. I've had that dream a million times. "When I finally found you, you couldn't speak," he said. "And no one believed me when I told them you were my mom."

I have to ask myself if our trips to New York exacerbate such anxieties, walking through a city where everyone is anonymous. I have to ask myself what it means if George feels safer in our small New England town than in a big, diverse city. Is that just because everyone there knows us, knows that we belong together? Or is the message deeper and more sinister than that? Is the message, imparted through all the avenues of white supremacy, that it's only in these little Whitopias, where they are such a minority they could never threaten the status quo, that my children feel safe? I have to ask myself if we're raising our children to believe that they are safest in the whitest of places.

Because isn't history unfolding to show us that they are safe nowhere in this impossible sea?

48

ONE NIGHT in my hotel room in Rome, with the window open to the cold air, I have the dream again. The one where my father is really alive. This time he isn't somewhere living happily without us. This time he's sick. Hospitalized, still, after all these years. Ngoni and I get the call that he is being discharged from Riggs. That we need to come for him. They need him gone. So we go, my husband and I, to collect a father I've thought dead for thirty-seven years.

I'm not surprised to learn he's alive. My dad is never dead in the dream. I'm just scared of the way he will reshape my life. We meet with a nurse to plan what it will be like to bring him home. The pills, the care, the disruption. The complexities of his disease. The way we'll have to fit him into the life I've made without him. I know I can't do it. I know I'm not equipped. I think of Ngoni's uncle Dakarai and our encounter in the doorway, of how unequipped I was just to inhabit a neighboring cottage after that. My whole body shakes as we climb the icy stairs to the next building. I need something to hold on to. Why don't I take Ngoni's hand?

Through and down a hallway, I look into one room and see a man so clearly mad, pasty skin and blond beard and dazed eyes raging at ghosts. *My father is sicker than this?* I think. *They can't handle him but they can handle this man?* I think. Then there in a corner up ahead on the left, in a corner of a hallway that ends there and not in any room because he isn't a patient here anymore, I see a skinny, shrunken black man. His untamed beard has gray sprinkled throughout. His untamed hair has gray sprinkled throughout. *This can't be him,* I say to myself. *My father isn't black,* I say to myself. Does he dream-blur into Dakarai?

But I am told this is my father, and there is no more hallway now, nowhere else to look. I go ahead anyway, past this man, my eyes seeking out another room, another father. The nurse grabs my arm to stop me, and I turn to see Ngoni standing in front of him already. Showing respect. Looking into my father's eyes. I move to stand in front of him. I move to stand next to my husband. My whole body hums.

"George," my father says to me, not looking at me. "George," my father says to me, looking only at my husband. "You brought a black man home." I wonder, right there in my dream, why my father calls me by his own name. I wonder, right there in my dream, if I am my father.

I will never have an answer to that question.

"George," my father says to me, holding Ngoni's hand. "You brought a black man home to marry."

I WAKE UP curled in a ball, alone in this strange hotel room in Rome, more afraid than I have ever been. For myself, for my children, for my husband. This legacy Ngoni and I bring with us through our genes—the ways in which madness snakes through our timelines and our histories—is something I can't look at head-on at home. When my children are with me in the house, or as they walk down the hill to the school bus, or as I watch them ricochet around a soccer pitch, this fear stays mostly away. Friends talk to me about their parenting worries—a child who isn't thriving at school, a kid who seems poised to make poor decisions—and I soothe them with stories from my own childhood, ways in which I was that kid, examples of the poor choices I made. I give them proof in my presence here now, solid and unshakable, that their sweet beloveds will push through. I soothe their anxieties because that is my role. I am the levelheaded friend, I cherish being the levelheaded friend.

But here in Rome, away from all that, I can see more clearly that the state of anxiety in which I operate when alone—the disasters I cook up in quiet moments, the racing pulse I conjure when someone is late, the visions of funerals for people not answering their phones—all comes from this fear I carry like a sack of rocks. My children are not the children of most of my friends, whose paths may get crooked but who will likely find their ways back. My children are not the children of most of my friends, whose white skin will armor them when they run a red light. My children have something deposited in their blood that the children of my friends do not carry. It comes from my father and from my father-in-law, it comes from my father's cousins and from my husband's uncle. It could boil over at any moment and take them from me. My children have something else deposited in their genes. It comes from their father and is imprinted on their skin, unhidable from the forces in this country that fight to abolish it. Here in this hotel room in Rome, alone with my fear, I see more clearly than I have before how race and mental illness could mix in my sons and be their undoing. I see more clearly than before what I fear. That I am my father. That Ngoni is my father. That my children will become my father, too. And that would be my final undoing.

"George," my father said to me in my dream. "You brought this man home to marry. Where will the children be?"

◆   ◆   ◆

IT IS TIME for bed and I have been told to go to bed and I am in my bed but I do not want to be in bed and I cannot sleep, will never sleep, cannot believe I have been sent up here alone to sleep.

Yesterday, and all of the nights before yesterday, my mother followed me up the stairs, sat on the end of my slim twin frame, listened as I recited the alphabet, the names of my stuffed animals, my spelling words, multiplication facts. Yesterday when her head bobbed back and her eyes closed and a loud snore escaped from her mouth before I was through, she snapped her head back up, gathered herself together, kissed my forehead, and left.

Tonight she sent me upstairs alone. Tonight she decided I am old enough to put myself to bed. I climbed the stairs alone and I brushed my teeth alone and now I am in this slim twin bed with only Edward Tedward, and he is not enough. Yesterday my mother pulled back the blanket and the sheets to form a V shape across my bed, so I could slide into the envelope. I did not pull the blanket back tonight, I just sat down on the top and fidgeted my way in, and the sheets are now tangled and I cannot cannot cannot kick my way through. The more I kick my legs down, the more twisted I become. The sheets are a Chinese finger trap like the one in my goodie bag at Katya's birthday party. I kick and I kick and I kick and with each kick the twisting is tighter. I kick in these sheets and I cannot get out and I am scared in my bed and my father is dead and there is nothing nothing nothing in this world I can change.

49

THE PENULTIMATE CHAPTER of *The Leopold Contract* begins, "I caught sight of him turning into Via Giulia when I came to the corner. I knew it was Via Giulia because beyond it were the steps which led to the river drive."

I read these words on my penultimate day in Rome, lying on my bed after lunch with the window open to the midafternoon air. I'm tired and ready to go home and after a morning with my dad's letters and the haunting hangover from the dream, after the adventure of the Coliseum and Forum the day before, I can't bear the sight of another tourist. I thank Dad for this scene set in what he promises will be a quiet street. "In the sixteenth century this street was supposed to have been what Via Veneto is today. Just now it was in deep dark. There wasn't a car parked on it or a dog on it or a sign that anything had happened on it since the ghost of Gregory XIII." I don't know why Pope Gregory's ghost might have inhabited this street, but after a week of walking in my father's footsteps I can say with confidence that Dad was running from ghosts all over this city, running from depression and disordered thinking and his own scared self. I put the book down, rub my hands over my face, climb into the shower, and set it to as hot as I can stand. Then I leave the hotel to find the final street my father describes in Rome.

Via Giulia is, according to the map I have folded and refolded every which way this week, somewhere behind my hotel. When I walk out the door this gray afternoon and turn left instead of right—I have not yet turned left—I discover that it's about five steps away. It runs parallel to Via del Pellegrino, where I'm staying and where one could eat or lodge or buy glass baubles or cheese or handmade furniture or leather purses or men's jackets. But though it's so close, Via Giulia is deserted. I don't know if it's siesta time and there are closed doors into places I cannot see, but there is barely another soul on Via Giulia today. Not a car parked on it or a dog on it or a sign that anything had happened on it since the ghost of George Wolk passed through. I turn left and walk in the direction I think I'm most likely to find those stairs Dad mentioned, and I soon come upon a fountain plastered into a wall that stops me in my tracks. It shows a woman's face, her eyes open wide, her mouth lazily agape with water trickling out of it like blood. She looks like she's been caught with a knife to the belly, like this is her last breath and she can't believe who her murderer was. I stand and look at her a while, troubled by the expression on her face, and wonder how old she is and who made her and what she's trying to say. After some time I walk on, find the steps Dad described in his book and read the graffiti in the stairwell and turn back the way I came because I thought I saw a quiet café and would love a cappuccino. Once I have one in hand, I sit outside on a cold chrome chair at a cold chrome table to finish Dad's book.

That's where I am when I read, "There is a fountain I like on the Via Giulia as you approach it from the north end of Piazza Farnese. It is an ugly mask with the water pouring haphazardly from its wide mouth, a grotesque like the sculpted mask still watching from the edge of this ancient orange building on the corner." She had stopped Dad in his tracks, too. And now we are together, Dad and I. Now we are the closest we will ever come to talking. We have seen some of the same things in this world. We have been awed by some of the same things.

I spoon up the last of the frothed milk stuck to the sides of my cup, resist the urge to lick the inside, and think about what it means to sit on a street with my own name, to sit on an ancient street that has changed very little in the fifty years since my father walked up and down it studying its contours for scene.

A woman with long auburn hair and an army-green jacket catches my attention and gestures to the empty chair at my table. I nod. She sits down and leans over to grab the ashtray near my cup and asks with her eyes if I need it. I shake my head. I am curled into the corner of this chrome chair cold through my jeans, I am curled over my father's book, and my cup is empty. I could get up and leave—in the U.S. I would get up and leave. This woman could have this table to herself. But she is my witness now. We sit together and I read the words my father wrote when he lived in this city fifty years ago, and for just a moment I want to look at her and smile, look at her and tell her about George, at home in his bed right now, sleep-clinging to Edward Tedward and wishing that when he woke up, I'd be home. I want to tell her that in 1974 my brother suggested to a tired family all out of ideas that they name me after that nice lady on TV. I want to tell her that maybe when his young son suggested that name, my father thought of this place, this street, the mask with the mouth agape, and said, *Yes, that's her name.* Maybe, after my father had rejected so many names, he said yes to this one because it reminded him of Rome. A city where he'd lived when he still thought he could outrun the ghost.

When I go back to his book, Dad's hero has turned away from the mask to assess if Via Giulia really is the street on which the action will unfold, if he really will find the villain in one of these houses. Dad writes, "'It was not this street,' I said softly but clearly, so that if you were standing next to me, on these dead stones, you would have heard it." It's the first time in the book my father uses the second person, and it feels as though he's talking to me. As though I am standing next to him on these dead stones.

"It was not this street," I say softly but clearly to the woman with the auburn hair as I get up to leave. If you were standing next to me on these dead stones, you would have heard it.

ON THE LAST pages of *Leopold,* the hero and his love interest—both spies—have not saved the world. The bad guy has gotten away, and now all that's left is for them to separate, too. Go their own spy ways.

"Before Christmas in this holy town they set up stalls around the inner edge of the piazza and every night for a month there is a carnival," Dad writes on the last page. Earlier this morning, I read similar words, a similar description, in a letter he sent my mother just before Christmas 1967, telling her he had finally finished "the spy thing." "This is a difficult town to leave," he wrote in his letter. "This has always been a difficult town to leave," he wrote in his book.

It's still dark when I climb into the cab the hotel calls for me the next morning. I don't ask this driver his name. I don't say much to him at all. We make our way out onto the Corso, and to my right I get one more look at Castel Sant'Angelo in the distance, lit from below. "The air is cold," my dad wrote in a letter to my mom. "Across the refuge of the river, the lit Castle of St. Angelo." It is all I can see of Rome at this hour, and my vision blurs with the angel on top. "This has always been a difficult town to leave," I whisper to this site that guided my father as he navigated the streets and the sycamore-lined sidewalks, to this site that guided me along those same lengths this week. The angel on the top of the castle waves goodbye, and I lean my forehead into the cold glass of the window and wonder what it is I've found.

50

WHEN I GET back from Rome, I say to my mother, as I show her the pictures of the city in which she loved my father, that I wanted to lie down on the floor of the Pantheon and look up through the oculus.

"Oh, we did that," she says, and I'm disappointed in myself.

"I finally read the letters he wrote to you," I say after a minute. "It took me a long time. I couldn't read his handwriting," I say. She gave me those letters more than two years ago.

"No one could."

"But I got so I could read his handwriting in Rome," I tell her. "He loved the shit out of you," I tell her. I don't tell her what else I think about the letters. How I'm even more convinced now that Dad was sick longer than we knew. How I think he worried about himself as early as 1967, how I think he didn't believe he'd live very long, even in 1967. That I think his preoccupation with his mental health contributed to his choice to write slavers under contract, so he could study people pushed to limits no humans should have ever had to endure. That I now also wonder if his study of witchcraft contributed to his delusions about me when I was born. I don't tell her that because what's the use, or because it's become obvious, or because it's all just too painful to mention. All of these reasons and ones I don't have access to, too, about shame and sadness and fear. I don't have an answer for why I am always scared to speak—have always been scared to speak. I just know it about myself now, and try to forgive myself for not being brave or fearless or able to confront the pain I keep hidden.

"Yes, he did love the shit out of me," she says, a small smile in her eyes.

"But you left him there. You told me you were fleeing a failing relationship."

She nods.

"What was it?" I ask, maybe hoping she'll say what I can't. A foolish hope after a lifetime of submerged emotions, of unspoken feelings that somehow therefore magnified the trauma. Magnified what I know she just hoped would disappear so we could move on without it.

"I was just sure it wasn't going to work out," is what she says. "Obviously I was wrong."

I want to say, *Obviously you were right. It didn't work out at all!*

"I'm glad you were wrong," is what I say instead. I want to live.

"Yes, me too," she says, but there's hesitation in her voice. She is acknowledging that she is glad because she has three children to love. She is acknowledging that not everything was a mess. But there is something else in her voice, something that hints at regret. Something that hints at the pain she endured. I want her to name it, but I don't know how to help her.

"He was so pissed when I got pregnant with you," she says after a time, words she has said to me before. "Another thing to take my attention away from him."

I think of his letters to her, of his admission that he needed her in order to stay sane. Those are not the words he uses, he doesn't call it 'sanity.' But he believed that with her he could stave something off. It makes Mom's words sting a little bit less, knowing that he was fragile. It helps me pack away all of the words we can't say, knowing why he needed her attention.

And anyway, now my mom is done with this conversation. She's changing the subject. She's telling stories about Rome she's never told me before. One is about a parked car, a tiny Fiat like all the cars in Rome, slowly rolling into them while they sat at the Pollarola one night, the emergency brake neglected. Dad and McNeill had to push it off her, back into its spot.

Then she laughs the way she laughs before she tells a good story, laughing through that moment when she's the only one who knows what's funny and you're left waiting. "Bruno used to call your father *Il professore*," she says out of nowhere, before I've told her that I met him or that he didn't recognize Dad in the picture. "It bothered your father that Bruno didn't understand what he really did. I would say to him, 'What, do you want him to call you *Il scrittore?*'" And she laughs again, harder this time, though I don't know why it would've been funny for Bruno to call my dad a writer.

Il professore. What would I have asked Bruno if I'd understood?

51

A WEEK LATER, I board the Amtrak in Albany for another trip to the city, this time to have lunch with my brother. He meets me at Penn Station and we walk to a burger joint on 6th Avenue. As Josh settles onto his barstool, he starts right in with his memories of Dad, with his version of Dad returning from the *sesshin*. Josh knows why I'm here.

"I came around the corner from school and saw Dad's car in the driveway and ran into the house," he says. In his eyes, he's six years old. He is open and excited and ready to see his dad, who was away for a week. I listen as though to a story, but I already know the end. "No one was in the kitchen and when I looked through into the living room, I saw a man there, but it wasn't Dad."

Josh pauses now and I shift on my own stool but refuse to look away. I focus on the dent in his chin when I can't look at his eyes.

"I thought, *Oh this must be family, Dad brought home family.*" Josh has been watching the fry cook in front of him, but now he looks at me to make sure I'm following. "I figured he had a brother I didn't know about, that this was some uncle. Because it looked like a guy related to Dad, but it wasn't Dad."

I'm willing the tears at the backs of my eyes to stay put because we're not here for grief. We're not here to mourn the little boy in the driveway—the one he was before he got to the kitchen—even if I've missed that boy all my life. That's not how we do it in the Wolk family. No, we're here for facts. Facts and memories. Nothing more.

"Where was Mom?" I ask.

"So," Josh says, looking back at the fry cook and nodding at my question like *Yeah, you're with me.* His hair is cut short around the ears and in back, but long enough on top for it to sweep back from his face when he runs a hand through it. It's grayer than mine, but not by much. The wrinkles around his eyes are deeper than mine, but not by much. He's the person on this earth I most resemble, and sitting alone with him like this, a couple of blocks from his office, is a rare gift. "I went to find her. As I walked through the living room and around the corner to go upstairs, I did that thing kids do, skimming the wall." Josh turns to me and opens his hazel-green eyes just like mine as wide as he can, and again he's six. I can see his small boy body sidestepping around our dad, his back against the wall that leads to the staircase behind which we used to play hide-and-seek. I can see his son's face in his face, I can see my father's face in his face. I can see my face in his face. I see us all in his face. "I got upstairs and asked Mom where Dad was, and she looked at me like *dummy.* 'Downstairs,' she said."

Josh's story of the first day we saw our father transformed, his first day home from the *sesshin,* couldn't have ended any other way. But this story doesn't actually end. Josh gives me no conclusion, no moment when he walks into the living room and says hello. No snap-action stop. Just the dawning awareness that nothing will ever be the same.

I've been looking for the demarcation point—the before/after that changed it all. Everyone has always said the *sesshin* is where he broke, but the facts I've been finding these last few years make me question that tale. I believe now that my father was sick longer than we knew, and I want to find a moment when we should have noticed, when we should have known not to let him go to that place. When we could have stopped it all before it happened. But Josh isn't having that.

"Before Dad left," he says now, "he was open and warm and kind and funny. He was *Daddy.*" And now there are tears in both our hazel-greens when they meet. "When he got back, he was not that man anymore."

I want to find a moment from before the *sesshin,* from way, way before, because if a week meditating can break a man, then we're all so much more vulnerable than I can bear. I want to prove that my father was always ill and that therefore none of us ever will be. I want my brother to stop tearing holes in my theory. But then I think about each of our different perspectives on history, each of our different interpretations. Maybe there is room for both of ours as we revisit the facts we know and try to make sense of them for ourselves.

I know that when he got back from that retreat, my father believed his publishers were stealing his money, but before he went away he believed he could control the movements of the people walking by across the street. And before that, he believed a woman he flirted with once in a bar communicated with him years later through newspaper advertisements. I know once he got back from the *sesshin* he believed his family were reincarnated Zen Buddhist masters and that I was a witch, but when he was in Rome ten years earlier, he was afraid of his brain seeping out from behind his ear, maybe even afraid he would cut off that ear if things got too bad, as Vincent had done. And I know that from at least the moment he started writing novels—and maybe before, there is no record—he studied the development of mental illness as the result of trauma, he studied how to make it stay at bay. I don't tell Josh any of this in the burger joint on 6th Avenue. That's not how we do it in the Wolk family, either. No, I'm here to listen, not question my brother's narrative. Which, as it emerges, reveals that Josh has a different interpretation from the rest of the family, too. He thinks that by the time Dad got to Riggs, he was no longer delusional, just depressed. As he talks, I realize our father's history is a complicated knot.

"Told me about his 'breakdown' at the Zen experience," wrote a nurse named A. Ryan on New Year's Eve 1979. "Much anguish exhibited when referring to his children, his marriage. Talked of feeling especially alienated at [Riggs]," she wrote. The next entry on the page is dated three days later. This nurse's note starts, "Spoke to me about much the same issues as noted above." This nurse has tidier handwriting than the other. I like her right away. I think she sees my father, I think she knows him. "Says he feels helpless about his depression ever lifting and the 'drain' he is in this condition on his family," she wrote. "He appeared *very* depressed with his head literally hanging down much of the day." The next entry comes the next day, January 4. He asked to play Boggle with a nurse whose name I can't read. I also can't read much of her note except for the last line: "He wondered if he should go to a closed hospital."

He'd be dead in a day.

I WATCH THE muddy Hudson out my train window and think that maybe Josh was right—maybe depression killed our father, not delusions. He told my mother in his letters from Rome that it lurked in the shadows of New York City subway stations and deep inside the Castel Sant'Angelo. He told her that it crippled him with fears of failure. Maybe depression is what brought him to carry out acts of cruelty on his little sister when they were children. Or maybe he was just a prick. Maybe depression made him seek out other women both times he was married. Or maybe he was just a philanderer. Maybe depression made him wonder what he and van Gogh had in common, with the sadness and the feeling behind the ears. Maybe all along it was depression, and the breakdown at the *sesshin* was the blip. Maybe the story would've ended with a belt strap even if he'd never gone away.

Maybe Dad *was* sick longer than we knew, but I no longer mean that he was psychotic and we didn't notice. I just mean maybe he was depressed all his life. He was magnanimous and gregarious and paranoid and charming and funny, and maybe he could hide his depression for longer periods or better than some other people can. But maybe when it fell on him so hard, it killed him.

DAD CAME HOME from the hospital for Christmas the year I was five. He'd been away less than a month, but he seemed like a stranger when he walked through the rust-red kitchen door even though I saw the wavy black hair on his head and the thick mustache on his lip. Even though I knew those heavy eyebrows, that square jaw. Even though he wore his glasses that turned from clear to dark when he walked out into the sun, turned from clear to dark some days in the living room, too, turned from clear to dark so easily and hid him from me so fast.

I can't remember what color his eyes were.

At some point during that visit, he must have walked along State Street for presents. I wonder now how much time he spent at Child's, the toy store down the street I was sure was named for its customers. Did he go there alone? How easy, how hard, was it for him to choose three identical bears, one for each of his children? Bears we each named with identical names.

Josh was sick, like he was sick every Christmas. In a picture in my mom's photo album, his feverish face sleeps on the red couch, his lips bright with heat, his pale arm tight around his tan bear, around his Edward Tedward.

There's a picture of me from that day, too. I stand in the living room holding a brand-new baby doll in one hand and a clear plastic umbrella open over my head in the other, a maniacal smile on my face.

"It was awful," Nan told me recently. "Dad just sat in the middle of the living room and didn't say anything. We tiptoed around him like Christmas was fun anyway."

It was awful, according also to his medical records. "A dazed, depressed, older-than-his-age looking man. Hasn't been able to write for a year."

What happened to the refuge he sought in his writing? Why couldn't he find it anymore? If he'd been able to keep writing, would he have found the path out of his illness? Or should I feel thankful that toward the end the production line stopped? That he could no longer find refuge in his own representations of interracial sex on the page? That there are only six slavers with my father's pseudonyms on their covers, not sixty?

52

"MY FEELING IS that somebody who writes slavers is not somebody who supports miscegenation laws," Ngoni says to me a couple of nights after my return from New York. "It's too intimate, crafting that kind of story."

My husband and I are perched on kitchen stools with our dinners, the kids in the other room watching a movie. He's helping me categorize the different interpretations of my father—his career, his illness, which begat what. I've just expressed my frustration that I can't find the key that will reveal why my dad could do what he did when he sat at his desk. How someone with his politics—he was liberal, supported the Civil Rights Movement, took pride in the fact that he and my mom lived in Mickey Schwerner's old apartment in Brooklyn—could write books so rooted in stereotype anyway. I know as I talk about all of this that I'm steering us away from the topic of Dad's depression, that I'm making a choice not to tell Ngoni what my brother thinks killed our father. Maybe I'm worried it will remind him of his own father, or of his uncle Dakarai, who's finally got a handle on his demons thanks to the right medications. Maybe I can't bring it all into one room right now, it's too much to bear with the kids just down the hall. Or maybe it's just still too raw after our fight a few nights ago—our first in a long time. It was about when we should tell the kids about their grandfathers' illnesses, about their possible inheritances, when we should tell them what the signs are and how to look for them. It's rare for me and Ngoni to disagree on how to parent these kids, but we disagree on this. So after leaving it unresolved a few nights ago, I'm not eager to return to the topic just yet. We won't solve this one so simply, so I'm making us talk instead about Dad's books, about his career.

"I know that some people think your father's career was scandalous," he says, "but for me, the scandal is the least interesting piece of it." He stops talking for a moment. Collects his thoughts. "It's really important to know where you come from, even when the story might not be pleasant."

The room shifts. "When I first visited the house on State Street soon after we met, to meet your mom, I felt this huge absence. Not your missing father, but the absence of grief," he says. "You hadn't mourned him, I could tell, so no one could face the fact that he had existed and shaped who you were and the fabric of the family. But what I never understood was that it felt like an intentional absence."

I hadn't thought about that before. That after an intentional death came an intentional absence. I've thought about how we each mourned my father independently, how his suicide fractured the family into individual parts, how my mother's emotional reserve might have influenced how free I felt to bring him up when I needed to. But I chalked all that up to her WASPy upbringing, to her Protestant beginnings. I haven't thought before about how much work she put into pretending she didn't need him after he died. Or how that was a model I followed.

"If you fundamentally believe, as I do, that the world of the living is intimately connected to the world of the dead," Ngoni says, "then you've got to give the dead permission to rest. In Zimbabwe, the Shona ritualize mourning for just this reason. Another way we do it is naming. Naming George after your father helped your dad know he had permission to rest."

I nod my head because I want him to keep talking, but I'm not sure I fully follow him. I don't fundamentally believe that the world of the living and the world of the dead are intertwined. I don't believe in an afterlife or that there's a higher power looking after us all in this one or that the dead have feelings that are influenced by decisions made by the living. But there's something in Ngoni's belief system I want to grab onto, something that soothes me and allows me to think it might be possible to believe more than one thing. And while I wasn't raised with it, the fact is that Jews also ritualize mourning, also honor the dead with names. When my husband talks this way, I don't *not* believe.

One morning last winter after Julius walked down the hill to the school bus, and while George still slept in his bed—his bus comes later—I strapped snowshoes to my boots and headed into the woods with the dog for our morning hike. It took me a moment to realize that something was different this morning, that this morning's hike didn't feel like any of the ones before. It took me a moment to realize that Dad was there in the woods with me that day. The air felt heavier, I think. So I talked to him a little. Said I was glad he'd come. But mostly we just enjoyed the winter quiet. When I came to the clearing that leads back to the house, I figured he would follow me home, but he didn't. After I woke George up and scrambled him some eggs, after I packed his snack and told him to put on his boots, I looked out the window and felt my dad out there, hovering around the orange Adirondack chairs, snow all around.

"Sometimes it feels like we made our home in this place by these woods to give my father that," I say to Ngoni in the kitchen that night. "To give him a place to rest. Sometimes I think that's what this whole life is. Mom was right, I never felt him at the cemetery. But in the mornings, sometimes, it feels like he's here."

THESE DAYS, STANDING at the stove next to Ngoni, laughing while we make the chili, I picture Dad stooped on a stool behind us, laughing too. Sometimes, when I fill the kettle in the darkness of an early morning while Ngoni irons his shirt, I picture Dad's handwriting on a note attached to a newspaper clipping he wants my husband to read and which he left on the counter for him to find. Sometimes, sitting in the passenger seat of Ngoni's car as we drive by Riggs on our way to a soccer tournament—the kids singing or laughing or fighting in the backseat—I picture Dad holding a worn lawn chair under his arm in the parking lot when we arrive.

"I've just come to watch the boys' games," he'll say when we smile at his appearance. "I wanted to surprise you." And he hugs me before we line up our chairs in a row and sit together, my sons warming up and showing off with shots on goal, turning to see if he's watching. My sons calling out his name.

Anna told me that day in Vermont that he would have been a good grandfather to my sons. Sometimes I believe her.

It's retrocausality. Letting the present affect the past.

53

MOM AND I were seated at the long butcher-block counter in the kitchen of the house on State Street with the small TV in the corner showing Jane Pauley and Bryant Gumbel speaking the news. The knives hung from the magnetic strip on the wall behind Mom's head, and the coffee carafe was full. On my side of the counter, tea and toast as I watched the clock tick closer to school. Is that when we first talked about Dad's books?

Or Mom and I were in the living room on a sunny Sunday morning, me on the floor in the warm spot with the blue-and-red Persian rug scratching the backs of my legs and my history textbook open and ignored by my side. Mom in the window seat they built together, her right foot resting on her left knee, her left hand picking at her toenails, her gaze going out the window or down at the crossword puzzle in her lap. Was it then?

Wherever we were, Dad was ten years dead and Mom was telling me how he made a living. It's a moment I have to invent because although I can now remember her words, I can't place the scene, cannot demonstrate its veracity and promise that it happened exactly this way.

"Those books were just a paycheck, Jules," she said, as though this justified their existence. As though this told me who my father was. "He wrote them under contract."

Did I come upon them and feel scandalized and angry and ask for an explanation? I don't remember such a moment. Did Josh or Nan bring them up, and I hung around longer to ask more questions? It's possible. What I do remember is holding onto those words "under contract," which were the only explanation I got, and were the only words I needed to spin a story: It wasn't my father's idea to write interracial pornography. It was the fault of the publishing houses, it was the fault of the contracts that helped him buy the house on State Street. It was his agent's fault, the market's fault.

"Those books don't tell you who he was," my mother said—that day, or yesterday. After that conversation, did I sneak back to the bookcase in the hallway to peek at the ones with Dad's real name on the spine, as I'd done when I was little? Maybe I pulled out my old favorite, *Jeremiah Painter,* and held it in my hands again like I used to and looked again at the face on the cover, the dusty black face of a cowboy with a rifle in his hand and two pistols in his jacket pockets, a large, flat-brimmed hat shading his eyes. Did I laugh at my childhood notion that he looked like my dad? Or did I focus on his mint-green shirtsleeve poking out from under his jacket, the flash of mint green again at his waist where his jacket is unbuttoned, and wonder if every character is in some small way a part of its creator? I don't think I wondered as a teenager the way I wonder today why my white father wrote so many books about black people. I think I was blind to all of that. All that mattered to me until I had my own children was the fact that my father was dead. The fact that he had chosen to die.

"*M*A*S*H* is almost on!" Josh called down to me as his feet pounded each stair above my head. "I get the brown chair!" I slid the book back into its place and climbed into the uncomfortable green chair and waited for Alan Alda to appear on the screen like he had been doing for all of these years since Dad died, to calm me down and make me laugh and help me believe the world was safe. Soon we were watching the opening credits and humming the tune that Josh swore, in the movie version where they played the song with its lyrics, says suicide is painless.

Who was Jeremiah Painter?

Who was George Wolk?

IT TOOK ME a second read of that slim novel to see that *Jeremiah Painter* is, at its core, a Reconstruction fantasy. It's a book whose white author purports to show that though times are hard for the black man after the Civil War, a new life is possible. Jeremiah goes on to save the town, avert a war between its two main families, and settle on the banks of the river with his common-law Native American wife. He's the local hero by the end of the book, and his new white friends have promised to protect him from the bandits out looking for him (for sleeping with their white sister) should they ever come to town. I don't think it's wrong to suggest that if a real-life black cowboy had wandered into a real-life Divide in real-life 1868, he wouldn't have been temporarily jailed by the sheriff, he would have been shot.

"[T]he Dream was gilded by novels and adventure stories . . . the brightly rendered version of [this] country as it has always declared itself," Ta-Nehisi Coates writes, reminding us that the America so many of us believe to be true is no more than a mirage. Reminding us that those novels and adventure stories support a dream that only exists for the white people among us, a dream world in which Jeremiah Painter can be the hero, but in which Julius and George Munemo will have to work twice as hard as their friends to make a life.

And George Wolk wrote that shit. My father might have left me a trail of breadcrumbs to follow and hoped that when I got to the end, I'd see he was a politically progressive awesome dude who would have loved my kids, but I just can't get away from the fact that he gilded that dream—the dream that forms the boot on my boys' necks as they're trying to grow into men.

"Your father would have been horrified to hear you call him a racist," my mother said to me last month. "He was pretty cold-blooded about exploiting the racial taboo so he could make a buck, but he was deeply ashamed of where he came from." She then repeated a story she'd told me before, about how my grandmother kept a separate set of dishes—a single plate, cup, and bowl—for the maid. "Your father was so ashamed when he realized I'd seen those dishes."

As she spoke, I began to see that writing *Jeremiah Painter* may have healed something in my father. That book could also be read as an inquiry into the making of a bigot, and maybe he was trying to figure out the same thing about his parents as I've been trying to figure out about him. Parlee, a secondary character with almost no relationship to the movement of the plot, has what my sons would call "an emotionally scarring backstory," as if he were a superhero whose sad past had turned him powerful. Dad explores it for some pages despite the fact that Parlee won't appear much in what follows. His home was burned down and his sons were killed in the war. It leads him to hate black people. It's almost as though Dad was trying to understand how surviving the Holocaust could turn some Jews into racists. Or how the manifestation of white supremacy could turn some folks into white liberals. Another minor character in *Jeremiah Painter* is the banker, Henry Morton. Could it be a coincidence that this was almost the name of the explorer of the Congolese forests I'm certain my dad read when he was doing research for *Black Scarab*, Henry Morton Stanley? But his Henry Morton couldn't do enough to try to make Jeremiah comfortable in Divide—that is, after all, why he offered him a job cleaning his mother's house.

AFTER ENCOURAGING the release of my father's books back into the world as e-books, after seeing their shameful covers, I told Ngoni that I believed my own whiteness is what allowed me not to think of the ramifications of that decision, what allowed me to think only of my parents, of my own sadnesses. What allowed me not even to think of my sons before making that call. Because in a world where white people believe we are always making the right choices, there is little room to question the decisions as they develop. And in a world where white liberals believe everything we do is for the greater good, questioning our decisions doesn't even occur to us.

"There's an expectation that people are not human beings," Ngoni said to me. "There is an idea that we always make decisions from the most informed place, from the most honest place, from the best possible place," he said. "Sometimes we make mistakes. Sometimes you make mistakes. You're a human being with complicated emotions, and most things are not so simple as people would like to think," my husband said to me.

I took solace in those words not because they absolve me of responsibility. They don't, nor would Ngoni ever want to do that. I took solace in those words because they reminded me that I married a man who sees all the parts of a person. He saw all the parts of my father when introduced to him through the covers of his slavers when we were dating. He sees all the parts of me today and loves me anyway.

I took solace in those words because after all of this, I get to come home to him.

54

IN EARLY 1999, a couple of months after my wedding, Rachel invited me out for lunch. I was in a graduate program in the city where she worked and she said she wanted to try to set things right. Make it possible for us to have a relationship now that we lived so close to one another. I didn't know whose side Rachel was on—though I did believe things had long been difficult between her and her mother—and I felt some hope in the possibility of staying connected to the other person on the planet so closely related to my dad. Despite everything, I still feel that hope.

So I arrived at her office early in the afternoon, and when she buzzed me up she announced that she'd made us tuna fish sandwiches because she'd recently had surgery and wasn't up for the uncomfortable chairs of a restaurant. I settled in the seat where I assumed her patients sat, and looked across at her, waiting for a signal.

"I don't believe my mother is racist, Jules," was how she began. This was followed by a history of our family—one Rose had never told me. My great-grandfather left Poland early in the century, but traveled back and forth from New York City to Zamość several times to see his wife, Malka. Each time she fell pregnant with another son. Each time he left her there, saying there wasn't enough money to bring the family across. "On his last visit, my great-uncle Ben took him aside and said it was time to take Malka and the boys back with him," Rachel told me. "Ben gave them the money for the journey."

Rose was born in New York soon after her mother had left her home behind forever. Once she got married, Malka lived with them; she and Rachel shared a bedroom until she died. But a couple of years before Rachel was born—when my dad was a baby—Ben and his family were killed in Zamość's town square, along with all of the other Jews from the ghetto. "We lived with that grief every day because of course Malka knew what happened to those left behind," Rachel told me. "My father's father fled Russian conscription when he was sixteen and lost many relatives in the Holocaust. One of the ways this generation of Jews dealt with surviving was to devote themselves to the continuation of the Jewish people. They were going to reproduce Jews who would be Jews. So no, she's not racist. She simply wanted you to marry a Jew."

I bristled at this last statement, not understanding why I was only hearing this history now, after marrying a black man. I couldn't square Rachel's argument that my grandmother wasn't prejudiced against my husband because of his race with this heartbreaking history she'd just reported. I didn't know why they were so connected in Rachel's mind. So I said, "It seems more complicated than that."

Rachel grew visibly frustrated and almost shouted, "It's not that Ngoni's black. It's that he's not a Jew."

I nodded, but stayed quiet in my seat. I didn't yet have the language to say how ironic it was, as Rose didn't consider me Jewish—so how could my children be? I didn't yet have the language to say that racism never springs from a void—it is complicated and messy in all of its forms. I didn't yet have the language to ask how Rachel could reconcile this story when she had seen how my grandmother treated Ngoni—how is it that being the victim of one kind of cruelty can beget another kind? Without the language to say any of that, I changed the subject, engaged in small talk, waited until it was time to go home to my husband. Rachel and I didn't see each other again for years.

◆　◆　◆

MOTHER'S DAY, 2002. I'm visiting from New York, standing in the kitchen of the house on State Street, my hand clutching the telephone receiver, fingers shaking as I dial. When I hear the ring across the line, I take a deep breath and wonder if Rose will slam the phone back down when she hears my voice. Wonder what I will do if she does.

"Hello?"

"Grandma, it's Jules." I wait. I breathe. "I'm calling to wish you a happy Mother's Day."

The pause is not very long.

"And to you, someday," she says. This is nowhere on the spectrum of possibilities I had envisioned. I don't really believe she's said it.

"Actually, Grandma, that's why I'm calling."

I tell her I'm due in December. I tell her we're living in New York now. I tell her I can't wait to become a mother.

Her congratulations sound sincere. I ignore that she doesn't ask after Ngoni.

◆　◆　◆

BETWEEN THAT DAY and her death in 2007, Rose and I maintained the barest of relationships. We rarely spoke on the phone, but exchanged occasional letters and cards. Ngoni and I took eight-month-old Julius to her eightieth birthday party—she held him on her lap briefly as I heard echoes of her question in my head, *Where will the children be?*, and believed for a moment that she had moved beyond it. Until I saw the look in her eye when she spotted my husband across the room.

We took the children there later, when she was dying, for what we knew would be our last visit. She was so frail that her caretaker, Eva, stood sentinel by her side and had for a moment blocked her view of Ngoni. When she saw him, the tenor of her voice shifted and when she said, "You're here, too?" I couldn't help—after all we had been through over the years—but hear the hate hot in her tone.

Ngoni didn't join me for the funeral. Josh, Nan, and I drove together, sat together, spoke to few. When the rabbi asked if anyone wanted to come up and share memories of Rose, Paul spoke eloquently about a woman who had accepted a son-in-law despite his religion, how she had welcomed him despite the fact that he wasn't Jewish. As I watched Rachel weep in the front row where she sat with her kids, I thought about what made us different. How her Christian husband was

allowed to be the father of Jewish children, and how mine never could
be. How Rachel was a Jew, how I was not. How the only world in which
Rose would really have welcomed me into her heart was one where I
married a Jew and converted. But if my conversion was what stood
between her having Jewish great-grandchildren, why did it matter who
I married? Ngoni would have welcomed being the father to Jewish children, if that had mattered to me. Sitting on that hard wooden bench
between my siblings, thinking back on all the things she'd said to me
over the years, listening to Paul's words, I knew that whatever recon-
ciliation we'd pretended at these last years was a lie. I knew that my
father's suicide broke her—and now that I was a mother myself I had
so much more sympathy for that. But I knew that the hatred she felt, or
the fear, was based on my husband's race, not his religion.

No one spoke for a long moment after Paul sat back down, and I felt
Josh next to me itching to get up and I knew he felt what I did—that the
sin of our mother's religion had scarred us to Rose, how she had never
truly seen us as her own. The irony of what Paul had said wounded our
hearts, because of course Rose never welcomed my mother as she had
welcomed Paul. But this wasn't our forum and I was relieved when Josh
didn't get up. The truth we knew about Rose wasn't welcome here, and
speaking it to this crowd would do no one any good. Soon Eva walked
to the front of the room, addressing those assembled in her thick Ugan-
dan accent. I know my siblings shared my sense of outrage, my sense
of heartbreak. That her black caretaker could love her, and that Rose
could love her black caretaker in return, revealed a complexity about
my grandmother's racism that was hard for all of us to swallow.

I believe Rose did not see Eva as a threat to Judaism because as a
black woman she could never be the mother of Jewish children. I believe Rose did see Ngoni as a threat to Judaism because, despite what
Paul just said about religion, as a black man his children would be black.
Even if I had converted to Judaism, I think Rose still wouldn't have seen
my black children as Jewish. Beliefs about race and religion and gender
mixed up in a mess inside my grandmother's heart, and the result was
a coldness, a bitterness she couldn't overcome.

As I sit with this all of these years later, what strikes me is that
we are all so broken. My grandmother lived in a world dominated by

division from and fear of the other. She cared more about the continuation of her tribe than about the happiness of her family. She passed something on to her descendants, something that had been passed on to her. I define that thing as racism, I see no difference between the fear she felt that her people would be wiped from the earth and the hatred she communicated to people she defined as outsiders. Maybe this is too simplistic a view, or maybe it's exactly the definition of racism that I've been seeking all along.

55

ON A SUNNY fall day in 2017, my mother sends me a text that reads, "Suddenly my money from the e-book people has jumped to $116. I'm horrified that Trump has caused this." In each of the months since the e-books went up, she has received somewhere in the vicinity of seven dollars. So this is a surprise. I don't know if she can tell which of his books are selling, if she gets an itemized list or just a direct deposit. I don't know if it's the other books in the George Wolk Collection that are bringing in those few bucks. But that's not what matters now.

"Do you want to ask them to pull the books?" I reply.

"Just the slavers," she texts back some minutes later.

I have not been on my mom's case about this. Several times in the last two years I've suggested there might be something to do. Convince them to change the cover images, maybe. But pulling the books seemed like a step beyond anything I could ask of her—I am, after all, the one who got her into this. And I had to check my own motivations. Wouldn't it have been easier to write this book if I knew no one would be able to Google my father and find his slavers? I could have pretended to be clean. Leave my analysis of his words to the hard copies, and let the artist's depictions from the sixties and seventies tell the story. Nothing to see here. But as I text with her, I know I've been waiting for this chance, for the opportunity to right this wrong.

My mom has been watching this world burn recently, just like the rest of us. She'd say it's burning differently now, more openly than it has since the sixties. She knows the white supremacists with their torches received a permission they had previously lacked to come out of their hidey-holes after the 2016 presidential election. She knows this world has just gotten more openly scary for so many of us. But my mother doesn't admit as readily that the peril is the same, she's just more aware of it now. She doesn't acknowledge as fast that those guys were just waiting in their hidey-holes all along. That they have been here since the beginning of this treasonous country. I think her hesitation comes from the anxiety I see spiking as her grandchildren get older, as they start to look like young black men. My mother knows what this world is, what it can do to her grandsons.

But the day after white supremacists stormed Charlottesville I didn't call her up to tell her that I couldn't sleep because I saw a pickup truck flying a Confederate flag down the street. I didn't call her up and tell her I was scared he followed us home or ask her how I would protect my children if he threw a brick through the front window or tried to burn the house down. I didn't call her up some weeks later when I read that an eight-year-old boy in New Hampshire was nearly hanged from a tree by a mob of white teenagers. I didn't call her up and ask her if she thought that could happen to my sons. Because we both know the answer. I don't ever call her up and cry about all the fears I carry in this country, I don't ever call her up and rage. It's more than anyone should have to bear—my anxiety, the truth of this country—and I won't ask her to try.

So when I respond, all I say is that I'll help her draft the e-mail if she'd like. But she doesn't need any assistance at all. "In the atmosphere of increased racial bigotry, promoted and encouraged by Mr. Trump," my mother writes to the e-book publisher that afternoon, "I find that profiting from the sale of my husband's novels exploiting slavery makes me feel complicit, dirty, and ashamed. I don't want to continue to be a part of Mr. Trump's active revival of bigotry and hate and so I am writing to ask you to remove those books from sale." I tell her this means the world to me. I tell her I think she is brave and that I love her.

I don't do the math until later. I don't really ever want to do the math. There is no number of sales of my father's slavers that I would be happy to know, other than zero. While this new amount of money is no seven grand like McNeill's, it is still more than zero, and I can't bear it. At $2.99 a book, with my mom getting almost half of the proceeds, it seems like about a hundred copies of my dad's slavers sold in the one month after cities in the South started taking down their Confederate monuments in the dark of night. In the one month after white supremacists stormed a city to celebrate their active revival of bigotry in this country. In the days after a mob of white teenagers nearly lynched an eight-year-old child before he could grow into a black man. What does this say about America in the twenty-first century, what does this say about the likelihood of ever overcoming the legacy of slavery, of ever living in a world where no one wonders what my children are?

Maybe my grandmother was right—where *will* the children be?

I TOLD NGONI recently that while I agree that race is a social construct that exists only in the face of difference, I don't agree with Ta-Nehisi Coates's categorization of people "who believe that they are white." I know he's taking from Baldwin, I know Baldwin described them as "people who think they are white," and I disagree with that, too.

"I feel this lets white people off the hook from really looking at their legacies, and from really considering what they are doing in the present moment," I said. "Because we are perceived as white, we get all of the privileges according to the white power structure," I said. "And until we own that, nothing will change."

Ngoni asked me what I meant by "own that," and I stumbled. What do I mean? Am I really owning my legacy by figuring out who my father was? If so, does that mean I believe every white person should look into her closet and expose her racist skeletons? You know what—I do want that. But I don't know if owning my father's racist career will make any goddamned difference at all in this world. I have no reason to believe that my story will do more than deepen the divide. No actual changes to the power structure will take place with the publication of this book, no actual Confederate monuments will fall because some unknown writer came along and said she thought they should never have been erected in the first place, no KKK grand wizards will look inward and discover how lost they really are and burn their robes in effigy to their newfound understanding. So what do I mean when I say we need to own our legacy as white people? I sighed and told my husband that I don't fucking know.

"Plus, by that thinking, there is no way forward," Ngoni said after a while. "I have seen that world," he said, invoking the racial divisions in Zimbabwe, in South Africa, in the America some of us can pretend doesn't exist. "And that's no future we want."

It seemed like here in our living room, here in this mixed-race family, Ngoni and I couldn't agree on a way forward that would allow for any solidarity between races, that would allow for us to become allies across the divide. I know that is not the interpretation he wanted me to walk away with, but it is, nonetheless, my interpretation.

IT'S HARD TO find hope these days. Hard to know if there is a way out of Julius's clock, if we are making any progress at all. Maybe the marches against white supremacy will fade away, maybe mobs of white boys will continue carrying ropes around in case they encounter black-ness on their afternoon. And maybe then my kids will grow up and move into a world where they are asked the same questions that Ngoni is often asked today. Questions like—from a white woman he does not know—"I see you at this coffee shop every morning. Are you working on something important?" As though only she has the right to be there every day, working on something important. Questions like—from a white colleague he has met one hundred times in his decade at the college—"Who are you, and why are you running this meeting?" As though only a white person could be recognized in such a role. Ques-tions like—from librarians and administrative assistants—"Are you a student?" Questions like—from students—"Are you a visiting profes-sor?" Questions that subtly support the white supremacy of this coun-try, questions that at their base translate to, *Who are you and can you justify for me why you're here?* Our kids will move into a world ruled by white people, defined by white attitudes, shaped by the white dream.

My mother pulling down those e-books won't make a bit of differ-ence, not really. But I'm still so glad she did it. So glad that some white man, a man who makes his living publishing e-books online, has to read those words my clear-eyed mother wrote and then go through the steps required to get those books off of the electronic shelves. So glad that you, dear reader, won't ever see the images that man had published as the covers after all. So ever-fucking glad that my children won't see those pictures or be able to download those words when they Google their grandfather. That this tiny little step has taken place. Because what it shows me is that no matter who my father was, my mother is willing to stand up in the face of this broken world and declare that it's not for her.

This river lined with trees is not for you and me, my father wrote to my mother fifty years ago. What is for you and me is clenched here in this fist, this raw stone of my engraving.

I feel a tiny morsel of hope now that my father's slavers really are dead. A tiny morsel of hope that what is clenched here in my fist might contribute to the conversation.

Epilogue

There's another Polaroid on our fridge now, this one also from a wedding, taken ten years after the first. We're all squished up together under the tent at the end of the night. George's shirt is untucked and his collar is up and his face is glistening—he's just been moonwalking across the dance floor. Julius's shoulders are hunched and his hands are clasped in front of him so that he fits between Ngoni and me. He's looking off to his right and smiling that smile he gets just after he's laughed so hard it makes him squeak a little. The illusion in the picture is that I'm the tallest among us, but in fact the lawn slopes down and I've found the high spot. By the time this picture was taken Julius had long since overtaken me. In a couple of weeks, he'd be taller than Ngoni.

"Where does he get his height?" people ask us all the time.

I used to answer, "My dad was six foot three," but I can't say that anymore. And I don't like revealing facts from my father's medical records in small talk on the street or the soccer sidelines, so now I just say, "Both our fathers were pretty tall," and people nod like they get it, unaware of the illnesses we hope our children won't inherit from the grandfathers they never knew. Unaware of the worry I carry about what will happen when my sons begin to explore the ramifications of my father's career. They're too young for that still. Still too loyal to me. But it'll come, that knowledge of all the terror in a world that once felt safe. It's already starting to come, but in pieces and not—just yet—accompanied by accusations about the betrayal that is my legacy. Some days it's possible to push it all aside and just look at this picture.

In this one, even Ngoni's smiling. His jacket is unbuttoned, his tie is crooked, and apples have formed on his cheeks just like they used to form on Sekuru's. Maybe this is a trait one grows into, or maybe he smiles more often now, I'm not sure. But the way his teeth reflect the camera's flash makes me remember those long-ago college nights when I was the only one who knew they weren't straight. It brings back that feeling at the backs of my knees, the one I used to get every time he walked into a room. How do people find each other in this enormous world—how did we? Sometimes it feels like a magic trick that we made this family at all.

Come look at the picture with me, will you? See how none of us shares an exact eye color or skin tone with anyone else? See how no two people in my family have the same arc of nose or curve of lip? See how neither of our sons resembles one of us really, or looks very much like the other? But I can trace for you the lines of connection, I can show you how we fit together like a puzzle.

When I look at this picture, I don't think about boundaries that were crossed or how we present to the world or what the world can do to us. I just think about how endlessly, ridiculously grateful I am that these are the people I get to love in this life.

Acknowledgments

Thanks go first to Dad's people. His friends who took my phone calls as though it hadn't been thirty years since they'd heard my name: Robert Corash, Bruce Cowan, Miriam Duhan, Sarah Ellsworth, Tracy Kidder, Mark Kramer, Charles McCarry, George McNeill. His colleagues, who had likely never heard my name at all: Robert Gleason, Henry Morrison, David Williams. His cousins whom I hadn't before met: Chuck, Dan, Ira, Nora, Robert. His first wife, whose warmth one fall day on a deck in Vermont astounds me still. And his sister, who opened her heart and home to me even though it hurt. Thank you.

Thanks also to the folks who spoke to me about Judaism, pulp fiction, pornography, the publishing industry in the sixties and seventies, the daily life of a patient at a small psychiatric facility, the daily life of a fiction writer: Gary Goldstein, Jeffrey Israel, Scott Krause, Josh Lambert, Robin Longo, Jim Shepard, Steve Zacharius. Thanks also to the folks at the Stockbridge town hall and police department and to my charming lawyer, Kevin Bopp. And for the other kinds of professional help a writer needs, thanks go to Jessika Drmacich, VaNatta Ford, Amy Lovett, Christine Ménard, Alfred Sapse, and Emery Shriver.

I am grateful for the time and space to deepen this manuscript afforded to me by a fellowship at the Oakley Center for Humanities and Social Sciences at Williams College, and for the unforeseen boon of a week in Rome that it allowed. To my cohort of fellows there, who tackled unfamiliar terrain with all the gusto and intelligence I could ask for, and to Krista Birch who made it all possible: Thank you.

At Swallow Press special thanks go to Gillian Berchowitz for her guidance, to Beth Pratt for her partnership, and to Nancy Basmajian,

Sebastian Biot, Rick Huard, Jeffrey Kallet, Samara Rafert, Sally Welch, and Stephanie Williams: my appreciation for your care is boundless.

To my friends who became readers, to my readers and teachers who became friends, to the ones who were there in the dark and in the light: Xochitl Bervera, Alison Bost, Daryle Bost, Breena Clarke, Cassandra Cleghorn, Jaed Coffin, Susan Conley, Marisa Daley, Carol Edelstein, T Clutch Fleishman, Sherine Gilmour, Stacie Goddard, Joe Johnson, Adrienne LeBas, Gretchen Long, Patricia MacLachlan, Debra Marquart, Christine McAlister, Wendy McWeeny, Bridget Ngcobo, Melanie Nicholson, Nimu Njoya, Paul Park, Rubin Pfeffer, Angela Paik Schaeffer, Suzanne Strempek Shea, Karen Shepard, Candis Watts Smith, Janneke van de Stadt, Peter Starenko, Leslie Tane, Rebecca Tucker-Smith, Melanie Viets, Carter Walker, Elizabeth Weiner, Lauren Benanti Wolk; also to Anne Fassett Casson, who found its heart; Rhon Manigault-Bryant, who found its beginning; Kenda Mutongi, who found its home; Shannon Ratliff, who found its purpose; and Stefanie Solum, who found its title. I'd be nowhere without any of you.

To my in-laws in Zimbabwe, who didn't know I was keeping notes: Thank you for welcoming me into your family twenty years ago; I hope I've done it justice.

To my family of origin, who would each tell it differently but who trusted me to tell it anyway: I love you Susan McKenzie Wolk, Susannah Wolk Rodriguez, Joshua Morgan Wolk.

And the most gratitude, which cannot be measured in a lifetime of giving thanks, goes to my husband, Ngonidzashe, who never much liked the idea of being in a book but didn't let that get in the way of his unending support; and to our beautiful sons, Julius and George, who partway through gave me permission to write about them, cracking open my world. As you are the heart of this story, you are also my heart. I don't do anything but for the three of you.

Bibliography

Achebe, Chinua. "An Image of Africa." In *Hopes and Impediments*. New York: Doubleday, 1989.

Baldwin, James. *The Fire Next Time*. New York: Dial Press, 1963.

————. "White Man's Guilt." In *The Price of the Ticket: Collected Nonfiction 1948–1985*. New York: St. Martin's / Marek, 1985.

Benjamin, Rich. *Searching for Whitopia: An Improbable Journey to the Heart of White America*. New York: Hachette, 2016.

Breines, Paul. *Tough Jews: Political Fantasies and the Moral Dilemma of American Jewry*. New York: Basic, 1990.

Coates, Ta-Nehisi. *Between the World and Me*. New York: Random House, 2017.

Conrad, Joseph. *Heart of Darkness*. San Francisco: Wadsworth Pub., 1960.

Daley, Brittany A., and Stephen J. Gertz. *Sin-a-rama: Sleaze Sex Paperbacks of the Sixties*. Los Angeles: Feral House, 2005.

Gordon, Emily Fox. *Book of Days*. New York: Spiegel & Grau, 2010.

hooks, bell. *ain't i a woman: black women and feminism*. Boston: South End Press, 1981.

Kileff, Clive, and Peggy Kileff. *Shona Customs; Essays by African Writers*. Gweìo, Rhodesia: Mambo, 1970.

Kimmel, Michael S. *Manhood in America: A Cultural History*. New York: Free Press, 1996.

Lambert, Joshua N. *Unclean Lips: Obscenity, Jews, and American Culture*. New York: New York University Press, 2014.

Milner-Thornton, Juliette Bridgette. *The Long Shadow of the British Empire: The Ongoing Legacies of Race and Class in Zambia*. New York: Palgrave Macmillan, 2012.

Morrison, Toni. *Playing in the Dark: Whiteness and the Literary Imagination*. Cambridge, MA: Harvard University Press, 1992.

Mura, David. *A Stranger's Journey: Race, Identity, and Narrative Craft in Writing*. Athens: University of Georgia Press, 2018.

Onstott, Kyle. *Mandingo*. Richmond, VA: Denlinger, 1957.

Painter, Nell Irvin. *The History of White People*. New York: W. W. Norton, 2010.

Raftopoulos, Brian, and A. S. Mlambo. *Becoming Zimbabwe: A History from the Pre-colonial Period to 2008*. Harare: Weaver, 2009.

Ranger, T. O. *Are We Not Also Men?: The Samkange Family and African Politics in Zimbabwe, 1920–64*. Harare: Baobab, 1995.

Rankine, Claudia, Beth Loffreda, and Max King Cap. *The Racial Imaginary: Writers on Race in the Life of the Mind*. Albany, NY: Fence Books, 2016.

Stanley, Henry M. *In Darkest Africa*. Santa Barbara, CA: Narrative Press, 2001.

Staunton, Irene. *Mothers of the Revolution: The War Experiences of Thirty Zimbabwean Women*. London: J. Currey, 1991.

Sundquist, Eric J. *Strangers in the Land: Blacks, Jews, Post-Holocaust America*. Cambridge, MA: Belknap, 2005.

Turnbull, Colin. *The Forest People*. New York: Simon & Schuster, 1961.

Watson, Veronica T. *The Souls of White Folk: African American Writers Theorize Whiteness*. Jackson: University of Mississippi Press, 2013.

Wolk, George, writing as Norman Gant. *Black Scarab: A Novel*. London: Mews Distributed by New English Library, 1976.

———. *Black Vengeance*. New York: Lancer Books, 1968.

———. *Chane*. New York: Lancer Books, 1968.

———. *Slave Empire*. New York: Lancer Books, 1968.

———. *Slave Queen*. New York: Dell, 1970.

Wolk, George, writing as Heinrich Graat. *The Devil and Ben Camden*. New York: Belmont Books, 1970.

———. *The Revenge of Increase Sewall*. New York: Belmont Books, 1969.

———. *A Place of Demons*. New York: Belmont/Tower Books, 1972.

Wolk, George, writing as Sebastian Watt. *Natchez Kingdom*. London: Sphere, 1980.

Wolk, George. *400 Brattle Street*. New York: Wyden Books, 1978.

———. *Jeremiah Painter*. New York: Dell, 1973.

———. *The Leopold Contract*. New York: Random House, 1969.

———. *The Man Who Dealt in Blood*. New York: Warner Paperback Library, 1974.